Oxford **Mathematics**
Primary Years Programme

4

Contents

OXFORD
UNIVERSITY PRESS
AUSTRALIA & NEW ZEALAND

Unit 1 Number and place value

Topic 1 Place value

Student Book pages 2–5

Learning focus

Model, read, write, compare and order whole numbers up to ten thousands and beyond

Materials

- scissors
- playing cards (with the face cards and tens removed)
- place value tools, such as number expanders and base-10 materials
- 10-sided dice (0 to 9) – enough for one between two
- poster paper or digital tablet
- online random number generator
- *BLM 1: Place value cards*
- *BLM 2: Australian births in 2009 and 2014*
- *Activity sheet 1: Number facts and fun*

Potential difficulties: Zero as a placeholder

Some students have difficulty reading and writing numbers that contain zeroes. It's important to explicitly address this in order to build understanding of zero as a placeholder.

- Use place value charts to give examples of numbers with a zero in the middle, and reinforce what this means. Add concrete materials or diagrams to the chart to enhance students' visualisation of numbers.
- Practise deconstructing and renaming numbers according to place value to help students develop a strong sense of how numbers work.

Daily practice activity

Challenge students to identify examples of large numbers in their everyday lives. Compare and order the numbers, discussing where they were found and what they're used for.

Session 1: Pre-assessment

Students to complete: Pre-test 1, Unit 1, Topic 1, p. 72.

Session 2: Topic introduction

WHOLE CLASS

Introductory activity: Ordering larger numbers

Provide each student with *BLM 1: Place value cards*. Ask them to cut out the cards and order them from largest to smallest, and then check with a partner to see if they have the same answers. Discuss any discrepancies as a class. Instruct students to find all the numbers with a 3 in them and order them using the place value of the threes. Repeat with other digits, ensuring that students understand, for example, that the value of 5 in 539 is greater than the 5 in 91 453, even though the latter number is larger. Extend students' thinking by including examples where they order the numbers from smallest to largest.

AT-STANDARD GROUP

Student Book

Students to complete: Guided and Independent Practice activities, pp. 2–4. Ask early finishers to find a partner. Each student in a pair should draw five playing cards from a deck with the face cards and tens removed and keep the cards in the order they were drawn to form a 5-digit number. The student with the highest number scores a point. Repeat until one student wins by scoring 10.

SUPPORT GROUP

Concept exploration and skill development: Practising renaming numbers

Students need plenty of practice renaming numbers to develop their understanding and application of place value. Invite students to make numbers according to criteria that you specify, e.g. five numbers under 1000 that have 17 tens, or five numbers over 1000 that have 24 hundreds. Support students' responses by representing the numbers in multiple ways, such as using number expanders, base-10 materials or on an interactive whiteboard. You can also do the activity in reverse by giving students a number and asking them to rename it in different ways.

Student Book with teacher support

Students to complete: Guided Practice activities, p. 2. Support students by discussing how the Student Book connects with the renaming activity they've just completed.

OXFORD UNIVERSITY PRESS

EXTENSION GROUP

Student Book

Students to complete: Guided and Independent Practice activities, pp. 2–4.

Activity sheet

Students to begin: *Activity sheet 1: Number facts and fun.*

Session 3: Instruction and consolidation

WHOLE CLASS

Topic exploration: **Writing and interpreting larger numbers**

In mixed-ability pairs, give students a 10-sided dice and ask them to roll it 5 times, recording each digit rolled in order to make a 5-digit number. Instruct students to make a poster or slide presentation about their number. This should show their number written in words and as a numeral, and include everything they know about their number, such as the different ways to partition it and some places they might encounter it in real life. Allow time for students to share their work with their classmates, and to reflect upon what was easy and what was difficult about the task.

AT-STANDARD GROUP

Teacher activity: **Comparing numbers**

Working with larger numbers in context allows students to make connections between their learning and the wider world. Enlarge a copy of *BLM 2: Australian births in 2009 and 2014*, or display it on the whiteboard, and ask students to share their observations about the births in various areas of Australia across the five years. In pairs, ask students to write five questions about the information, recording the answers on a separate sheet of paper. Questions might be general, such as "Which states or territories had an increased number of registered births between 2009 and 2014?", or specific, such as "In which state or territory did the number of registered births decrease by 691 between 2009 and 2014?", depending on students' preferences and abilities. Allow pairs to swap with other groups and answer their questions.

SUPPORT GROUP

Student Book with teacher support

Students to complete: Independent Practice activities, pp. 3–4. Check in with students and discuss any difficulties, supporting them by using place value charts or other visual aids as needed.

EXTENSION GROUP

Student Book

Students to complete: Extended Practice activities, p. 5.

Activity sheet

Students to continue: *Activity sheet 1: Number facts and fun.*

Session 4: Instruction and consolidation

WHOLE CLASS

Topic exploration: **Number line estimation**

Draw an empty number line on the board with a range of 5000 to 6000. Mark a place on the line to represent a specific number such as 5252, but do not write the number in (see below for example).

5000   6000

In mixed-ability pairs, ask students to estimate what number they think the marker is pointing to. Discuss the guesses as a group, encouraging students to share the options they considered in choosing their answer. You may want to give a round of applause for the pair who got the closest to the actual number! Repeat with number ranges in the ten thousands, giving clues to help students narrow their guesses, such as indicating whether the number is larger or smaller than their estimates, if they're a long way off. If students' guesses are close, you can also introduce clues to help them get the exact number, such as letting them know the number in a particular place value column or telling them which place value column they need to alter. Extend students' thinking by allowing them to mark numbers on the number line for their classmates to estimate.

AT-STANDARD GROUP

Student Book

Students to complete: Extended Practice activities, p. 5. Ask early finishers to write in words the unrounded and rounded numbers from question 5 of the Extended Practice.

SUPPORT GROUP

Concept exploration and skill development: **Before, after and between**

In the early years, students tend to have plenty of opportunities to identify the numbers that come before and after a number, or to choose a number that falls between two given numbers, but this happens less as students move up through school. Generate a random number between 1 and 1000 using an online tool. Alternatively, invite a student to choose three playing cards from a deck with the face cards and tens removed, using them to form a 3-digit number. Ask students to suggest what number comes before and after the chosen number, encouraging them to explain how they knew. If they respond well to this activity, instruct them to nominate what is 10 more and 10 less and what is 100 more and 100 less than the start number.

When students are ready, move on to 4- and 5-digit numbers, discussing the effect of adding 1 and powers of 10 to each number. If necessary, draw a place value chart on the board to help students visualise and isolate the relevant place value column, and to help explain what happens when adding 1 to 9 in a place value column, or when taking 1 from a 0. Extend students' thinking by generating two 3-, 4- or 5-digit numbers and challenging them to suggest a number that falls between the two.

Student Book with teacher support

Students to complete: Extended Practice activities, p. 5. Use number lines or charts to support students with rounding numbers as needed.

EXTENSION GROUP

Activity sheet

Students to complete: *Activity sheet 1: Number facts and fun.*

Practice and Mastery Book

The Practice and Mastery Book can be used as a homework activity or during class time. The Practice activities support the Independent Practice activities in the Student Book; the Challenge activities support the Extended Practice activities in the Student Book; and the Mastery activities allow students to demonstrate their proficiency by applying their knowledge in open-ended and/or real-life problem solving contexts.

Session 5: Post-assessment

Students to complete: Post-test 1, Unit 1, Topic 1, p. 73.

OXFORD UNIVERSITY PRESS

Unit 1 Number and place value
Topic 2 Odd and even

Student Book pages 6–9

Learning focus

Understand the properties of odd and even numbers and how this knowledge can help with calculations

Materials

- online random number generator
- variety of counting materials, such as counters and Unifix cubes
- two 6-sided dice
- base-10 materials (or an online interactive base-10 materials app – see link in session 2)
- calculators (optional)
- *BLM 16: Odd and even conditions*
- *Activity sheet 2: That's odd!*

Potential difficulties: Place value

If students don't have a sound understanding of place value, they may struggle with the idea that the ones column determines whether a number is odd or even.

- Use base-10 materials or other manipulatives, connected with written numbers, to reinforce the idea that all tens, hundreds and thousands by themselves (e.g. 20, 500, 7000) are always divisible by 2.
- Give students plenty of opportunities to physically investigate the odd and even properties of single-digit and larger numbers.

Daily practice activity

Collect numbers through the day as a class – for example, the number of library books the class borrowed, the number of characters in a particular book – and conduct a quick "odd or even" analysis of each, inviting students to share the rationale for their choices.

Session 1: Pre-assessment

Students to complete: Pre-test 1, Unit 1, Topic 2, p. 72.

Session 2: Topic introduction

WHOLE CLASS

Introductory activity: Odd and even concept

In mixed-ability pairs, ask students to discuss what an odd number is and how you can tell if a number is odd. Share ideas as a class and formulate a working definition of odd numbers. How are odd numbers different from even numbers? Write a brief definition of an even number together.

Access a random number generator. Generate a list of 3-digit numbers and allocate a number to each pair of students. Students should write down their number and predict whether the number is odd or even, then work out a way to check if their prediction is correct. Provide a variety of materials for students to use in their investigations. Each pair should prepare a poster or short presentation to prove whether their number is odd or even. Return to your working definitions of the two terms and ask students to suggest ways you could make the descriptions more accurate.

AT-STANDARD GROUP

Student Book

Students to complete: Guided and Independent Practice activities, pp. 6–8. Ask early finishers to roll two 6-sided dice and predict whether the sum of the numbers will be odd or even. Students should then calculate the answers to check if they were correct.

SUPPORT GROUP

Concept exploration and skill development: Are you odd?

Students need to understand that the digit in the ones column determines whether the number is odd or even. Model the number 5 and ask students whether it's odd or even – you can use either base-10 materials or an online interactive base-10 materials app. Invite a student to manipulate the blocks to prove to you that the number is odd. Add 4 tens to the number to make 45, then ask students if they think 45 is odd or even. Remind students that even numbers can be exactly halved, and model halving the 4 tens. Can they be evenly split into two groups? Can the remaining five blocks be evenly split into two groups? What does this tell students about whether the number is odd or even? Add 3 hundreds to the number to make 345 and repeat the process.

Can 300 be halved? If students are ready, add 6 thousands and repeat the process.

Write an even single-digit number on the board, such as 8, and ask students to predict if it's odd or even, then check together with base-10 materials. Add a ten to the front to make a number such as 48, and follow the same process. Keep building the number, checking each time to make sure it's still even. Ask students what this tells you about odd and even numbers, working through other examples to consolidate the concept as needed.

Student Book with teacher support

Students to complete: Guided Practice activities, p. 6, linking the examples with the activity that students have just completed, and using base-10 materials to reinforce their understanding as required.

EXTENSION GROUP

Student Book

Students to complete: Guided and Independent Practice activities, pp. 6–8.

Activity sheet

Students to begin: *Activity sheet 2: That's odd!*

Session 3: Instruction and consolidation

WHOLE CLASS

Topic exploration: Odd and even numbers in skip counting patterns

Revise odd and even numbers with students, then apply this knowledge to counting patterns. Make a statement such as, "I'm counting by four from 8. Will my next number be odd or even?" Designate one side of the room odd and the other even and ask students to position themselves according to their predictions. Select a student from the correct side to explain why they made their choice. Continue with more difficult statements that encourage students to think about particular number patterns. For example, "I'm counting by eight from 24. Will the fifth number I count be odd or even?" In mixed-ability pairs, ask students to write their own odd or even clues and choose some to try out with the whole class.

AT-STANDARD GROUP

Teacher activity: Exploring odd and even conditions

In pairs, give students *BLM 16: Odd and even conditions* and ask them to write a number sentence that meets each of the criteria listed, but not to write the answers. Instruct students to swap their sheet with another pair and work out the answers to the problems. (It may be appropriate for students to use

calculators for the more complex equations.) Students should then note whether the answers meet the criteria. Discuss the task as a group when students have finished, sharing strategies used for choosing numbers and for making the calculations.

Student Book

Students to complete: Extended Practice activities, p. 9.

SUPPORT GROUP

Student Book with teacher support

Students to complete: Independent and Extended Practice activities, pp. 7–9. Check in with students as they work through the Independent Practice activities, discussing any difficulties, before supporting them to complete the Extended Practice activities, using manipulatives to assist as needed.

EXTENSION GROUP

Student Book

Students to complete: Extended Practice activities, p. 9.

Activity sheet

Students to complete: *Activity sheet 2: That's odd!*

Practice and Mastery Book

See page 4 for information about how to use the Practice and Mastery Book activities.

Session 4: Post-assessment

Students to complete: Post-test 1, Unit 1, Topic 2, p. 73.

OXFORD UNIVERSITY PRESS

Unit 1 Number and place value
Topic 3 Addition mental strategies

Student Book pages 10–13

Learning focus

Explore and choose appropriate mental addition strategies and develop strategies for memorising addition number facts

Materials

- 14 pencils
- counters
- 10-frames (optional)
- blank pieces of card to write numbers on
- playing cards (with face cards and tens removed)
- *Activity sheet 3: Rounding, estimating and calculating*

Activity sheet materials

- a calculator

Potential difficulties: Too many strategies?

It can sometimes be overwhelming if students are exposed to a large range of strategies but don't have a solid understanding of how and when to use them.

- Encourage students to choose the method that they find easiest, and provide opportunities to consolidate their skills until they're confident with that strategy. Slowly extend the range of strategies as students master each one.
- Allow students to use concrete materials while they're learning a strategy. This will help them develop visualisation skills, which will ultimately build their proficiency with mental arithmetic.

Daily practice activity

Ask students to share their experiences of watching or playing a team sport such as basketball, football or cricket. Challenge students to add the final scores of both teams together in their heads. Encourage students to share the strategies they used to get the answer.

Session 1: Pre-assessment
Students to complete: Pre-test 2, Unit 1, Topic 3, p. 74.

Session 2: Topic introduction

WHOLE CLASS

Introductory activity: Choosing effective strategies

Write three sets of numbers on the board, such as 16 and 30, 32 and 18, and 6, 12 and 14. Direct students to look at the first pair and ask them to work out the answer in their heads. Students should then share their answer with a partner and discuss how they got it. Allow time for the strategies to be shared with the whole class and list them on the board. Repeat the process for the remaining sets of numbers, prompting students to recall a range of strategies including the jump strategy, doubles and near doubles and reordering numbers. Divide students into small, mixed-ability groups, and ask each group to choose one strategy and write instructions explaining how to use it and the combinations of numbers it would work best with. Groups may also include illustrations or diagrams. Display the responses as a guide for students to refer to.

Introductory activity: Memorising addition number facts

Being able to quickly access number facts can help students to focus on the operational aspects of addition, and it is therefore worthwhile taking the time to build their automatic recall in a systematic way. Write the number fact 1 + 1 on the board and ask students to suggest what the answer is. Repeat with 1 + 2, 1 + 3 and 1 + 4. What do students notice about the answers? Continue until you have reached 1 + 10 and invite students to share any patterns that they can see or anything interesting they notice, such as the fact that when two odd numbers are added the answer is even and when an odd and an even number is added, the answer is odd. In pairs, allocate students a number between 2 and 20 and ask them to make their own automatic recall chart for their given number. Students should highlight any patterns that they see with their own number, and add in any hints and tips they have for remembering particular addition number facts. Display the finished charts around the room.

AT-STANDARD GROUP

Student Book

Students to complete: Guided and Independent Practice activities, pp. 10–12. Ask early finishers to choose pairs of numbers from their answers to question 4 on p. 12 and choose appropriate strategies to add them mentally, recording the equations and their responses.

SUPPORT GROUP

Concept exploration and skill development: Getting to a 10

Choose two students to stand up. Give one student 8 pencils and the other 6 pencils, verbally describing what you are doing. Take two pencils from the student who has 6 and give them to the student who has 8. Ask students if the total number of pencils has changed. Write the original problem on the board (8 + 6) and the new problem (10 + 4) and give students a short period of time to work out the answers. Discuss which was quicker to calculate and why, to demonstrate how getting to a 10 can make mental calculations easier. Spend some time exploring the strategy with students using counters, with or without 10-frames, by adding 2-digit numbers with 1-digit numbers. When they have had some practice, challenge students by getting them to try the strategy without materials.

Student Book with teacher support

Students to complete: Guided Practice activities, p. 10. Link the rearranging of the numbers with the getting-to-10 strategy, helping students to identify pairs of numbers that get to a 10 more easily.

EXTENSION GROUP

Student Book

Students to complete: Guided and Independent Practice activities, pp. 10–12.

Activity sheet

Students to begin: *Activity sheet 3: Rounding, estimating and calculating.*

Session 3: Instruction and consolidation

WHOLE CLASS

Topic exploration: Splitting numbers

The idea of splitting numbers to add comes naturally to many students, but some will need explicit instruction and practice. To reinforce the concept, write a 2-digit addition problem, such as 25 + 13, on the board. Give one student two pieces of card and ask them to split the first number by place value and write the tens part on one card (20) and the ones on the other (5). Repeat with a different student for the second number. Invite four students to stand at the front of the room and hand one card to each of them. Order the students first according to the original numbers (20, 5, 10, 3), then ask them to regroup as tens and ones. Choose another student to add the tens and ones and find

the final answer. Repeat the activity with 3- and 4-digit numbers.

AT-STANDARD GROUP

Teacher activity: Building mental addition fluency

Have two students each draw three playing cards from a deck with the tens and face cards removed, to form two 3-digit numbers. Ask students to identify the lower of the two numbers. The aim is to use addition to get from the lower to the higher number in exactly five steps. Give students some time to find a solution, completing the calculations mentally, but writing down the steps they took. Allow students to share their answers, focusing on the strategies they used.

In pairs, ask students to continue the activity by each drawing three cards from their decks to form the two numbers to use each time. To make the activity more difficult, don't allow students to add numbers that end in a zero, or vary the number of steps required to get from one number to another. Encourage pairs to check and compare their responses and discuss why they chose to use particular numbers within their steps.

Student Book

Students to complete: Extended Practice activities, p. 13.

SUPPORT GROUP

Student Book with teacher support

Students to complete: Independent and Extended Practice activities, pp. 11–13. Check in with students as they work through the Independent Practice activities, discussing any difficulties, before supporting them to complete the Extended Practice activities, helping them identify appropriate strategies for each number set.

EXTENSION GROUP

Student Book

Students to complete: Extended Practice activities, p. 13.

Activity sheet

Students to complete: *Activity sheet 3: Rounding, estimating and calculating.*

Practice and Mastery Book

See page 4 for information about how to use the Practice and Mastery Book activities.

Session 4: Post-assessment

Students to complete: Post-test 2, Unit 1, Topic 3, p. 75.

OXFORD UNIVERSITY PRESS

Unit 1 Number and place value
Topic 4 Addition written strategies

Student Book pages 14–18

Learning focus

Explore and select efficient written addition strategies for solving addition problems

Materials

- A4 paper
- highlighters of different colours
- scissors
- glue
- base-10 materials
- class set of 10-sided dice
- Unifix cubes
- *BLM 4: Splitting sums*
- *BLM 5: Find the answers*
- *BLM 6: Addition place value chart*
- *Activity sheet 4: Working with large numbers*

Potential difficulties: Where to start

It can be counterintuitive to start calculations from the right when students begin working with vertical algorithms, as they're used to starting from the left with horizontal addition.

- Take the time to ensure students understand that starting from the right allows for trading and regrouping more easily. Use concrete materials to demonstrate how trading across columns works, recording each step as you go.

- Help students develop ways to remember how to approach vertical addition algorithms, highlighting that the smallest place value column is always the starting point. This will also support them when they come to add decimal numbers.

Daily practice activity

Have a race between students using different addition strategies, including written split strategy, vertical addition and mental strategies. Write an addition problem on the board and ask a different student to try each strategy. Compare speed and accuracy and discuss the kinds of problems that are suited to particular methods.

Session 1: Pre-assessment

Students to complete: Pre-test 2, Unit 1, Topic 4, p. 74.

Session 2: Topic introduction – Split strategy

WHOLE CLASS

Introductory activity: Commutative property

Students' understanding of the commutative property can help them understand how to rearrange numbers to make them easier to work with. Write a 3-digit addition problem on the board, such as 435 + 284. Ask students how to partition the first number by place value and write each of the separate numbers (400, 30 and 5) on an A4 piece of paper. Repeat with the second number, and also write five "+" signs on individual sheets of paper. Choose students to hold each number and sign, and ask them to stand across the front of the room to make an addition problem (i.e. number + number + number, etc.) with the numbers in any order. Invite a student to suggest how the numbers could be rearranged to make them easier to add, and physically rearrange the students holding the numbers in that order. Guide the class to carry out the calculation and record the answer.

Ask for another way that the numbers could be reorganised, and move the students into the selected order. Ask the class to predict what they think the answer to the new problem will be. Do they recognise that it will be the same? Carry out the calculation and compare the two answers. Ask students which order they found easiest to add, allowing for other suggestions and encouraging students to articulate why a particular arrangement was easier for them.

AT-STANDARD GROUP

Student Book

Students to complete: Guided and Independent Practice activities, pp. 14–15. Ask early finishers to recalculate their answers to question 1 on p. 15, by starting with the highest place value column instead of the ones. Students should check to see if they got the same answers.

SUPPORT GROUP

Concept exploration and skill development: Hands-on split strategy

As calculations become more complex, it's important to ensure that students understand the concepts underpinning the strategies they're using. Give each student *BLM 4: Splitting sums* and three different-coloured highlighters. Ask them to highlight the hundreds in each number in the first equation in one colour, the tens in another and the ones in a third colour. After checking they are correct, ask them to now cut out the hundreds digits. Discuss what these digits mean. Do students understand that the 1 is 100 and the 5 is 500? Ask students to cut two A4 pieces of paper in thirds lengthways and glue each hundreds digit on the left of a piece. Students can then write in the zeroes to represent the rest of the number. Repeat for the tens and ones numbers. Ask students to group their numbers according to place value and then write the new addition sum. Guide students to find the answer.

Follow the same process for the remaining two problems in BLM 4. Discuss the effect of regrouping in the second one, and examine what happens when students are splitting 4-digit numbers.

Student Book with teacher support

Students to complete: Guided Practice activities, p. 14. Support students by following the splitting sums process for any activities that they have difficulty with.

EXTENSION GROUP

Student Book

Students to complete: Guided and Independent Practice activities, pp. 14–15.

Activity sheet

Students to begin: *Activity sheet 4: Working with large numbers.*

Session 3: Topic introduction – Vertical algorithm

WHOLE CLASS

Topic exploration: Trade or no trade

Model a 2-digit plus 2-digit addition problem with trading in the ones column, such as 43 + 68, inviting students to suggest each step in the process. Talk them through what you are recording and why. You may want to use base-10 materials or model the process on an interactive whiteboard to help students visualise what to do.

Choose a student to roll two 10-sided dice and record the results as a 2-digit number, then repeat to get a second number. Write the two numbers as a vertical addition algorithm and ask students if they think you will need to trade, and how they

know. Complete the calculation as a class. If no trading was involved, repeat until you have worked through an example with trading. Split the class into two mixed-ability teams to play *Trade or no trade*. Each team rolls two 10-sided dice twice and records the resultant numbers one above the other on the board as a vertical addition algorithm. One player from each team must then suggest whether trading will be required to add their two numbers. If they are correct, they score a point. (There's no need to complete the calculations if the students can justify their responses, unless you want to.) As students become more proficient at identifying whether a trade is required, increase the number of digits in the numbers being used. You may also like to give bonus points if students identify when more than one trade would be required for a calculation. The first team to score seven points is the winner.

AT-STANDARD GROUP

Teacher activity: Experimenting with trading

Draw two sets of vertical additional algorithms to write two 3-digit numbers in on the whiteboard, as shown below.

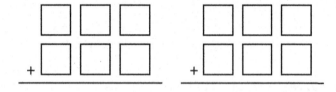

Explain that students will be playing against you to try and make the highest total possible. Roll a 10-sided dice and choose one of the boxes in the algorithm to write the number in. Articulate your thinking to students as you go, for example: "This is an 8, which is a fairly high number, so I am going to put it in the hundreds column". Choose a student to roll the dice and to place their digit in the other algorithm template. Continue playing until all six boxes in each algorithm are filled, then ask students to predict who won the game before totalling the numbers. Invite a student to add the students' numbers together, talking through what they're doing. Add your numbers together to see who won.

Instruct students to play the game in pairs, starting with making 3-digit numbers, then continuing to 4- and 5-digit numbers if they're able. You can also vary the rules by challenging students to make the lowest total possible, or by asking them to add three or four numbers together instead of two.

Student Book

Students to complete: Guided and Independent Practice activities, pp. 16–17.

OXFORD UNIVERSITY PRESS

SUPPORT GROUP

Student Book with teacher support

Students to complete: Independent Practice activities, p. 15, and Guided Practice activities, p. 16. Check in with students and work through the examples, supporting them with materials as required.

EXTENSION GROUP

Student Book

Students to complete: Guided and Independent Practice activities, pp. 16–17.

Activity sheet

Students to continue: *Activity sheet 4: Working with large numbers.*

Session 4: Instruction and consolidation

WHOLE CLASS

Topic application: Find the answers

This game will give students the opportunity to practise their reasoning, build fluency with addition and use the strategies they've learned. Divide students into mixed-ability pairs and ask them to find another pair to play against. To play *BLM 5: Find the answers*, the four students will need one set of the game cards between them (cut out), and one game board for each pair. Students should lay the game cards face down in a pile. The team with game board 1 takes the top card and works out the answer. If that answer is on their game board, they keep the card and put it on top of the correct number. If it's not, they return it to the bottom of the pile. Play continues until one team has their board covered. Encourage the pairs to discuss how to find the answer, and to choose the most efficient strategy for each problem, whether written or mental.

At the end of the session, ask students to share how they approached the game and the addition strategies that they used.

AT-STANDARD GROUP

Student Book

Students to complete: Extended Practice activities, p. 18. Ask early finishers to recalculate the examples in question 1 on p. 15 using a vertical algorithm, and to write about which method they found easier and why.

SUPPORT GROUP

Concept exploration and skill development: Consolidating vertical addition skills

The leap from mental addition to written addition requires a solid understanding of the concepts of adding and place value. Concrete materials are still useful at this stage to build students' understanding.

Give each student an enlarged copy of *BLM 6: Addition place value chart* and put one up on display. Write a single-digit addition problem on the board that involves trading, such as 8 + 5. Ask students to represent the numbers to be added using two Unifix cubes towers, and to place each set of cubes in the correct column of the place value chart, modelling with your copy at the front. Instruct students to join their two towers together and tell you the total. Ask them where the tower should go on the place value chart, guiding them to realise that we can't put more than 9 in any column, so ten of the cubes will need to be traded for 1 ten. Model this in the answer box, putting one Unifix cube in the tens section and 3 in the ones section.

Set students a similar one-digit problem to model and solve independently, then record the matching vertical algorithm as a group. Repeat with two-digit numbers involving no trading, and then with trading just in one column. You may like to move to adding hundreds, but be sure students are confident with modelling the problems and articulating the process before you do this.

Student Book with teacher support

Students to complete: Independent and Extended Practice activities, pp. 17–18, modelling the regrouping process as required.

EXTENSION GROUP

Student Book

Students to complete: Extended Practice activities, p. 18.

Activity sheet

Students to complete: *Activity sheet 4: Working with large numbers.*

Practice and Mastery Book

See page 4 for information about how to use the Practice and Mastery Book activities.

Session 5: Post-assessment

Students to complete: Post-test 2, Unit 1, Topic 4, p. 75.

Unit 1 Number and place value
Topic 5 Subtraction mental strategies

Student Book pages 19–22

Learning focus

Explore and choose appropriate mental subtraction strategies and develop strategies for memorising subtraction number facts

Materials

- counters and number charts
- interlocking cubes
- base-10 materials
- *BLM 10: Think board*
- *Activity sheet 5: Unlocking your subtraction skills*

Potential difficulties: Concept consolidation

It's important that students completely understand the concept of subtraction before they attempt subtraction with larger numbers.

- Start with smaller numbers to consolidate the concept before moving on to subtracting 2-digit numbers mentally. For example, ask students to try the compensation strategy with 13 take away 8 to demonstrate how it works using easily manageable numbers, with visual aids such as counters and number charts.
- As students' confidence grows, gradually decrease reliance on concrete materials and introduce larger numbers.

Daily practice activity

Instead of giving points for good behaviour or work, use subtraction as a class-management strategy. Give each group or individual 1000 points to start with, and subtract points as a reward. Students need to keep track of their own scores, with the aim of reaching zero.

Session 1: Pre-assessment

Students to complete: Pre-test 3, Unit 1, Topic 5, p. 76.

Session 2: Topic introduction

WHOLE CLASS

Introductory activity: Using the compensation strategy

Students may not have been explicitly taught the compensation strategy, although many may use it naturally in mental calculations. It's useful to begin with concrete materials so students develop an understanding of the strategy. In mixed-ability pairs, ask students to collect 24 interlocking cubes and organise them into two sticks of 10 and four loose cubes. Write the problem on the board: 24 – 9. Instruct students to take away one stick of 10 and ask them how many cubes are left. Discuss how many you have taken away and how many you needed to take away, and invite students to suggest what you could do to complete the equation. Ask students to explain the process to their partner.

Still in their pairs, give students *BLM 10: Think board* and pose a word problem for students to solve using the compensation strategy. For example: *Aminah blew 55 bubbles. 29 of them popped. How many are left?* Ask students to represent solving the problem with materials, by drawing it and with a number sentence. Discuss why the compensation strategy was a suitable choice for this problem, and what other strategies could have been used.

Introductory activity: Memorising subtraction number facts

Students often have more difficulty with subtraction facts than with addition facts, possibly because they are used less frequently. Linking subtraction facts with known addition facts can therefore be a good strategy to build students' fluency with subtraction. As a class, work to list the addition number facts from 1 + 1 through to 1 + 19. Discuss what the related subtraction facts are and list them next to the addition facts. Reinforce the idea that one addition fact can help students know two subtraction facts – for example, if they know 1 + 17 = 18, they also know both 18 – 1 = 17 and 18 – 17 = 1.

In pairs, have students construct a chart showing addition number facts for a number between 2 and 9, along with the two related subtraction facts. Allow time for students to share their work, and challenge them to link other number facts with known subtraction facts. For example, if students know that 18 – 1 = 17, can they tell you what 18 – 2 is?

OXFORD UNIVERSITY PRESS

AT-STANDARD GROUP

Student Book

Students to complete: Guided and Independent Practice activities, pp. 19–21. Ask early finishers to find the correct answers to any incorrect problems they identified in question 3 on p. 21, using a mental strategy of their choice.

SUPPORT GROUP

Concept exploration and skill development: Empty number lines

Empty number lines are a good tool to help students move from concrete representations of subtraction to performing calculations in the abstract. Write a subtraction problem on the board, such as 34 – 13, and give students time to work out the answer. Select a student to describe how they solved the problem, illustrating their strategy on an empty number line as they articulate it. Allow students who used different strategies to also share their thinking, modelling their approaches on an empty number line to compare the process and the answer. Write some more problems on the board for students to solve in pairs on an empty number line, and share strategies and responses when they have finished.

Student Book with teacher support

Students to complete: Guided Practice activities, p. 19, modelling the problems with base-10 materials as needed.

EXTENSION GROUP

Student Book

Students to complete: Guided and Independent Practice activities, pp. 19–21.

Activity sheet

Students to begin: *Activity sheet 5: Unlocking your subtraction skills.*

Session 3: Instruction and consolidation

WHOLE CLASS

Topic exploration: Exploring mental subtraction strategies

Brainstorm subtraction strategies that students are familiar with and discuss each one. Write three subtraction problems on the board, such as 485 – 39 =, 537 – 526 =, and 753 – 512 =. In mixed-ability pairs, ask students to work out the answer to each problem using two different strategies, and record what they did with words, diagrams or number sentences. Allow time for students to discuss which strategies they found easier for each problem and why.

AT-STANDARD GROUP

Teacher activity: Building mental subtraction fluency

Students tend to be more familiar with mental addition than mental subtraction. Giving them lots of opportunities to practise their mental subtraction skills will help build fluency. Call out a subtraction "fact" such as 23 take away 14 is 9 (or write it on the board, if students in the group have short term-memory issues). Give students some time to think. If they believe the answer is correct, they should raise both hands and shout "Bingo!", but if they think it's incorrect, they should cross their arms and shout "No bingo!" Give further examples using combinations of numbers that lend themselves to particular strategies. Invite students to prove why their decision was correct by explaining the strategy they used.

Student Book

Students to complete: Extended Practice activities, p. 22.

SUPPORT GROUP

Student Book with teacher support

Students to complete: Independent and Extended Practice activities, pp. 20–22. Check in with students as they work through the Independent Practice activities, discussing any difficulties, before supporting them to complete the Extended Practice activities, helping students choose appropriate strategies and using visual tools such as empty number lines as appropriate.

EXTENSION GROUP

Student Book

Students to complete: Extended Practice activities, p. 22.

Activity sheet

Students to complete: *Activity sheet 5: Unlocking your subtraction skills.*

Practice and Mastery Book

See page 4 for information about how to use the Practice and Mastery Book activities.

Session 4: Post-assessment

Students to complete: Post-test 3, Unit 1, Topic 5, p. 77.

Unit 1 Number and place value

Topic 6 Subtraction written strategies

Student Book pages 23–27

Learning focus

Explore and select efficient written subtraction strategies for solving subtraction problems

Materials

- base-10 materials
- six 10-sided dice
- playing cards from ace to 9 (one set per pair)
- Unifix cubes
- *BLM 13: Digit cards* (two copies photocopied onto card and cut out)
- *BLM 14: Subtraction ladders*
- *BLM 15: Subtraction place value chart*
- *Activity sheet 6: Using your subtraction skills*

Potential difficulties: Regrouping

Understanding regrouping can be a stumbling block for students as they work towards calculating with larger numbers.

- Avoid the temptation to take away concrete materials too early, and help students articulate their thinking as they tackle problems.
- Continue to offer activities that build students' understanding of the underlying place value concepts until they can fluently regroup numbers in multiple ways.

Daily practice activity

Each day, ask students to look at the total number of pages in the book they are currently reading, and to subtract the number of pages they have read so far to find out how many are left. You could also do this as a class if you're reading a class novel together.

Session 1: Pre-assessment

Students to complete: Pre-test 3, Unit 1, Topic 6, p. 76.

Session 2: Topic introduction – Split strategy

WHOLE CLASS

Introductory activity: Exploring the split strategy

This activity supports students' understanding of place value in the context of the split strategy. On the board, write a 3-digit subtraction equation that doesn't involve regrouping, such as 548 – 325. Make the two numbers by choosing six students to hold one each of the digits from *BLM 13: Digit cards*, emphasising the correct place value language as you do, e.g. "You are the 500, you are the 40 and you are the 8". Invite students to suggest the first step using the split strategy, and have the "hundreds" from the first number step forward and state what their number is, i.e. 500 rather than 5. Choose a student to work out 500 – 300, recording the equation on the board, and replacing the 5 in the original number with a 2 representing 200. Repeat with the other place values until you have arrived at the final answer, "taking away" the digit cards from the students as you go.

Practise as a class with equations that involve regrouping/trading, and work up to modelling the problems with 4-digit numbers. In pairs, encourage students to discuss the process they had to follow to use the split strategy.

AT-STANDARD GROUP

Student Book

Students to complete: Guided and Independent Practice activities, pp. 23–24. Ask early finishers to write three subtraction word problems and swap with a partner to solve them.

SUPPORT GROUP

Concept exploration and skill development: Reinforcing the split strategy

For students who are struggling with the split strategy, a subtraction ladder with concrete materials can provide good visual reinforcement. Show students an enlarged copy of *BLM 14: Subtraction ladders* and write a 2-digit subtraction problem above the first ladder, such as 56 – 37. Invite a student to make both numbers in the problem using base-10 materials, and ask the rest of the students in the group to identify how you would split 37 by place value. How many tens are there? Choose a different student to take the correct amount of tens away from the base-10 model of 56 and discuss the number that remains. Write this stage of the calculation on the subtraction ladder (see below). Repeat with the ones to find the final answer, again recording the amount taken away, as well as the answer, on the bottom rung of the ladder. Is the number at the bottom larger or smaller than the number at the top? Why?

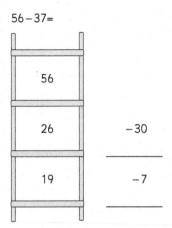

$56 - 37 =$

In pairs, give students their own copy of BLM 14 and set another 2-digit subtraction problem for them to solve using the same process, including modelling with base-10 materials. Monitor how they're going before giving them further 2- and then 3-digit examples to try.

Student Book with teacher support

Students to complete: Guided and Independent Practice activities, pp. 23–24, drawing a subtraction ladder with an extra rung to support students if required.

EXTENSION GROUP

Student Book

Students to complete: Guided and Independent Practice activities, pp. 23–24.

Activity sheet

Students to begin: *Activity sheet 6: Using your subtraction skills.*

Session 3: Topic introduction – Vertical algorithm

WHOLE CLASS

Topic exploration: Trade or no trade

Model a 2-digit minus 2-digit subtraction problem with trading in the ones column, such as 72 – 38, and invite students to suggest each step in the process. Talk them through what you're recording and why. You may want to use base-10 materials or model the process on an interactive whiteboard to help students visualise what to do.

Choose a student to roll three 10-sided dice and record the numbers rolled as a 3-digit number,

then repeat with two 10-sided dice to get a 2-digit number. Write both numbers as a vertical subtraction algorithm, asking students how to align the numbers in place value columns. Ask students if they think you'll need to trade, and how they know. Complete the calculation as a class, talking through how to correctly record each step. If no trading was involved, repeat until you have worked through an example with trading.

Split the class into two teams to play *Trade or no trade*. Each team rolls three 10-sided dice to get a 3-digit number and then two 10-sided dice to get a 2-digit number, and records the numbers as a vertical subtraction algorithm on the board. One player from each team must say "Trade" or "No trade" to indicate whether trading will be required to complete the subtraction calculation. If they're correct, they score a point. (There's no need to complete the calculations if the students can justify their responses.) As students become more proficient at identifying whether a trade is required, increase the number of digits in the numbers being used. If students are coping well, you may also like to give bonus points if they identify when more than one trade is required. The winning team is the first to score seven points.

AT-STANDARD GROUP

Teacher activity: Experimenting with vertical subtraction

In pairs, give students a set of playing cards from ace to 9 (ace is equal to 1). Ask each pair to draw three cards from their set to form a 3-digit number, such as 674. Next, reverse the number to make a second number, e.g. 476, and then make a vertical subtraction algorithm with the larger number at the top, e.g. 674 – 476. Ask each pair to work out the answer, then use that new number to form a second number by reversing the digits and repeating the subtraction process. Students continue until they reach zero.

Bring the group back together to see who needed the greatest amount of steps to reach zero, and check the calculations as a group. Extend students' thinking by trying the activity with 4-digit numbers.

Student Book

Students to complete: Guided and Independent Practice activities, pp. 25–26.

SUPPORT GROUP

Student Book with teacher support

Students to complete: Guided Practice activities, p. 25, using concrete materials and assisting with recording as needed.

EXTENSION GROUP

Student Book

Students to complete: Guided and Independent Practice activities, pp. 25–26.

Activity sheet

Students to continue: *Activity sheet 6: Using your subtraction skills.*

Session 4: Instruction and consolidation

WHOLE CLASS

Topic exploration: Applying subtraction skills

Open-ended problems give students the opportunity to access the task at their level of understanding. Give students a contextualised problem, such as the following:

My next-door neighbour left some cookies for the school fete on my doorstep. Unfortunately, before I got home from work, some birds got into the packaging and ate a lot of the cookies. There are 113 left, but I know she was planning to bake at least 200. How many might there have been in the first place, and how many might the birds have eaten?

In pairs, ask students to find as many answers to the problem as they can within a defined time period, recording their workings out. Allow time for each pair to share their responses with another pair. As a class, discuss the different strategies students used to solve the problem.

AT-STANDARD GROUP

Student Book

Students to complete: Extended Practice activities, p. 27. Ask early finishers to plan a 5000 km journey from where they live, using the internet to research possible destinations, and recording subtraction calculations to show how many kilometres they would have left to travel after each stop along the way.

SUPPORT GROUP

Concept exploration and skill development: Consolidating vertical subtraction

As with addition, concrete materials can be used effectively alongside the vertical algorithm for subtraction to support students' understanding of place value and regrouping. Give each student *BLM 15: Subtraction place value chart* and put one up on display. Write a simple 2-digit subtraction problem on the board that involves trading, such as 31 – 17. Model writing the two numbers as a vertical subtraction problem on your place value chart, and make each number with Unifix cubes, then ask the students to do the same. Next, ask students where you start in vertical subtraction, and what the first

calculation will be. Discuss the fact that since you can't subtract 7 from 1, you'll have to take 1 ten from the tens column and break it into 10 ones to place in the ones column. Guide students to do this with their Unifix cubes, and discuss how to record it. Complete the rest of the calculation together, both with the Unifix cubes and in writing.

Set students a similar 2-digit problem to model and solve independently, recording the matching vertical algorithm as they go. Repeat with 3-digit numbers involving no trading, and then with trading just in one column. If students are coping well, you may like to move to subtracting thousands, but be sure that they are confident with modelling the problems and articulating the process before you do this.

Student Book with teacher support

Students to complete: Independent and Extended Practice activities, pp. 26–27, using subtraction place value charts and concrete materials to support students' understanding as needed.

EXTENSION GROUP

Student Book

Students to complete: Extended Practice activities, p. 27.

Activity sheet

Students to complete: *Activity sheet 6: Using your subtraction skills.*

Practice and Mastery Book

See page 4 for information about how to use the Practice and Mastery Book activities.

Session 5: Post-assessment

Students to complete: Post-test 3, Unit 1, Topic 6, p. 77.

OXFORD UNIVERSITY PRESS

Unit 1 Number and place value
Topic 7 Multiplication and division facts

Student Book pages 28–31

Learning focus

Explore the connection between multiplication and division and develop strategies for memorising multiplication and division facts

Materials

- counters, grid paper, craft sticks, glue
- decks of playing cards with face cards removed
- large pieces of paper
- craft materials such as glitter, sequins, small mosaic squares
- paper supermarket catalogues or access to an online supermarket catalogue
- *BLM 20: 10-frames*
- *Activity sheet 7: Getting organised*

Activity sheet materials

- a large piece of paper

Potential difficulties: Dividing by zero

Although it's important to understand that multiplication and division are inverse operations, this can cause confusion when a zero is involved. Students may recognise that 4×2 is 8 and $8 \div 2$ is 4, and then assume that because 3×0 is 0, $0 \div 0$ is 3.

- Discuss the effect of multiplying and dividing by zero and emphasise how this is similar and different to operations with whole numbers.
- Concrete materials can demonstrate to students that if they start with nothing, they can't divide it and end up with an answer such as 3.

Daily practice activity

Ask students to identify representations of multiplication or division facts in your immediate environment and share them each day. For example, the windows in your classroom might show that 4×2 is 8 and the lockers might show that 20 bags divided by 10 is 2. List the facts on a class chart.

Session 1: Pre-assessment

Students to complete: Pre-test 4, Unit 1, Topic 7, p. 78.

Session 2: Topic introduction

WHOLE CLASS

Introductory activity: Using multiplication facts for division

Take time to ensure that students understand why multiplication and division are inverse operations. This will help them apply this knowledge in unfamiliar situations. Write a statement on the board such as, "If $8 \times 10 = 80$, then $80 \div 8 = 10$". In mixed-ability pairs, challenge students to prove whether the statement is true. Provide a range of materials, such as counters, grid paper and *BLM 20: 10-frames* for students to use. Discuss their findings as a group, then ask students if they can suggest one more related multiplication and division fact, using their materials as a visual model. Connect the concept to number facts that the students already know to find related multiplication and division facts.

AT-STANDARD GROUP

Student Book

Students to complete: Guided and Independent Practice activities, pp. 28–30. Ask early finishers to find a partner and collect a deck of playing cards with the face cards removed. Students turn over two cards at a time and give the related multiplication fact, including the answer. The first to identify the correct fact and answer gets to keep the cards. Once the students have gone through the entire deck, the one with the most cards is the winner.

SUPPORT GROUP

Concept exploration and skill development: Exploring related number facts

For students who are less confident with numbers and number facts, it's important to continue using concrete materials to reinforce their understanding. Write a multiplication problem on the board, such as 3 groups of 5 is 15, and ask students to model it using craft sticks. Do students make the groups in piles, or organise the sticks in an array? Model setting the sticks out in an array with 3 columns and 5 rows, talking through how to do this by lining up the sticks both vertically and horizontally.

Introduce the idea that multiplication is commutative – i.e. the order doesn't make any difference. This means that the answer to 5 × 3 will be the same as the answer to 3 × 5 so if students know one multiplication fact, they get another one free!

Look at the division facts that the array shows. Ask students what 15 divided by 5 is, inviting one student to show you on the array. What about 15 divided by 3?

Ask pairs of students to make arrays to show some other multiplication or division facts using their knowledge of inverse operations, such as 6 groups of 3 or 28 divided by 7. For each one, discuss the other multiplication and division facts that are also represented by the array.

Student Book with teacher support

Students to complete: Guided Practice activities, p. 28. Link the examples with the activity that the students have just completed, allowing them to model the arrays with concrete materials if required.

EXTENSION GROUP

Student Book

Students to complete: Guided and Independent Practice activities, pp. 28–30.

Activity sheet

Students to begin: *Activity sheet 7: Getting organised.*

Session 3: Instruction and consolidation

WHOLE CLASS

Topic exploration: Remembering difficult facts

There are often one or two number facts that students have trouble getting into their heads. Ask each child to nominate a multiplication fact they have difficulty remembering. It doesn't matter if several students choose the same fact – it may be one that many children struggle with. Ask each student to write their fact on a large sheet of paper. Provide a variety of materials, such as glitter, sequins, small mosaic tiles, and have students decorate the numbers and symbols in the fact to make it stand out. Students might also like to draw an array or represent the number fact in another visual way. Display the finished pieces or send them home to help the students remember their facts.

Topic exploration: Using number facts

Show students a supermarket catalogue online or give pairs of students a copy of the same paper catalogue. Turn to a particular page and choose an item that has a price in whole dollars of $10 or less and ask students to tell you as quickly as they can how much it would cost to buy 5 of them. How about

8 of them? Repeat with several other items in the catalogue. Return to the original page you chose and nominate a dollar amount that represents a multiple of one of the items. For example, if there is an item for $6, you might suggest a total price of $24. Challenge students to find the item you are thinking of and to tell you how many of it you could buy with that amount as quickly as they can.

For further practice, ask pairs of students to make a shopping list for another group to identify prices and quantities. The list should include items and quantities for students to work out how much multiples of an item would cost, and totals for students to work out how many of a particular item were bought.

AT-STANDARD GROUP

Teacher activity: Doubling and doubling again

As students learn their multiplication facts, it's helpful for them to have some strategies they can use if they forget one. One method is using doubles facts as a base, as most students have good recall of these. Provide counters and ask students to show 2 groups of 2 as an array. Next, ask them to make 4 groups of 2 underneath and compare the two representations. Can they identify that the second group is double the first? Extend this idea to show that fours facts are double the twos facts, using concrete materials to consolidate the concept. Ask questions such as, "If 2 times 5 is 10, what will 4 times 5 be?" Challenge more capable students to consider that the eight facts are the twos facts doubled, then doubled again, and have them represent the fact sets with counter arrays.

Student Book

Students to complete: Extended Practice activities, p. 31.

SUPPORT GROUP

Student Book with teacher support

Students to complete: Independent and Extended Practice activities, pp. 29–31. Check in with students as they work on the Independent Practice activities, discussing any difficulties, before supporting them to complete the Extended Practice activities, talking through the requirements of each question and modelling with concrete materials as needed.

EXTENSION GROUP

Student Book

Students to complete: Extended Practice activities, p. 31.

Activity sheet

Students to complete: *Activity sheet 7: Getting organised.*

Practice and Mastery Book

See page 4 for information about how to use the Practice and Mastery Book activities.

Session 4: Post-assessment

Students to complete: Post-test 4, Unit 1, Topic 7, p. 79.

OXFORD UNIVERSITY PRESS

Unit 1 Number and place value
Topic 8 Multiplication written strategies
Student Book pages 32–36

Learning focus

Describe and choose appropriate written multiplication strategies such as extended multiplication to solve problems involving 1- and 2-digit numbers

Materials

- large pieces of paper
- 10-sided dice
- video cameras or tablets
- base-10 materials
- virtual base-10 materials (optional)
- manipulatives such as Unifix cubes
- *BLM 24: Tens cards*
- *BLM 25: Contracted multiplication game*
- *Activity sheet 8: Using your multiplication skills*

Activity sheet materials

- a calculator (optional)

Potential difficulties: Multiplicative thinking

Many students need help making the transition from additive thinking, which often sees students rely on strategies such as repeated addition, to multiplicative thinking, which allows more flexible manipulation of numbers and groupings.

- Give students time to work through multiplication problems, allowing them to verbally explain the steps and to represent them with materials.

- Build students' knowledge of number facts and number patterns to enable greater fluency when working with multiplication problems.

Daily practice activity

Each day, give students a multiplication word problem that relates to their daily lives. For example, if there are 24 students in your class, ask them to work out how many pencils there would be if each student was given a box of 6. Give students the opportunity to work out the answer with a partner, then share their responses as a class.

Session 1: Pre-assessment

Students to complete: Pre-test 5, Unit 1, Topic 8, p. 80.

Session 2: Topic introduction – Extended multiplication

WHOLE CLASS

Introductory activity: Beginning with extended multiplication

Students need to be familiar with extended multiplication before introducing contracted multiplication, as it reinforces the role of place value in the calculation. Write a 1-digit by 2-digit multiplication problem on the board, such as 3×32, and ask students to talk with a partner about how they would solve it. Share students' strategies as a class. Rewrite the problem in a vertical layout on a large piece of paper and explain that splitting the larger number by place value can make it easier to multiply. Show students an online number expander and enter the number 32 with the expander closed. Click to open the expander and explain that the first step in expanded multiplication is to multiply by the rightmost column, which in this case is the ones. Invite a student to tell you what 3 times 2 ones is, and to record the answer immediately below the multiplication problem. Repeat with the next step, emphasising that you are multiplying 3 by 3 tens, and invite a different student to record the answer. Allow a third student to add the two answers together to get the final total. Repeat the activity using another number.

Write two more examples on the board, such as 5×42 and 6×57. Ask students to work in pairs to lay out and then complete each problem. Talk through the process for each problem as a class, again reinforcing the place value elements of the calculation.

AT-STANDARD GROUP

Student Book

Students to complete: Guided and Independent Practice activities, pp. 32–33. Ask early finishers to write word problems to match the calculations in questions 1a–f on p. 33.

SUPPORT GROUP

Concept exploration and skill development: Practising with multiples of 10

Students need fluency in multiplying by multiples of 10 before they start to learn extended multiplication and other formal multiplication strategies. Write 5 problems that involve multiples of 10 on the board, including their answers, such as $3 \times 40 = 120$, $5 \times 80 = 400$ and $4 \times 50 = 200$. Ask students to suggest what they notice about the equations, prompting them to recognise that each one has a smaller multiplication problem within it, e.g. $3 \times 4 = 12$. Write another problem, such as 2×60 on the board, without its answer, and invite a student to underline the first number in each part of the problem. What do you get when you multiply those two numbers? How can this help you get the final answer?

Take a set of *BLM 24: Tens cards* and a 10-sided dice. Choose a student to turn over the top card and roll the dice, then multiply the two numbers together. Record the equation and its answer on the board. Put students into pairs and have them practise their extended multiplication facts in the same way.

Student Book with teacher support

Students to complete: Guided Practice activities, p. 32. Support students by rewriting the equations using extended number facts as needed.

EXTENSION GROUP

Student Book

Students to complete: Guided and Independent Practice activities, pp. 32–33.

Activity sheet

Students to begin: *Activity sheet 8: Using your multiplication skills.*

Session 3: Topic introduction – Contracted multiplication

WHOLE CLASS

Topic exploration: Comparing extended and contracted multiplication

On a large piece of paper, use contracted multiplication to work through the same 1-digit by 2-digit multiplication problem that you used in the session 2 class activity, such as 3×32. Talk through each stage of the calculation, and as with extended multiplication, emphasise that in the second stage you are actually multiplying 3 by 30, not by 3. Bring out the piece of paper you recorded the problem on when using extended multiplication and ask students to suggest similarities between the two methods, and then differences, listing their ideas on the board.

Write another multiplication problem on the board, such as 6×45. Ask students to solve it in pairs, first using extended multiplication, and then using contracted multiplication. Did they get the same answer for both? Repeat with another example, then

encourage students to discuss what they learned about both methods.

AT-STANDARD GROUP

Teacher activity: Practising contracted multiplication

Display two enlarged copies of *BLM 25: Contracted multiplication game board* and play a game against the students. The aim of the game is to have the highest answer possible. Invite a student to roll a 10-sided dice and write the number in one of the three shaded squares on the game board. Take your turn at rolling the dice and recording the number on your game board. Continue play until each of you has your three shaded squares filled, then work through the calculations to find the answers. The player with the highest answer scores a point.

In pairs, give students BLM 25 and ask them to play the game against each other. When they've finished, discuss the strategies they used to ensure they had the highest answer possible.

Student Book

Students to complete: Guided and Independent Practice activities, pp. 34–35.

SUPPORT GROUP

Student Book with teacher support

Students to complete: Independent Practice activities, p. 33 and Guided Practice activities, p. 34. Work through the examples supported by materials as required.

EXTENSION GROUP

Student Book

Students to complete: Guided and Independent Practice activities, pp. 34–35.

Activity sheet

Students to continue: *Activity sheet 8: Using your multiplication skills.*

Session 4: Instruction and consolidation

WHOLE CLASS

Topic application: Explaining extended multiplication

Having to explain a mathematical concept to someone else is an effective way of consolidating it in your own mind. Put students into small groups and ask them to make a video explaining how to do contracted multiplication. Make concrete materials such as base-10 materials, Unifix cubes and other manipulatives available, and encourage students to be creative. When they've finished, organise a screening for parents or another class.

OXFORD UNIVERSITY PRESS

AT-STANDARD GROUP

Student Book

Students to complete: Extended Practice activities, p. 36. Ask early finishers to find a partner and use BLM 25 to play a game where the object is to get the lowest answer possible.

SUPPORT GROUP

Concept exploration and skill development: Consolidating contracted multiplication skills

Before students are ready to tackle multiplication with larger numbers, it's important to consolidate their understanding with 1- and 2-digit numbers. Write a multiplication problem on the board, such as 4×22, and invite a student to model it with concrete materials or virtual base-10 materials. Do students try to model the 4 and the 22, or do they understand that the problem means 4 groups of 22? Guide the students to make 4 groups of 22 if they haven't already, then talk about how to find the final answer. Invite a student to rearrange the materials so the tens are together and the ones are together. What is the total? Work through the same problem on the board using contracted multiplication, linking each step to what was done with the base-10 materials.

Write another problem on the board, such as 3×45, and ask pairs of students to model it in the same way with base-10 materials. Check that everyone has made three groups of 45, then ask them to talk you through the next step. Keep working through the problem with materials until it has been solved, then ask the students to write a contracted multiplication version. Repeat with other problems to build students' understanding.

Student Book with teacher support

Students to complete: Independent and Extended Practice activities, pp. 35–36, using base-10 materials to model the problems as required.

EXTENSION GROUP

Student Book

Students to complete: Extended Practice activities, p. 36.

Activity sheet

Students to complete: *Activity sheet 8: Using your multiplication skills.*

Practice and Mastery Book

See page 4 for information about how to use the Practice and Mastery Book activities.

Session 5: Post-assessment

Students to complete: Post-test 5, Unit 1, Topic 8, p. 81.

Unit 1 Number and place value
Topic 9 Division written strategies
Student Book pages 37–40

Learning focus

Describe and choose appropriate written division strategies such as short division to solve problems involving 1- and 2-digit numbers

Materials

- 10-sided dice
- poster paper or tablet
- base-10 materials
- scissors
- *BLM 30: Division and multiplication Venn diagram*
- *BLM 31: Missing number division*
- *BLM 32: Division think board*
- *BLM 33: Sequencing division*
- *Activity sheet 9: Share and share alike*

Potential difficulties: Concept consolidation

Students sometimes need extra support to develop their understanding of division from solely repeated subtraction, or sharing out amounts singly, to being able to conceptualise the groups, allowing them to more fluently calculate with division.

- Scaffold students' understanding by using appropriate language, such as describing 6 ÷ 3 as "How many groups of 3 in 6?", supporting them with visual aids such as manipulatives and number lines.
- Explicitly link division and multiplication as inverse operations to help students see the connection, e.g. 2 groups of 3 is 6 and 6 divided by 3 is 2.

Daily practice activity

Each day, ask a student to give you a random 2-digit number, which will be the dividend. Roll a 10-sided dice to find the divisor. In pairs, students can use any method they like to work out if the 1-digit number divides evenly into the 2-digit number. Share students' answers and their strategies.

Session 1: Pre-assessment

Students to complete: Pre-test 5, Unit 1, Topic 9, p. 80.

Session 2: Topic introduction

WHOLE CLASS

Introductory activity: Written division calculations

Draw a division bracket (see below) on the board and ask students if they know what it is. Have they seen it used before? Represent a division problem that will have no remainder, such as 36 ÷ 2, using the symbol:

$$2\overline{)3\ 6}$$

Explain that although the symbol does not have an official mathematical name, the numbers represented on it do. The number inside the symbol is called the dividend and the number outside the symbol is the divisor. Write these terms on the board and give pairs of students time to discuss what they think they mean. As a class, write a brief definition of each. Work through the short division process to find the answer to 36 ÷ 2, linking the trading aspects with what students know about written methods for other mathematical operations.

Have each pair prepare a poster or digital presentation to explain the short division process for a problem such as 36 ÷ 4, which does not have a remainder. Encourage students to label the different parts of their algorithm with the terms they've just learnt, then allow them to share their work.

AT-STANDARD GROUP

Student Book

Students to complete: Guided and Independent Practice activities, pp. 37–38. Ask early finishers to work in pairs and describe how the process would be different if they were dividing a 1-digit number into a 3-digit number. The pairs should then add 200 to each dividend in Guided Practice questions 1a, b & c on p. 37, and try to solve the problems using short division.

SUPPORT GROUP

Concept exploration and skill development: Modelling division

As with other concepts, concrete materials are important in helping students understand division in a more abstract written form. Write a simple division

OXFORD UNIVERSITY PRESS

problem on the board that does not involve trading, such as 64 ÷ 2. Invite a student to rewrite the problem as a short division algorithm, reinforcing what the divisor and dividend are and where to place them. Give pairs of students base-10 materials and ask them to make 64. Remind them that for short division, you start with the tens, then ask them to divide the tens into two groups. How many tens are in each group? Where do we record this? Repeat with the ones.

If students are coping well, show them question 2a from the Guided Practice activities on p. 37 (75 ÷ 5), which involves trading. Have them make the larger number with base-10 materials, then ask them which part of the number to divide first. Instruct students to divide their tens into five equal groups, then ask what they should do with the leftover tens. How could they divide these into five groups? Guide students to trade the two leftover tens for 20 ones and show them how to record this part of the calculation on the algorithm. Then complete the calculation and record the final answer.

Student Book with teacher support

Students to complete: Guided Practice activities, p. 37, using base-10 materials to support their working as needed.

EXTENSION GROUP

Student Book

Students to complete: Guided and Independent Practice activities, pp. 37–38.

Activity sheet

Students to begin: *Activity sheet 9: Share and share alike.*

Session 3: Instruction and consolidation

WHOLE CLASS

Topic exploration: Multiplication and division

To consolidate students' understanding of the short division algorithm, it can be useful to compare it with the multiplication process. Briefly revise the contracted multiplication process, using a simple 1-digit by 2-digit problem, such as 4 × 37. Put students into small groups and give each group an enlarged copy of *BLM 30: Division and multiplication Venn diagram*. The groups should discuss and record the similarities and differences between the two processes. When they have finished, allow time for each group to make a short presentation of their ideas. Consolidate these into a whole-class Venn diagram and display it in the classroom.

Topic exploration: Solving division problems

Word problems can be a challenge for students learning written division methods, as they require identification and correct placement of the divisor

and the dividend. Present students with a word problem such as, "I bought a jar with 96 jelly beans in it. If I am sharing them equally between 6 people, how many will each receive?" Allow students to work on the problem individually for five minutes, then invite them to partner up and check the way they have laid out the division algorithm and their answers. As a class, ask how they knew where to place the numbers. Challenge students to find other numbers that the jelly beans could be divided equally into and have them represent their solutions using a division algorithm.

AT-STANDARD GROUP

Teacher activity: Missing number division

Missing number activities can be a good way to consolidate students' understanding of a concept, and to uncover any misconceptions. Show students an enlarged copy of *BLM 31: Missing number division* and talk through the first question together. What do you need to know in order to find the answer? What process will you use? How will you know you have it right? In pairs, ask students to complete the remaining examples, allowing collaboration between groups. Share students' answers at the end of the session, prompting them to justify their reasoning and to explain the processes they used.

Student Book

Students to complete: Independent Practice activities, p. 39.

SUPPORT GROUP

Student Book with teacher support

Students to complete: Independent Practice activities, pp. 38–39. Discuss any areas of difficulty and support students to complete the activities, using base-10 materials to model the problems as needed.

EXTENSION GROUP

Student Book

Students to complete: Independent Practice activities, p. 39.

Activity sheet

Students to continue: *Activity sheet 9: Share and share alike.*

Session 4: Instruction and consolidation

WHOLE CLASS

Topic exploration: Refining division skills

It's important that students can link the written division algorithm with what they already know about division. Show students an enlarged copy of *BLM 32: Division think board* and write a horizontal division problem, such as 56 ÷ 4, in the centre. Start with the Short division box and work through rewriting and solving the problem using short division. Ask students what multiplication facts helped them solve the problem, and what multiplication problems their knowledge of inverse operations can now help them solve. Record these in the Related multiplication facts box. Repeat this process to complete the Related division facts box. Finally, ask students to suggest a word problem that matches the equation and record this in the Word problem box.

Give students (in pairs or individually) BLM 32 and ask them to fill in the boxes to solve a division problem that you set them (choose one that has no remainders). You may like to extend students to try a 3-digit divided by 1-digit problem, either giving the whole class the same problem, or tailoring the problems to where students are at. Finish by inviting students to share everything they know about division.

AT-STANDARD GROUP

Student Book

Students to complete: Extended Practice activities, p. 40. Ask early finishers to write their own missing number division problems and swap with a partner to solve.

SUPPORT GROUP

Concept exploration and skill development: Sequencing the division process

This activity aims to reinforce the order of the steps in the short division process. Give pairs of students a copy of *BLM 33: Sequencing division* and have them cut out the cards. Ask students to remind you what the key terms mean – dividend, divisor, and divide. How are they similar? How are they different? Write a horizontal division problem on the board, such as 84 ÷ 7, and ask students to sequence the six steps on their cards as they solve it. You may want to start by asking students to describe what the first step would be and what would come next. When everyone has finished, ask each pair to team up with another pair and compare their order. If there are any differences, the pairs should talk through the calculation to try and sort out the correct order. Invite the students to tell you how to do short division in their own words, using their cards as prompts.

Student Book with teacher support

Students to complete: Extended Practice activities, p. 40, supporting students to set out the problems and work through the steps to solve them as needed.

EXTENSION GROUP

Student Book

Students to complete: Extended Practice activities, p. 40.

Activity sheet

Students to complete: *Activity sheet 9: Share and share alike.*

Practice and Mastery Book

See page 4 for information about how to use the Practice and Mastery Book activities.

Session 5: Post-assessment

Students to complete: Post-test 5, Unit 1, Topic 9, p. 81.

OXFORD UNIVERSITY PRESS

Unit 2 Fractions and decimals
Topic 1 Equivalent fractions

Student Book pages 41–44

Learning focus

Write and compare fractions, and model and identify equivalent fractions

Materials

- sheets of white paper
- interlocking cubes
- pan balance
- digital camera or tablet (optional)
- scissors
- *BLM 7: Blank fraction wall*
- *BLM 8: Make mine equivalent*
- *Activity sheet 10: Half of a half*

Activity sheet materials

- two pieces of coloured paper
- a sheet of poster paper
- scissors
- glue
- a piece of A4 paper

Potential difficulties: Fractions in the written form

Students may recognise equivalent visual representations of fractions but have difficulty with numeric forms.

- Spend time reinforcing the function of the numerator and denominator to give students a basis for comparing written representations of fractions.
- Allow opportunities to match a fraction's written form with corresponding visual representations, to consolidate interpretation of different forms of fractions.

Daily practice activity

On the first day, discuss the meaning of the word *equivalent* and write a definition as a class. Ask students to bring in or discuss examples of equivalence, such as one $5 note being equivalent to five $1 coins, or jandals in one country being the equivalent of flip-flops in another. Encourage students to articulate what makes the items equivalent, to build their understanding of the broader concept.

Session 1: Pre-assessment

Students to complete: Pre-test 6, Unit 2, Topic 1, p. 82.

Session 2: Topic introduction

WHOLE CLASS

Introductory activity: Exploring equivalence

Give each student a sheet of white paper and ask them to fold it in half, then to unfold it and colour one of the halves red. Instruct students to refold the paper in half, then fold it in half again the other way. Once they've reopened the paper, ask them to talk to a partner about how many parts the fold marks now show and how many of those parts are coloured in. Guide the students to fold the paper once again so that they've made eighths. Discuss how the size of the area they coloured in has not changed, but the name of the fraction that is coloured in has. Write $\frac{1}{2}$, $\frac{2}{4}$ and $\frac{4}{8}$ on the board and present them as equivalent fractions, encouraging students to identify the relationship between the numerators and denominators in the three fractions.

AT-STANDARD GROUP

Student Book

Students to complete: Guided and Independent Practice activities, pp. 41–43. Ask early finishers to identify as many pairs of equivalent fractions as they can from the fraction wall on p. 43.

SUPPORT GROUP

Concept exploration and skill development: Understanding equivalence

Students are likely to have heard the term *equal* or *equals*, but may be less familiar with the term *equivalent*. Revisit the class definition of equivalent from the Daily practice activity and brainstorm situations when students have encountered something that is equivalent to another thing, such as buying the same product in a different brand in the supermarket.

Demonstrate equivalence by asking students to create two sticks of eight interlocking cubes and asking them to break one of them in half. How many halves are equivalent to a whole? Ask one student to put their two halves on one side of a pan balance and the one whole on the other to show that they're equivalent. Ask students to break their whole into four equal pieces. What is each piece called? How many of the quarters are equivalent to one of the halves? Invite a student to use the pan balance to check if their guess is correct. Repeat with different numbers of interlocking cubes, listing the equivalent fractions that you find together on the board and encouraging students to use the physical fractions and the pan balance to check their hypotheses about equivalent fractions.

Student Book with teacher support

Students to complete: Guided Practice activities, p. 41. Support students by modelling the fractions with interlocking cubes and allowing students to check equivalence with the pan balance as needed.

EXTENSION GROUP

Student Book

Students to complete: Guided and Independent Practice activities, pp. 41–43.

Activity sheet

Students to begin: *Activity sheet 10: Half of a half.*

Session 3: Instruction and consolidation

WHOLE CLASS

Topic exploration: Representing equivalent fractions

Providing students with the opportunity to experience many representations of equivalent fractions can help consolidate the concept in their minds. In pairs, give students *BLM 7: Blank fraction wall.* Look at the top row and ask students what fraction of the whole one part of that row is. How do students know? Ask them to label one fraction in the top row, then continue down, identifying the fraction sizes and labelling one unit fraction in each row.

Choose one example of an equivalent fraction from the wall, such as $\frac{1}{12} = \frac{2}{24}$. Represent the two equivalent fractions using interlocking cubes, draw them, write the numerical form for each and write the name for each in words. Point out the numerator and the denominator in each of the two fractions and discuss the relationships between the numbers in each. Have each pair of students choose another pair of equivalent fractions they can see from the wall and represent them in as many ways as they can. Take photos of their work to display, or allow time for students to walk around and view each other's work.

AT-STANDARD GROUP

Teacher activity: Working with equivalent fractions

Show students an enlarged copy of *BLM 8: Make mine equivalent* and colour in the leftmost column

of the square divided into 100, so that 10 hundredths are shaded. Invite students to suggest what fraction the coloured section represents, and write the fraction in the box beneath it. Ask students how many sections of the top line of the next square would need to be coloured to make a fraction equivalent to the first one. Choose a student to come and colour in that number of sections, and to fill in the written form of the fraction. Repeat for the remaining two large squares.

Give each student their own copy of BLM 8 and ask them to choose a fraction of their own to represent in each of the four squares. Instruct students to cut their sheets in four so that each fraction is separate, then ask them to arrange the four pieces of paper in front of them. Offer them some prompts to help them compare the relative size of different fractions, e.g. "Bring all the fractions that are smaller than $\frac{7}{10}$ out the front". If students are coping well, ask them to focus on one set of fractions, e.g. the twentieths, and challenge them to decide whether the fraction they made is larger or smaller than a hundredths or a fiftieths fraction. Allow students to make visual comparisons of the fractions to consolidate their understanding.

Student Book

Students to complete: Extended Practice activities, p. 44.

SUPPORT GROUP

Student Book with teacher support

Students to complete: Independent and Extended Practice activities, pp. 42–44. Check in with students as they work through the Independent Practice activities, discussing any difficulties, before supporting them to complete the Extended Practice activities. If required, cut a copy of the hundredths grid from BLM 8 into tenths to give visual reinforcement.

EXTENSION GROUP

Student Book

Students to complete: Extended Practice activities, p. 44.

Activity sheet

Students to complete: *Activity sheet 10: Half of a half.*

Practice and Mastery Book

See page 4 for information about how to use the Practice and Mastery Book activities.

Session 4: Post-assessment

Students to complete: Post-test 6, Unit 2, Topic 1, p. 83.

OXFORD UNIVERSITY PRESS

Unit 2 Fractions and decimals

Topic 2 Improper fractions and mixed numbers

Student Book pages 45–48

Learning focus

Model and convert between fractions and mixed numbers using number lines and diagrams

Materials

- paper circles
- scissors
- 6-sided dice
- adhesive
- sheets of A3 paper
- *BLM 9: Scone recipe*
- *Activity sheet 11: More than a whole one*

Potential difficulties: Equivalence in collections

Students may have experience dividing up and comparing equivalent fractions of wholes, but can become confused when asked to identify multiples of fractions of collections.

- Use concrete materials and number lines to connect counting by fractions with the number of items that are in each fraction: for example, one third of 9 chocolates is 3, and two thirds is 6.
- Use everyday situations to demonstrate how multiples of unit fractions relate to collections as well as wholes.

Daily practice activity

Each day, ask students to get into groups of a specific number. As a class, count how many "whole" groups are made and what fraction of a group is left over. For example, you might have four groups of five and four students left over representing another $\frac{4}{5}$ of a group. Write the fraction that you have as a mixed number and as an improper fraction.

Session 1: Pre-assessment

Students to complete: Pre-test 6, Unit 2, Topic 2, p. 82.

Session 2: Topic introduction

WHOLE CLASS

Introductory activity: Introducing improper fractions and mixed numbers

Students may assume that you can't have a fraction with a numerator that's larger than the denominator. To build a good understanding of this concept, give students the opportunity to connect different representations of mixed numbers. Ask students if they would rather have $1\frac{3}{4}$ pieces of pizza or $\frac{7}{4}$. Give each student two paper circles and instruct them to fold and cut each one into quarters.

In mixed-ability pairs, ask students to make $1\frac{3}{4}$ with their pieces and then make $\frac{7}{4}$. What do they notice? Ask students to draw the two fractions, write the numeric form of each and represent them on a number line. Allocate different improper fractions to each pair and ask them to make it, draw it, write it and represent it on a number line, and to find the equivalent mixed number.

AT-STANDARD GROUP

Student Book

Students to complete: Guided and Independent Practice activities, pp. 45–47. Ask early finishers to look for real-life examples of mixed numbers and improper fractions in the classroom, such as three half bottles of paint ($\frac{3}{2}$ bottles), to share with the rest of the class.

SUPPORT GROUP

Concept exploration and skill development: Identifying improper fractions

As students work with improper fractions, it's important that they understand what both the numerator and the denominator are telling them. Roll a 6-sided dice twice and record the first number as the numerator of a fraction and the second as the denominator. Draw a simple number line from 1 to 6 on the whiteboard and ask students whether the fraction is larger or smaller than one. Model where to place the fraction on the number line, explaining that the denominator tells you how many parts each whole or "1" is divided into, and the numerator tells you how many of each part you have.

Give each student a dice and ask them to roll it twice to make their own fraction, recording it on a piece of paper. Using adhesive, instruct students to stick their fraction on the number line. As a group, review the placements and decide if they're accurate. Use the activity to help students write a rule about how to identify when a fraction is larger than one.

Student Book with teacher support

Students to complete: Guided Practice activities, p. 45. Discuss which parts of the fraction change and which stay the same when counting by unit fractions, using the number line to support students' learning.

EXTENSION GROUP

Student Book

Students to complete: Guided and Independent Practice activities, pp. 45–47.

Activity sheet

Students to begin: *Activity sheet 11: More than a whole one.*

Session 3: Instruction and consolidation

WHOLE CLASS

Topic exploration: Counting with fractions

Students may be used to counting fractions to one, but may not have experienced how to count beyond one with either mixed numbers or improper fractions. Divide students into mixed-ability groups and allocate each group one of the following fractional parts: quarters, halves or thirds. Model for students how to rule a 36 cm line on a piece of A3 paper, marking off 12 cm and 24 cm and labelling them as 1 and 2, with zero on the ruler being 0 and 36 cm being 3. Instruct students to make their own number line in the same way, then label counting by their given fractional part from 0 to 3. Did students use mixed numbers or improper fractions? Were they able to identify whole numbers as improper fractions (e.g. 2 as $\frac{6}{3}$)? Discuss the spacing of fractions on the number line to ensure that students understand that the fractions represent equal parts or distances. Challenge students to count by a different fractional part on the same number line, and to share the strategies they used to place and label the second set of fractions.

AT-STANDARD GROUP

Teacher activity: Recipe quantities

Understanding the real-life applications of mathematics is critical to building students' interest and understanding. One area in which fractions are often used is cooking. Give each student a copy of *BLM 9: Scone recipe* and explain that as you're cooking for a large group, you need to double the recipe. Students must write the quantities required for each ingredient in order to make a double batch, using a number line to support their thinking, if

necessary. Discuss the results, particularly what to do when the self-raising flour quantity of 2 cups is doubled. You may also like to actually make the scones as a group or with the whole class using the adjusted quantities.

Student Book

Students to complete: Extended Practice activities, p. 48.

SUPPORT GROUP

Student Book with teacher support

Students to complete: Independent and Extended Practice activities, pp. 46–48. Check in with students as they work through the Independent Practice activities, discussing any difficulties, before supporting them to complete the Extended Practice activities, using number lines or other materials to support them as required.

EXTENSION GROUP

Student Book

Students to complete: Extended Practice activities, p. 48.

Activity sheet

Students to complete: *Activity sheet 11: More than a whole one.*

Practice and Mastery Book

See page 4 for information about how to use the Practice and Mastery Book activities.

Session 4: Post-assessment

Students to complete: Post-test 6, Unit 2, Topic 2, p. 83.

Unit 2 Fractions and decimals
Topic 3 Decimal fractions

Student Book pages 49–52

Learning focus

Model, compare and order fractions to hundredths, and convert between decimals and fractions

Materials

- base-10 materials
- virtual base-10 materials (optional)
- scissors
- *BLM 21: Decimal place value chart*
- *BLM 22: Decimal number expanders*
- *BLM 23: Decimal fractions snap cards* (multiple sets, copied onto card and cut up)
- *Activity sheet 12: Working with decimals*

Activity sheet materials

- a digital stopwatch

Potential difficulties: Zero as a placeholder

As with whole numbers, zero can cause confusion when it comes to decimal notation.

- Use place value charts and concrete materials to build students' confidence with reading decimal numbers involving zero, so they can understand and explain the difference between numbers such as 0.4 and 0.04.
- Consolidate the concept through simple activities such as regularly asking how many decimal places a tenths or hundredths number has.

Daily practice activity

Each day, write the price of an item, such as food from the school canteen or from a supermarket catalogue on the board and discuss how the decimal amounts relate to hundredths, e.g. $1.95 is one whole dollar and 95 hundredths.

Session 1: Pre-assessment

Students to complete: Pre-test 7, Unit 2, Topic 3, p. 84.

Session 2: Topic introduction

WHOLE CLASS

Introductory activity: Introducing tenths and hundredths

While students probably have experience of tenths in the form of fractions, and of hundredths in terms of money, they may not have been formally introduced to them as part of the decimal system. Base-10 materials are ideal for helping students experience and visualise decimals and connect them with their fractional forms. Show students a base-10 hundred block, either with concrete materials or using a virtual version. Tell them that the block represents one whole and ask them how many of the small squares make up the whole. Write $\frac{1}{100}$ as a fraction on the board. Next, show students a ten stick and ask how many make up a whole. Write $\frac{1}{10}$ as a fraction on the board. Explain that tenths and hundredths can also be written as decimals, and write the decimal form of each next to the fractions.

Distribute base-10 materials to pairs of students and give them time to test how many tenths fill one whole and how many hundredths fill a tenth. Ask each pair to show you what two tenths looks like by holding up the corresponding materials. How would you write it in decimal notation? Repeat with other tenths and hundredths numbers, talking through and recording the fraction and decimal representations of each.

AT-STANDARD GROUP

Student Book

Students to complete: Guided and Independent Practice activities, pp. 49–51. Ask early finishers to take a small handful of base-10 tens and ones and work out what fraction of a base-10 hundred (or whole) it is and how to write it as a decimal. Repeat with other amounts.

SUPPORT GROUP

Concept exploration and skill development: Reinforcing decimal place value

Students may not be used to thinking of place value as extending beyond ones. A place value chart can help students read, write and interpret decimal numbers. Show students an enlarged copy of *BLM 21: Decimal place value chart* and ask them what they notice about it. Ask students where $\frac{1}{10}$ might go on the chart. Use base-10 materials to reinforce that a tenth is less than a whole or one, and so is written after the decimal point on the place value chart. Repeat with $\frac{1}{100}$, modelling with base-10 materials and asking students where to write it on the place value chart. Discuss the role of the zero in the tenths column to help students understand and remember how to write hundredths. Practise writing some decimal fractions, with and without whole numbers, on the chart with students.

In pairs, give students BLM 21, then write some fractions involving tenths and hundredths on the board for students to represent on the chart. Discuss each example as a group, clarifying any areas of misunderstanding.

Student Book with teacher support

Students to complete: Guided Practice activities, p. 49. Use base-10 materials to model the numbers as required.

EXTENSION GROUP

Student Book

Students to complete: Guided and Independent Practice activities, pp. 49–51.

Activity sheet

Students to begin: *Activity sheet 12: Working with decimals*.

Session 3: Instruction and consolidation

WHOLE CLASS

Topic exploration: Understanding decimals

Give each student a copy of *BLM 22: Decimal number expanders* and explain how to cut each one out and fold it so the place value headers can be hidden or revealed as required. Tell students that you have 4 ones and 5 tenths, modelling with base-10 materials if needed, and ask them to suggest how this would be written in decimal notation. Guide students to write a 4 in the ones section of their expander and a 5 in the tenths section, then experiment with different ways to rename the number, such as 45 tenths and 450 hundredths. Let students choose their own numbers to fill in their remaining number expanders, recording the decimal notation and different ways of renaming each one. Discuss students' findings, linking the renamed numbers with fractional representations: e.g. 45 tenths is the same as $\frac{45}{10}$.

AT-STANDARD GROUP

Teacher activity: Matching fractions and decimal representations

Students need to practise converting from fractions to decimal numbers and back again. Give pairs of students a set of *BLM 23: Decimal fractions snap cards* copied onto card and cut up. Students can play a traditional game of *Snap*, with the aim of finding pairs of matching fractions and decimal places. The cards can also be used to play *Concentration* by laying them face-down in an array and having students try to find matching pairs. Allow time to discuss any difficulties students encountered.

Student Book

Students to complete: Extended Practice activities, p. 52.

SUPPORT GROUP

Student Book with teacher support

Students to complete: Independent and Extended Practice activities, pp. 50–52. Check in with students as they work through the Independent Practice activities, discussing any difficulties, before supporting them to complete the Extended Practice activities, using a decimal place value chart and/or base-10 materials to support their understanding as needed.

EXTENSION GROUP

Student Book

Students to complete: Extended Practice activities, p. 52.

Activity sheet

Students to complete: *Activity sheet 12: Working with decimals*.

Practice and Mastery Book

See page 4 for information about how to use the Practice and Mastery Book activities.

Session 4: Post-assessment

Students to complete: Post-test 7, Unit 2, Topic 3, p. 85.

OXFORD UNIVERSITY PRESS

Unit 3 Money and financial mathematics

Topic 1 Money and money calculations

Student Book pages 53–56

Learning focus

Round and calculate with money amounts and use decimal fractions in real-life situations

Materials

- school canteen menu or supermarket catalogues
- calculators
- supermarket receipts
- *BLM 35: 0–99 chart* (optional)
- *BLM 38: Change scenarios*
- *BLM 39: Money pathways*
- *BLM 40: Rupees and yen*
- *Activity sheet 13: Money then, now and around the world*

Potential difficulties: Decimal place value

Students who do not have a sound understanding of decimal place value may struggle with rounding and money calculations as they get more complex.

- Support students' understanding with visual aids such as place value charts and number lines.
- Link activities to real life as much as possible to help students make connections to contexts in which they may already have experienced decimals and money.

Daily practice activity

Practise calculating with money by presenting two options and asking students which they would rather have, e.g. three $10 notes or two $20 notes. Challenge students by making the examples more complex, incorporating decimal points as their proficiency grows.

Session 1: Pre-assessment

Students to complete: Pre-test 8, Unit 3, Topic 1, p. 86.

Session 2: Topic introduction

WHOLE CLASS

Introductory activity: Calculating change amounts

The strategies used to calculate change can vary depending on the situation. Discuss the rules for rounding to the nearest five cents and ask students to suggest when this might be necessary. Brainstorm and record the calculation strategies students think they might use in change situations, then give each pair of students a copy of *BLM 38: Change scenarios*. Ask the pairs to work out how much change would be given in each of the situations, encouraging them to record their working out and the strategy they used. Also have them describe which amounts they rounded up or down, and why. Draw on their responses to make a class guide to giving change that lists which methods are useful for particular situations. For example, counting up might be a useful strategy when there is little difference between the purchase price and the amount being handed over.

AT-STANDARD GROUP

Student Book

Students to complete: Guided and Independent Practice activities, pp. 53–55. Ask early finishers to choose what they would buy at Dean's Ice Creams (on p. 55) if they had $8.50 to spend. How much change would they get?

SUPPORT GROUP

Concept exploration and skill development: Consolidating counting with money amounts

Students are often well-drilled in skip counting by common numbers such as 2 and 5, but have had less practice in counting by multiples of 10, particularly off the decade. This is a necessary skill to have when counting from and by denominations such as 20 cents or 50 cents. Give students a copy of *BLM 39: Money pathways* and work through the first example together, using *BLM 35: 0–99 chart* for extra support if needed. Ask students to work through the next example individually, then pair them up to compare answers and discuss the strategies they used. Repeat for the remaining examples.

Have pairs of students make their own number paths. Students should then swap with another pair and solve each other's. As a group, discuss and list the key things to remember when counting with money.

Student Book with teacher support

Students to complete: Guided Practice activities, p. 53. Use a number line to help students identify the closest number to round to as needed.

EXTENSION GROUP

Student Book

Students to complete: Guided and Independent Practice activities, pp. 53–55.

Activity sheet

Students to begin: *Activity sheet 13: Money then, now and around the world.*

Session 3: Instruction and consolidation

WHOLE CLASS

Topic exploration: Adding and subtracting money using an algorithm

Students may need to use their knowledge of vertical algorithms to help them with money calculations. Write two money amounts on the board that won't require trading when they're added, such as $2.53 and $4.25. Invite students to suggest how you might rewrite the problem as a vertical algorithm, discussing how the decimal points in the two amounts must be aligned, just as the place value columns are aligned. Work through the problem as a class, and then model the use of a subtraction algorithm to check the answer.

Have pairs of students choose two items with two decimal places from the school canteen menu or from a supermarket catalogue. Students should add the two prices using a vertical algorithm, then swap with another pair to check the calculations using subtraction. As a class, discuss similarities and differences in using vertical algorithms for numbers with and without decimal places.

Topic exploration: Adding money using calculators

The ability to accurately use a calculator is an important skill for students to develop, especially when decimals are involved. Ask students to bring in supermarket receipts from home. Cut off the total, but retain and number both pieces so you can easily match them again later. Give pairs of students a calculator each and a receipt between them and have them add the amounts listed to find the total. Did both students get the same answer? Give them time to check their total against the actual total, then discuss possible errors, such as forgetting to put in the decimal point, or missing a digit. Swap the

receipts between the pairs and give students another turn. Challenge students by suggesting how much they might have paid with, and asking them to use the calculator to work out the change.

AT-STANDARD GROUP

Teacher activity: International change

Ask students if they have ever seen money from other countries. What did it look like? How was it similar to the local currency? How was it different? Explain that you are going to look at money from two different countries – rupees from India and yen from Japan.

In pairs, give students *BLM 40: Rupees and yen* and ask them to look at the rupees. What do they notice about them? How are they similar to our money? What does the rupees symbol look like? Repeat with the Japanese yen, drawing students' attention to the different denominations of each currency, and to the fact that neither yen nor rupees have a smaller unit such as cents.

In their pairs, ask students to suggest what change they might get if they bought an item for 400 rupees with a 1000 rupee note, and if they bought something for 400 yen with a 1000 yen note. Repeat with different purchase prices and payment amounts to give students a feel for calculating with international currency. To finish, ask them to make 20 rupees and 2000 yen in five different ways and share their responses.

Student Book

Students to complete: Extended Practice activities, p. 56.

SUPPORT GROUP

Student Book with teacher support

Students to complete: Independent and Extended Practice activities, pp. 54–56. Check in with students as they work on the Independent Practice activities, discussing any difficulties, before supporting them to complete the Extended Practice activities, helping them to relate the South African money to their knowledge of the local currency, and using visual aids such as number lines as appropriate.

EXTENSION GROUP

Student Book

Students to complete: Extended Practice activities, p. 56.

Activity sheet

Students to complete: *Activity sheet 13: Money then, now and around the world.*

Practice and Mastery Book

See page 4 for information about how to use the Practice and Mastery Book activities.

Session 4: Post-assessment

Students to complete: Post-test 8, Unit 3, Topic 1, p. 87.

Unit 4 Patterns and algebra
Topic 1 Number patterns
Student Book pages 57–60

Learning focus

Analyse patterns and identify rules for number patterns and identify multiples of given numbers

Materials

- blank calendar page for the current month, one per pair (or access to an online version)
- hundred chart and counters (optional)
- craft sticks or similar construction materials
- glue
- *BLM 18: Exploring number patterns*
- *BLM 19: Number pattern record sheet*
- *Activity sheet 14: Patterns with numbers*

Activity sheet materials
- a calculator
- a pencil and ruler

Potential difficulties: Number knowledge

Students who have difficulty recalling skip-counting patterns and tables may also have trouble when it comes to number patterns.

- Encourage students to refer to number charts, and teach them how to use their knowledge of repeating digits to find the next number in a pattern.
- Help students develop better recall of number facts by playing games and conducting other activities that make practice enjoyable. Group students in a way that ensures everyone will experience success.

Daily practice activity

At the start of the week, ask students what a rule is and why we have rules. Start with a simple number pattern on the board, such as 1, 3, 5, 7, and ask students to suggest what the rule is for the pattern. Repeat this activity each day, with more difficult patterns.

Session 1: Pre-assessment
Students to complete: Pre-test 9, Unit 4, Topic 1, p. 88.

Session 2: Topic introduction
WHOLE CLASS
Introductory activity: Number patterns in real life

In mixed-ability pairs, give students a blank calendar page for the current month, or display one on the interactive whiteboard. Ask students to work with their partner to identify as many different patterns as they can in the numbers on the page, and record the rules for each pattern. Encourage them to be creative in their search, looking for diagonal patterns as well as horizontal and vertical ones. Challenge students to identify the next five numbers in one of their patterns. Share students' discoveries as a class, recording the different types of patterns that were found.

AT-STANDARD GROUP
Student Book

Students to complete: Guided and Independent Practice activities, pp. 57–59. Ask early finishers to use different colours to explore the multiples of 3, 6 and 9 on one of the hundred charts on p. 59.

SUPPORT GROUP
Concept exploration and skill development: Exploring number patterns

Most students will have some knowledge about number patterns from their experiences with skip counting. This makes counting patterns a good place to start when exploring multiplication patterns. Enlarge a copy of *BLM 18: Exploring number patterns* and use the first circle to demonstrate how to record the number pattern made by counting by twos. What shape does it make? Will it make the same pattern if you start at 1 instead of 0?

Give students their own copy of BLM 18 and *BLM 19: Number pattern record sheet*. Ask students to count on by the numbers listed in the record sheet, representing each one on a circle to see what pattern shape it makes and recording their findings. Discuss the results, asking students to identify the longest and shortest patterns and the rule that would be used to describe each counting pattern.

Student Book with teacher support

Students to complete: Guided Practice activities, p. 57, using a hundred chart with counters to mark the numbers in each pattern as needed.

EXTENSION GROUP

Student Book

Students to complete: Guided and Independent Practice activities, pp. 57–59.

Activity sheet

Students to begin: *Activity sheet 14: Patterns with numbers.*

Session 3: Instruction and consolidation

WHOLE CLASS

Topic exploration: Applying multiplication patterns

It's helpful for students to understand the relevance of patterns in everyday life. Brainstorm different situations when number patterns are used. You may need to make some suggestions to get students started, e.g. how many packs of 12 chocolate frogs might you need if there are 18 people at your party? Or how many nails might you need to construct 10 chairs that each require 40 nails? Set students a "mass production" craft project to give them hands-on experience with multiplication patterns, e.g. ask students to make a village using craft sticks, with each house identical. Students would need to work out how many craft sticks they'll need for one house, and use this number to identify how many sticks they'll need for two, five or 10 houses. Instruct students to record their patterns in words, in symbols and in a table showing the relationships between the number of houses and the number of sticks required, and then allow them to complete the project in small groups. Ensure each group writes a brief summary of the rule for the pattern, and how they used the pattern to work out how many sticks they needed. Display students' work and give them time to view what other groups have done.

Topic exploration: Repeated addition and subtraction

Draw a Venn diagram on the board and write *multiplication* on one side and *repeated addition* on the other side. As a class, complete the diagram to show the similarities and differences between the two operations, encouraging students to consider aspects such as the speed of calculation, the answers and the equality of the groups being put together. Write a repeated addition problem such as $4 + 4 + 4 = 12$ on the board and ask students to give you the two related multiplication facts. Model the problem with an array and on a number line to reinforce the concepts in a visual way and discuss in what situations you might use each process.

In pairs, have students complete their own Venn diagrams comparing division and repeated subtraction. Students should also include two examples of repeated subtraction problems and the matching division facts, and draw arrays to illustrate each of their problems. Ask students to report back to the class and complete a consolidated repeated subtraction/division Venn diagram based on their findings. Again, discuss in what situations you might use both processes.

AT-STANDARD GROUP

Teacher activity: Describing and creating number patterns

Pose the following scenario to students:

Samuel's grandmother gives him eight presents every year for his birthday. He turned nine yesterday. How many birthday presents has he received from his grandmother in his lifetime?

Discuss different ways to represent and solve the problem, such as drawing the solution using repeated addition or multiplication. Model representing the rule using symbols (e.g. $1 \times 8 = 8$ for his first birthday; $2 \times 8 = 16$ by his second birthday) and in a table. How could you use this information to predict how many presents Samuel would receive at any age?

Ask students to write their own number pattern stories, then swap the stories around the group so students work on each other's problems. Encourage students to describe the strategies they used and represent the rule in multiple ways to show how they could apply the rules for the pattern to find the solution for any number.

Student Book

Students to complete: Extended Practice activities, p. 60.

SUPPORT GROUP

Student Book with teacher support

Students to complete: Independent and Extended Practice activities, pp. 58–60. Check in with students as they work through the Independent Practice activities, discussing any difficulties, before supporting them to complete the Extended Practice activities, using manipulatives to model the shapes as needed.

EXTENSION GROUP

Student Book

Students to complete: Extended Practice activities, p. 60.

Activity sheet

Students to complete: *Activity sheet 14: Patterns with numbers.*

Practice and Mastery Book

See page 4 for information about how to use the Practice and Mastery Book activities.

Session 4: Post-assessment

Students to complete: Post-test 9, Unit 4, Topic 1, p. 89.

OXFORD UNIVERSITY PRESS

Unit 4 Patterns and algebra
Topic 2 Problem solving
Student Book pages 61–64

Learning focus

Interpret, represent and solve word problems involving the four processes

Materials

- cards to write word problems on
- pan balances
- interlocking cubes
- poster paper
- highlighters
- playing cards
- *BLM 29: Long word problems*
- *Activity sheet 15: Mystery numbers*

Potential difficulties: Reading comprehension

A degree of reading comprehension is involved when students are solving word problems. For students who are struggling readers, this can add an extra layer of confusion.

- Pair weaker readers with stronger readers during activities, or check on struggling readers and read the problems with them. This ensures that they have adequate opportunities to develop and demonstrate their mathematical skills.
- Co-constructing and displaying charts listing words that are often associated with particular mathematical symbols can also help support these students.

Daily practice activity

At the start of the week, have pairs of students write one word problem on a card. Each day, share the cards around and have each group solve someone else's problem. Share strategies and answers as a class.

Session 1: Pre-assessment

Students to complete: Pre-test 9, Unit 4, Topic 2, p. 88.

Session 2: Topic introduction

WHOLE CLASS

Introductory activity: Problem solving strategies

Present students with a simple open-ended problem, such as: *Liam has an odd number of pencils and Lara has an even number. If they have fewer than 20 pencils between them in total, how many might they each have?* As a class, brainstorm and record the different strategies that students could use to approach solving the problem. If necessary, prompt them to consider strategies such as estimating and checking, using a calculator, drawing a diagram or writing a number sentence. Work through each method together, discussing the accuracy of the answers and which method suited the problem the best.

Present a similar problem, such as: *When the number of pencils Miro owned was subtracted from the number of pencils Skye owned, the answer was 9. How many pencils might they each have owned?* In pairs, ask students to choose one method to solve the problem. Each group should then find a group who used a different strategy and compare their answers. Discuss as a class which strategies students chose and why or why not they were good strategies to use for the problem.

Introductory activity: Equivalent number sentences

Students' experience of number sentences is often restricted to two numbers, the required operation between them, followed by an equals sign. For example, $23 + 13 =$. It's important that students understand what the equals sign means; that is, that what is on one side of the sign is equal to what is on the other. Write a word problem on the board such as, "When a number is taken away from 25, the answer is the same as 8 plus 5. What is the number?" Give students time to think about it, then have them discuss their responses with a partner. As a class, talk about how to approach the problem. Do students realise that two steps are required? Write the problem as an equivalent number sentence with a missing element: $25 - \square = 8 + 5$. Does this make it easier to solve? Use a pan balance to demonstrate the equivalence with interlocking cubes by putting 13 on one side and 25 on the other, and taking away cubes until it balances. Discuss with students how using inverse operations is another way to find the answer and restate the problem as 13 + □ = 25. Invite students to suggest which method they find easier and why.

Write some more examples on the board, such as □ + 15 = 14 × 2 and 46 – 19 = □ × 3, and ask students to work in pairs to solve them using their preferred method. Discuss the strategies and answers as a class, modelling with the pan balance and interlocking cubes to check if the two sides are equal.

AT-STANDARD GROUP

Student Book

Students to complete: Guided and Independent Practice activities, pp. 61–63. Ask early finishers to use a pan balance and interlocking cubes to check their answers to question 2 on p. 62.

SUPPORT GROUP

Concept exploration and skill development: Using the four operations

By now, students should have some experience with solving word problems and the language that helps identify which operation is required. Write a number problem for each of the four operations on the board (e.g. 34 + 57 =, 85 – 38 =). In pairs, ask students to choose two of the number problems and make a small poster with a matching word problem. The poster should also include the solution and a diagram or other visual to illustrate the problem. Students could link their problems to a current theme you're investigating, or use their imaginations. Share the stories with the rest of the class and allow students to provide feedback on the problem solving methods used.

Student Book with teacher support

Students to complete: Guided Practice activities, p. 61. Use a pan balance and interlocking cubes or other manipulatives to model the problems as required.

EXTENSION GROUP

Student Book

Students to complete: Guided and Independent Practice activities, pp. 61–63.

Activity sheet

Students to begin: *Activity sheet 15: Mystery numbers*.

Session 3: Instruction and consolidation

WHOLE CLASS

Topic exploration: Problem solving strategies

Brainstorm different problem solving strategies that students are familiar with, such as drawing a diagram, making a number sentence, making a table, estimating and checking or acting it out. Pose a short, open-ended problem, such as, "Jamie had jotted down the number of year 3s and the number of year 4s attending a mathematics awards ceremony, but he put the piece of paper in his pocket, and some of the numbers got smudged. Here's what he has: 3□ + □9 = 1□□. He needs to work out how many students from each year level are coming, and the total number of chairs needed. What might the missing numbers be?" Write the missing number equation on the board and read the scenario to students for a second time. Write each of the problem solving strategies that students identified in their brainstorm on a separate piece of card. Put students into mixed-ability pairs or small groups and allocate each group a different strategy. (It doesn't matter if multiple groups end up with the same strategy.) Students must use their allocated strategy to find possible answers to the problem, recording their efforts on a piece of paper. If any groups finish quickly, encourage them to try a different strategy.

Bring students back together and discuss their responses. Which strategies worked well with this problem? Were there any strategies that weren't really suitable? Use students' responses to write some brief guidelines for when you might and might not use each of the strategies.

Topic exploration: Associative property

Understanding the properties of the four operations can help students build fluency, problem solving and reasoning skills. Ask students to suggest what the word *associate* means and use the discussion as a springboard into introducing the associative property. Draw three playing cards from a deck with the face cards removed and give one each to three students. Choose two other students to each hold a card with + on it and another student to hold one with = on it. Arrange the students along the front of the room to form a horizontal algorithm, e.g. 5 + 3 + 4 =. Move the first three students closer together and as a class, add 5 and 3 and then add 4 and record the answer. Adjust the position of the students so those holding 3 + 4 are closer together and add these first before adding 5 to the answer. Is the total the same or different? Why? Explain that the associative property means that it doesn't matter how you associate or group the numbers in addition, you will still get the same answer.

Organise students into small groups and allocate each group one of the remaining operations – subtraction, division or multiplication. (It doesn't matter if multiple groups work on the same operation.) Task the groups with finding out if the associative property also works with their given operation. Encourage students to use materials and provide examples to support their conclusions. Ask each group to share their findings with the class to build understanding that the associative property works with addition and multiplication but

OXFORD UNIVERSITY PRESS

not with subtraction and division. Extend students' thinking by trying a few examples of multiplication and subtraction together that involve four different addends or factors.

AT-STANDARD GROUP

Teacher activity: Interpreting word problems

In real life, we are rarely presented with word problems of only one or two sentences in isolation. Instead we have to sort through lots of information to work out what's important. To develop this ability, read students the first story from *BLM 29: Long word problems*. When you have finished, invite students to suggest which pieces of information are important to solving the problem. Have they identified the key elements? In pairs, give students BLM 29 and allow them to read the problem for themselves, highlighting the key words and numbers that will help them find the answer. Ask each pair to solve the problem and write a matching number sentence to go with it. Share their responses as a group. Were students able to recognise the information that was not important to solving the problem?

Ask each pair to solve the second problem, finding and highlighting the key pieces of information and the second word problem, again providing a matching number sentence. Invite students to share the words that they highlighted, as well as their responses.

Student Book

Students to complete: Extended Practice activities, p. 64.

SUPPORT GROUP

Student Book with teacher support

Students to complete: Independent and Extended Practice activities, pp. 62–64. Check in with students as they work through the Independent Practice activities, discussing any difficulties, before supporting them to complete the Extended Practice activities, using visual strategies such as drawing a diagram or making a model to help students interpret the problems as needed.

EXTENSION GROUP

Student Book

Students to complete: Extended Practice activities, p. 64.

Activity sheet

Students to complete: *Activity sheet 15: Mystery numbers.*

Practice and Mastery Book

See page 4 for information about how to use the Practice and Mastery Book activities.

Session 4: Post-assessment

Students to complete: Post-test 9, Unit 4, Topic 2, p. 89.

Unit 5 Using units of measurement

Topic 1 Length and perimeter

Student Book pages 65–68

Learning focus

Estimate, measure and compare lengths and perimeters using standard units of measurement and convert between the units

Materials

- three large sheets of paper
- selection of magazines
- 30 cm rulers
- selection of measuring instruments such as tape measures and metre rulers
- chalk
- poster paper or tablets
- selection of books
- *Activity sheet 16: The importance of accuracy*

Potential difficulties: Conceptualising formal units

Some students find it difficult to estimate length with formal units or to picture how big a given measurement is.

- Establish familiar reference points to help students conceptualise formal units. For example, if students know that their classroom ruler is 30 cm long, they can then identify other lengths as longer or shorter than 30 cm.
- Provide students with plenty of hands-on experience working with formal units to estimate lengths and then measure the objects to check the accuracy of their guesses.

Daily practice activity

Nominate a different length each day and ask students to suggest objects or items that are about the same length. Choose a variety of lengths in millimetres, centimetres and metres to consolidate students' understanding of the different units. Repeat the same activity with perimeters.

Session 1: Pre-assessment

Students to complete: Pre-test 10, Unit 5, Topic 1, p. 90.

Session 2: Topic introduction

WHOLE CLASS

Introductory activity: Comparing formal units

Take three large sheets of paper and label them *millimetres*, *centimetres* and *metres* respectively. Provide students with magazines and ask them to cut out pictures of items and paste them on the appropriate sheet according to the unit that they would best be measured in. Which unit has the most pictures? Why do you think this is? Ask students whether they think any of the pictures are in the wrong place, and to explain why they think the item would be better measured using another unit. Discuss the importance of choosing the most appropriate unit of measurement to get an accurate and usable result and talk about the most appropriate measuring tool to find the length of each item.

AT-STANDARD GROUP

Student Book

Students to complete: Guided and Independent Practice activities, pp. 65–67. Ask early finishers to draw two different shapes with a perimeter of exactly 30 cm, then two shapes with a perimeter of exactly 26 cm and two shapes with a perimeter of exactly 190 mm.

SUPPORT GROUP

Concept exploration and skill development: Exploring length

Revise measuring conventions with students, such as starting from the zero mark on the ruler. Ask students to rule a line exactly 6 cm long using a 30 cm ruler, monitoring and assisting them to ensure accuracy. Ask students to look at the small marks between the centimetres on their rulers. What are they called? How many of them are there in each cm? Support students to rule a line that is 60 mm long beneath their first line. What do they notice about the two lines?

Ask each student to rule a line of any length and record the measurement on a separate piece of paper. Pair up students and ask them to measure each other's lines. Did they agree on the line lengths? Repeat the activity several times, challenging students to use millimetres or a combination of millimetres and centimetres as they measure.

OXFORD UNIVERSITY PRESS

Student Book with teacher support

Students to complete: Guided Practice activities, p. 65. Support students to use their rulers as number lines for the calculations, as appropriate.

EXTENSION GROUP

Student Book

Students to complete: Guided and Independent Practice activities, pp. 65–67.

Activity sheet

Students to begin: *Activity sheet 16: The importance of accuracy.*

Session 3: Instruction and consolidation

WHOLE CLASS

Topic exploration: Experimenting with length

Students need lots of practice using rulers, tape measures and other scaled instruments to measure length. Take the class outside onto a basketball court or similar area with a flat surface. Organise students into small groups and give each group a metre ruler and some chalk. Ask each group to mark a line exactly 3 m long. Have groups check each other's lines for accuracy. What makes it hard to make the line exactly that length? Allow students to use tape measures and other measuring instruments, as well as the metre rulers, to make lines of different lengths and record their measurements. Encourage students to consider how lengths that are slightly over or under a precise measurement such as 1 m or 30 cm can be measured and recorded.

Inside the classroom, challenge students to draw a line of exactly 1 m in length on an A4 sheet of paper using a 30 cm ruler. Share strategies for how to fit the line on the paper and how to ensure that the measurements are accurate. Brainstorm solutions as a class, and list students' observations and tips for accurate measuring.

Topic exploration: Understanding perimeter

It is important to ensure that students understand the concept of perimeter as the sum of all the lengths around the outside of an area. Model measuring the perimeter of a book with students, recording each of the four lengths on the board, then adding them. What do students observe about the lengths of the sides? Provide a good selection of books of different sizes and ask pairs of students to choose one that they think has a perimeter closest to 75 cm. Invite students to measure the actual perimeter and see which pair got the closest. Repeat with different target perimeters, encouraging students to think about how to make a reasonable estimate before selecting their book.

Ask students to identify non-rectangular objects in the classroom. As a class, estimate and measure the perimeters, recording the lengths of each side before adding them to help students consolidate their understanding of perimeter.

AT-STANDARD GROUP

Teacher activity: Comparing lengths

Ask students to suggest two items in the classroom that are similar lengths, preferably items that aren't directly next to each other. Which of the two items do students predict is longer? Ask students to choose an appropriate measuring instrument to check the lengths of the items. Which was longer? By how much? With a partner, ask students to find five other pairs of items with similar lengths, recording their estimated lengths before conducting their measurements. Encourage them to use different units of length such as millimetres and centimetres. Students can make a poster or multimedia presentation of their findings, recording the comparisons between the lengths of various items and reflecting on whether their estimation skills improved.

Student Book

Students to complete: Extended Practice activities, p. 68.

SUPPORT GROUP

Student Book with teacher support

Students to complete: Independent and Extended Practice activities, pp. 66–68. Check in with students as they work through the Independent Practice activities, discussing any difficulties, before supporting them to complete the Extended Practice activities, helping them with conversions between units as required.

EXTENSION GROUP

Student Book

Students to complete: Extended Practice activities, p. 68.

Activity sheet

Students to complete: *Activity sheet 16: The importance of accuracy.*

Practice and Mastery Book

See page 4 for information about how to use the Practice and Mastery Book activities.

Session 4: Post-assessment

Students to complete: Post-test 10, Unit 5, Topic 1, p. 91.

Unit 5 Using units of measurement
Topic 2 Area

Student Book pages 69–72

Learning focus

Estimate, measure and compare areas using standard units of measurement

Materials

- 30 cm rulers
- metre rulers
- large sheets of newspaper or other paper
- base-10 materials
- centimetre grid paper
- *BLM 17: Investigating area*
- *Activity sheet 17: An even shorter shortcut*

Potential difficulties: Area in context

Students may have had few opportunities to investigate area in genuine contexts, which can make it difficult to build a solid understanding of the concept.

- Involve students in situations where it is necessary to know the area of a space. For example, if the oval is being resurfaced with artificial grass, find out how much needs to be purchased and check the measurements together.
- Use mathematical reasoning to work out how to rearrange the classroom. For example, you might calculate how much floor space you would need for storage of a particular resource, or for a particular piece of furniture.

Daily practice activity

To consolidate students' understanding of square centimetres, give them a target area each day, such as 8 cm^2, and challenge them to draw a shape with that area. Encourage students to find and share effective strategies to measure how close they got to the target.

Session 1: Pre-assessment
Students to complete: Pre-test 10, Unit 5, Topic 2, p. 90.

Session 2: Topic introduction

WHOLE CLASS

Introductory activity: Square centimetres and square metres

It's important for students to develop an understanding of the size of common formal units of area. Ask students to draw a square centimetre on a piece of paper. Show students the size of a centimetre using a 30 cm ruler, then draw a square centimetre on the board. How close were students' approximations?

In small mixed-ability groups, ask students to make a square metre out of newspaper or other paper. Instruct students to fold the square metre in half and then into quarters and open it out again. Groups should estimate how many base-10 hundreds they would need to cover one quarter of the square metre, then test their prediction and record the results. Repeat with one half of the metre. Do students recognise that the measurement for the half metre should be double the measurement for the quarter? Ask students how many base-10 hundreds would be needed to cover the whole square metre and to write a short explanation for their solution. Give students time to share their ideas, and challenge them to suggest how many square centimetres are in a square metre.

AT-STANDARD GROUP

Student Book

Students to complete: Guided and Independent Practice activities, pp. 69–71. Ask early finishers to find an illustration in a book and identify which surfaces shown in the picture would best be measured in square centimetres, and which they would measure in square metres.

SUPPORT GROUP

Concept exploration and skill development: Measuring and comparing areas

Set students a series of challenges that will allow them to explore and connect informal units of area with formal units. For example, working in pairs, ask students to find a surface with an area of exactly 8 tiles, a surface that has an area larger than 1 square metre, and an item with an area that is smaller than 6 of a different informal unit. Guide students to use base-10 materials to help them check the areas in square centimetres. Are square centimetres larger or smaller than the other units students used? Will

OXFORD UNIVERSITY PRESS

they need more or fewer of them to find the area? Have students write their own challenges based on area and swap with other students in the group to find objects that have areas larger, smaller or similar to particular dimensions.

Student Book with teacher support

Students to complete: Guided Practice activities, p. 69. Use base-10 ones and the square metres that students made in the whole-class activity to help them visualise the probable areas for each item.

EXTENSION GROUP

Student Book

Students to complete: Guided and Independent Practice activities, pp. 69–71.

Activity sheet

Students to begin: *Activity sheet 17: An even shorter shortcut.*

Session 3: Instruction and consolidation

WHOLE CLASS

Topic exploration: Investigating area

In mixed-ability pairs, give students a 30 cm ruler and *BLM 17: Investigating area*. Instruct them to estimate the area of the first rectangle using base-10 tens as a unit, and then to check the actual area using base-10 materials. Discuss the importance of exactly covering the area, with no bits hanging over and no overlaps of materials. Ask students to record the area of the rectangle in square centimetres. How do they know? As a class, talk about the connection between square centimetres and the area of a base-10 ten, allowing students to use their rulers to check the measurements for themselves. In their pairs, ask students to estimate and check the area of the second rectangle, then come back together as a class to compare responses.

AT-STANDARD GROUP

Teacher activity: Measuring the bits

Many of the areas that need to be measured in real life can't be measured neatly using square centimetres or square metres. Give each student a piece of centimetre grid paper and ask them to trace around one hand on it. Encourage students to find the area of their hands, either in pairs or individually. Allow them time to formulate and test their own strategies for doing this, then bring the group back together to share ideas. How did students start the task? What tools did they use? What can they do about the parts of the outlines that run through the middle of a centimetre square? Give students more time to apply new strategies they heard discussed, then spend time comparing students'

measurements. How accurate do they think their calculations are? Why? Did the students with visibly larger hand outlines reach a larger total in their area calculation? Encourage students to share strategies for calculating irregular areas with the whole class.

Student Book

Students to complete: Extended Practice activities, p. 72.

SUPPORT GROUP

Student Book with teacher support

Students to complete: Independent and Extended Practice activities, pp. 70–72. Check in with students as they work through the Independent Practice activities, discussing any difficulties, before supporting them to complete the Extended Practice activities.

EXTENSION GROUP

Student Book

Students to complete: Extended Practice activities, p. 72.

Activity sheet

Students to complete: *Activity sheet 17: An even shorter shortcut.*

Practice and Mastery Book

See page 4 for information about how to use the Practice and Mastery Book activities.

Session 4: Post-assessment

Students to complete: Post-test 10, Unit 5, Topic 2, p. 91.

Unit 5 Using units of measurement

Topic 3 Volume and capacity

Student Book pages 73–76

Learning focus

Estimate, measure and compare volume and capacity using standard units of measurement. Convert between litres and millilitres

Materials

- interlocking cubes
- a variety of different measuring jugs with scales
- water
- empty containers with capacities marked on, such as a soft drink bottle or liquid soap bottle
- a 200 g yoghurt container (with the capacity information on the label concealed)
- sour cream, cream, juice and water containers
- tape measures
- 1 L container, such as a milk carton
- a 250 mL container, such as a yoghurt container
- *BLM 28: Comparing capacity*
- *Activity sheet 18: Volume of a rectangular prism*

Potential difficulties: Conceptualising volume and capacity

It can be difficult to distinguish between the concepts of volume and capacity.

- Directly compare the concepts to help students understand the differences. Discuss the fact that capacity is usually measured using something that can be poured, whereas volume is measured using solid cubes, and link this with the formal units that are commonly associated with each property.
- Use gestures such as cupping your hands to represent capacity, and moving your hands outwards to show that space is being taken up for volume.

Daily practice activity

Each day, suggest a container or vessel and ask students if you would measure its capacity in millilitres or litres. Have them stand on one side of the room if they choose millilitres, and on the other side for litres. Allow students to justify their choices.

Session 1: Pre-assessment

Students to complete: Pre-test 11, Unit 5, Topic 3, p. 92.

Session 2: Topic introduction

WHOLE CLASS

Introductory activity: Exploring volume

Revise the idea of volume as the amount of space that an object takes up. Where have students heard the term before? In mixed-ability pairs, give students six interlocking cubes and instruct them to make a 3D shape using all their cubes. Choose some different arrangements to display at the front of the room. Explain that although the objects look different, each has a volume of 6 cubes. Distribute two more interlocking cubes to each pair, then ask students to construct an object with a volume of 8 cubes. Students should draw their object and record its volume. Compare the different objects, then repeat with other volumes.

Introductory activity: Measuring capacity with formal units

In mixed-ability pairs or small groups, distribute measuring jugs with scales marked on them and instruct students to fill the jugs up to halfway with water. Ask students how they knew how much water to put in. Did they try to fill half of the entire jug, or fill to the halfway point of the scaled section? Ask students to put exactly 200 mL in the jug, then look at where the water level is on the scale when they are standing above it, when they have their eyes level with the 200 mL mark and when they are crouching down to look up at it. Which do they think is the best position to be in to get an accurate reading? Why? As a class, discuss how to read measurements that fall between the numbers on the scale. Ask one student in each group to fill the jug with an amount of their choice, and have their partner read the scale. The student who filled the jug should check to make sure they agree with the reading. Students then swap roles.

AT-STANDARD GROUP

Student Book

Students to complete: Guided and Independent Practice activities, pp. 73–75. Ask early finishers to choose an empty container and check if the capacity marked on the outside matches the amount that it holds.

SUPPORT GROUP

Concept exploration and skill development: Comparing capacity

Revise the concept of capacity as the amount that a container can hold. Give small groups of students a copy of *BLM 28: Comparing capacity*, a 200 g yoghurt container (with the capacity information on the label concealed), and a variety of other containers as listed on the sheet. Students should estimate how many yoghurt containers of water will be required to fill each of the other containers, then check the actual number. Students should also record the difference between their estimates and the actual amounts. Allow students to use formal or informal units, depending on their level of understanding.

Student Book with teacher support

Students to complete: Guided Practice activities, p. 73. Model the objects in question 1 to help the students work out the volume as needed.

EXTENSION GROUP

Student Book

Students to complete: Guided and Independent Practice activities, pp. 73–75.

Activity sheet

Students to begin: *Activity sheet 18: Volume of a rectangular prism.*

Session 3: Instruction and consolidation

WHOLE CLASS

Topic exploration: Millilitres and litres

It may have been a while since students last worked with capacity, so it can be helpful to revise the two common units of litres and millilitres. Ask students whether millilitres or litres are larger. Show students an empty 1 L container, such as a milk carton, and an empty 250 mL container, such as a yoghurt container, to demonstrate the relative size of each unit. Ask students to show you how big 1 mL might be using their hands. Reinforce the idea that 1000 mL make up 1 L.

In mixed-ability pairs, ask students to select an appropriate measuring instrument and use water to fill it to 500 mL. How does this compare with 1 L? How do students know? How much more water would they need to add to make 1 L? Discuss whether students' choice of measuring instrument allowed them to accurately measure and compare the amounts, and allow them to choose a more appropriate instrument if they feel they need to.

Have each pair team up with another pair and combine their water in one jug. How much water do they have altogether? Ask students to start again

and this time have each pair fill their jugs to 250 mL. How does this compare with a litre? How many pairs will need to combine their water to make 1 L? Again, invite students to buddy up with other pairs to check their estimates. Repeat with other, smaller amounts, such as 200 mL and 100 mL. You could also challenge groups to work out how much water they have altogether if they have two lots of 750 mL or two lots of 800 mL, testing out their responses by measuring out the smaller amounts and combining them.

AT-STANDARD GROUP

Teacher activity: Problem solving with volume and capacity

Students encounter examples of volume and capacity in their everyday lives without realising it, so it's easy to tie topics to real-life examples. Ask students to imagine that you're going to have a class party. First, tell them you want to buy enough soft drink to ensure that everyone can have at least one cup. Students need to work out how many bottles will be needed, based on a uniform cup size of 250 mL and considering different possible soft drink bottle sizes, such as 1.25 L or 2 L.

Once students have worked out the capacity challenge, ask them to first estimate and then work out how much storage space you will need for the bottles. Students may use formal or informal methods for this task, but will have to measure the dimensions of one bottle in order to work out how much space is needed for several bottles.

Student Book

Students to complete: Extended Practice activities, p. 76.

SUPPORT GROUP

Student Book with teacher support

Students to complete: Independent and Extended Practice activities, pp. 74–76. Check in with students as they work through the Independent Practice activities, discussing any difficulties, before supporting them to complete the Extended Practice activities, assisting students to convert between formal units of capacity as needed.

EXTENSION GROUP

Student Book

Students to complete: Extended Practice activities, p. 76.

Activity sheet

Students to complete: *Activity sheet 18: Volume of a rectangular prism.*

Practice and Mastery Book

See page 4 for information about how to use the Practice and Mastery Book activities.

Session 4: Post-assessment

Students to complete: Post-test 11, Unit 5, Topic 3, p. 93.

Unit 5 Using units of measurement

Topic 4 Mass

Student Book pages 77–80

Learning focus

Estimate, measure and compare standard units of measurement. Convert between the units

Materials

- a selection of different mass measurement instruments, e.g. bathroom scales, digital kitchen scales, graduated kitchen scales and pan balances
- Unifix cubes
- items of varying masses (five per group)
- 200 g bag of flour and 200 g bag of breadcrumbs
- a range of materials such as interlocking cubes, rice, pasta, base-10 ones, paper clips and marbles (to measure mass)
- lunch boxes
- *Activity sheet 19: Worth your weight in gold*

Potential difficulties: Conceptualising formal units

Students often have difficulty estimating the mass of an item or group of items when formal units are introduced.

- Choose a familiar object such as a tennis ball and suggest a list of options for its mass, such as 60 g, 60 kg or 60 t. Discuss which alternative is likely to be correct and why.
- Vary the items and the options, and allow students to check the actual mass of some items to help them develop a sound understanding of mass concepts.

Daily practice activity

Ask students to bring in examples of full packets of items with the mass written on them. As a class, use a scale to check a few each day and see if the marked mass is accurate.

Session 1: Pre-assessment

Students to complete: Pre-test 12, Unit 5, Topic 4, p. 94.

Session 2: Topic introduction

WHOLE CLASS

Introductory activity: Comparing measuring instruments

Gather a collection of different instruments that can be used to measure mass, such as digital bathroom scales, digital kitchen scales, graduated kitchen scales and pan balances with Unifix cubes to use on one side. Divide students into groups so that each group is using one instrument type at a time, and provide a collection of the same five items with different masses for each of the measuring stations. Students should find and record the mass of each item using their allocated instrument, then rotate to the next apparatus until they have used them all. Ask the groups to report back to the class on which instruments were the easiest, most difficult and most accurate to use, and why. Ensure students understand how to read and interpret the scales or displays on each instrument, including when measurements fall between numbers on the scale.

AT-STANDARD GROUP

Student Book

Students to complete: Guided and Independent Practice activities, pp. 77–79. Ask early finishers to find single items or groups of items in the classroom that have masses equivalent to each of those in question 2, p. 79.

SUPPORT GROUP

Concept exploration and skill development: Mass and size

It's not uncommon for students to assume that larger objects have a greater mass, as this is often, although not always, the case. Show students two items of the same mass with obviously different volumes, such as a 200 g bag of flour and a 200 g bag of breadcrumbs, and ask them to guess which has the greater mass. Allow some students to heft both items and see if this changes their perception. Use a scale to find the mass of both items and discuss the results. Were students surprised? Put the items on a pan balance to confirm that they have the same mass.

Provide students with a range of objects such as interlocking cubes, rice, pasta, base-10 ones, paper clips and marbles. In pairs, ask students to measure out a mass, such as 250 g, of each material and record the observations, sharing them with the rest of the class.

OXFORD UNIVERSITY PRESS

Student Book with teacher support

Students to complete: Guided Practice activities, p. 77. Help students to read, interpret and record the numbers on the scale as required.

EXTENSION GROUP

Student Book

Students to complete: Guided and Independent Practice activities, pp. 77–79.

Activity sheet

Students to begin: *Activity sheet 19: Worth your weight in gold.*

Session 3: Instruction and consolidation

WHOLE CLASS

Topic exploration: Understanding grams and kilograms

Students will have had experiences with formal units of mass, but may not have consciously thought about what each unit means. Divide the class into two teams. Choose a member of the first team to find an item in the classroom that they believe has a mass of 1 kg. Ask the student to bring the item out the front and check its actual mass using a scaled instrument. How much over or under 1 kg was the object? You may like to allow students to use a calculator to find the difference; this becomes the team's score. Continue with each team taking turns to find objects of the target mass. The winning team is the team with the lowest score.

Change the parameters of the game to allow students to conceptualise different masses by, for example, asking them to find an item that has a mass of 10 g or 100 g. Allow several turns for each target mass so that students have an opportunity to refine and consolidate their understanding of how different masses feel.

AT-STANDARD GROUP

Teacher activity: Investigating mass

Ask students, "If everyone had the same lunch box, would their lunches have the same mass?" In pairs, instruct students to write their response and the reasoning behind it. Give each group a lunch box of the same size, a set of scales and a variety of materials with which to fill it, such as marbles, Unifix cubes and rice. Allow students some time to investigate the question, then come together as a group and share their observations. What methods have students used to try and prove their answer? Have they changed their initial thoughts? Give students a little more time to experiment with the materials, encouraging them to refine their thinking based on the group discussion. Ask each group to present their findings, then come to a group consensus to answer the question.

Student Book

Students to complete: Extended Practice activities, p. 80.

SUPPORT GROUP

Student Book with teacher support

Students to complete: Independent and Extended Practice activities, pp. 78–80. Check in with students as they work through the Independent Practice activities, discussing any difficulties, before supporting them to complete the Extended Practice activities, using tools such as a decimal place value chart to help with the conversions between units.

EXTENSION GROUP

Student Book

Students to complete: Extended Practice activities, p. 80.

Activity sheet

Students to complete: *Activity sheet 19: Worth your weight in gold.*

Practice and Mastery Book

See page 4 for information about how to use the Practice and Mastery Book activities.

Session 4: Post-assessment

Students to complete: Post-test 12, Unit 5, Topic 4, p. 95.

Unit 5 Using units of measurement

Topic 5 Temperature

Student Book pages 81–84

Learning focus

Read and record temperatures on thermometers and measure and compare the temperature of familiar items and places using standard units of measurement

Materials

- ice cubes
- thermometers
- digital cameras or tablets (optional)
- six clear bowls of water of different temperatures (make sure the hottest one is comfortable to touch)
- *BLM 43: Thermometer template*
- *Activity sheet 20: Keeping it cool and hot*

Potential difficulties: Reading scales

Thermometers often have physically smaller scales than many other instruments, with increments that are not marked on them.

- Give students plenty of experience using different thermometers, and explicitly teach them how to interpret the scales, especially when measures fall between the standard markings.
- Draw parallels with instruments that students are familiar with, such as clock faces, which often don't have the individual minutes marked on them, to help them understand how temperature scales work. Also introduce the use of digital thermometers.

Daily practice activity

Take the temperature at different times of the day and mark it on an enlarged copy of *BLM 43: Thermometer template* with the scale drawn in. Repeat each day and compare the temperatures at the same time across different days.

Session 1: Pre-assessment

Students to complete: Pre-test 13, Unit 5, Topic 5, p. 96.

Session 2: Topic introduction

WHOLE CLASS

Introductory activity: Experimenting with temperature

Discuss the fact that we commonly measure temperature in degrees Celsius, and ask students to suggest where they have seen different temperature measurements. Put students into pairs and provide each pair with three ice cubes and a thermometer. The challenge is for students to keep the ice cubes from melting for as long as possible. Children may use any resources in the room that they like, and can either keep the cubes together or separate them. Every five minutes, students should take the temperature near their ice cubes and record what the ice cubes look like, either in writing, or using a digital camera or tablet to take pictures. When the experiment is over, allow the most successful groups to share their strategies and make a list of conclusions about temperature.

AT-STANDARD GROUP

Student Book

Students to complete: Guided and Independent Practice activities, pp. 81–83. Ask early finishers to list as many different cold, cool, warm and hot items or places as they can.

SUPPORT GROUP

Concept exploration and skill development: Estimating and checking temperature

Although students have probably encountered situations involving temperature in their everyday lives, it's important that they have some direct personal experience of temperature under safe conditions. Fill six clear bowls with water of different temperatures (make sure the hottest one is comfortable to touch) and arrange them in random order so students can see them. Ask students to predict which bowl has the coldest and which has the warmest water in it, encouraging them to justify their responses by discussing indicators such as steam or condensation. Ask a volunteer to feel the water in each bowl and order them from coldest to hottest. What words can be used to describe the temperature of each one? How easy is it to tell the difference? Invite another student to check, to see if they agree. Guide students to use thermometers to check the actual water temperature of each bowl. Did the student place the bowls in the correct order?

Invite students to make any adjustments to the order based on the measured temperatures.

Student Book with teacher support

Students to complete: Guided Practice activities, p. 81. Discuss the scales on the thermometers with students, ensuring that they understand what each of the increment markings represents.

EXTENSION GROUP

Student Book

Students to complete: Guided and Independent Practice activities, pp. 81–83.

Activity sheet

Students to begin: *Activity sheet 20: Keeping it cool and hot.*

Session 3: Instruction and consolidation

WHOLE CLASS

Topic exploration: Understanding thermometer scales

Enlarge a copy of *BLM 43: Thermometer template* and discuss which numbers might be appropriate to mark on the scale if you were to use the thermometer to record the daily temperature. Discuss what each of the major and minor intervals marked on the template represents, and mark in the numbers on the major intervals. In pairs, give students BLM 43 and ask them to work together to complete their own scale. Choose one pair and guide them to mark the predicted temperature for the current day in blue. The next day, have them mark the actual temperature in red, while another pair marks the predicted temperature for that day in blue. Discuss with students how to record and interpret temperatures that fall between the intervals marked on the scale, such as 24.6°C. Continue until all the thermometers are complete, then display them around the room.

AT-STANDARD GROUP

Teacher activity: Temperature in students' lives

From hot soup to melted ice-cream, temperature probably plays a greater role in students' lives than they realise. As a group, brainstorm the different situations in which temperature plays an important role. In pairs, students should choose five situations and conduct some internet research into ideal temperatures associated with each. For example, what is the ideal temperature for soup to be served at, or for ice-cream to be stored at? Encourage students to present their findings in a way that their classmates will find interesting.

Student Book

Students to complete: Extended Practice activities, p. 84.

SUPPORT GROUP

Student Book with teacher support

Students to complete: Independent and Extended Practice activities, pp. 82–84. Check in with students as they work through the Independent Practice activities, discussing any difficulties, before supporting them to complete the Extended Practice activities, assisting them to accurately use and read the thermometers as needed.

EXTENSION GROUP

Student Book

Students to complete: Extended Practice activities, p. 84.

Activity sheet

Students to complete: *Activity sheet 20: Keeping it cool and hot.*

Practice and Mastery Book

See page 4 for information about how to use the Practice and Mastery Book activities.

Session 4: Post-assessment

Students to complete: Post-test 13, Unit 5, Topic 5, p. 97.

Unit 5 Using units of measurement

Topic 6 Time

Student Book pages 85–88

Learning focus

Read and write digital and analogue am and pm time to the minute. Convert between units of time

Materials

- 10-sided dice (one for each pair)
- teaching clock or real analogue clock
- cards with *am* and *pm* written on them
- printed or online version of a TV guide
- *BLM 11: Race to two minutes*
- *BLM 12: Clock anatomy*
- *Activity sheet 21: Why do we have am and pm times?*

Potential difficulties: Experience of analogue time

Most students are told when they need to get ready or when it's time for bed, so they don't need to read a clock for themselves. Given this, and the fact that most devices such as mobile phones and computers use digital time, students' access to analogue time can be limited.

- Make students who are struggling with analogue time responsible for helping to manage time in the classroom. For example, a student could ring a bell at a particular time to let the class know to pack up or move to a new activity.
- Display and regularly refer to an analogue clock in the classroom, relating the time to digital time as appropriate.

Daily practice activity

At different times during the day, stop and ask students to tell the exact time on an analogue clock, designating whether it's am or pm. Ask them to convert this to digital time and describe the differences.

Session 1: Pre-assessment

Students to complete: Pre-test 14, Unit 5, Topic 6, p. 98.

Session 2: Topic introduction

WHOLE CLASS

Introductory activity: Converting time

Students are used to hearing common conversions of time units, such as half an hour being the same as 30 minutes, but less commonly used times can be trickier to convert. Revise the main units of time and how they relate to each other, such as 60 seconds in a minute and 60 minutes in an hour. To practise converting from seconds to minutes, have students play a game of *Race to two minutes* with a partner. Give each student *BLM 11: Race to two minutes* and each pair a 10-sided dice. Students take turns rolling the dice and colouring the corresponding number of squares on the seconds grid. Students should then write the time in seconds in the "Time tally". Play continues, but as students get beyond 60 seconds, they need to express their tally in minutes and seconds, e.g. 65 seconds would be 1 minute, 5 seconds. The winner is the first to reach exactly two minutes. You can also play the game racing backwards from 2 minutes to zero. When students have finished, encourage them to share their ideas about how to convert between seconds and minutes, and relate this to converting between minutes and hours.

AT-STANDARD GROUP

Student Book

Students to complete: Guided and Independent Practice activities, pp. 85–86. Ask early finishers to find a partner and play *Race to two hours*, where the number rolled on a 10-sided dice represents minutes and the aim is to get to exactly two hours.

SUPPORT GROUP

Concept exploration and skill development: Revising time

Some students will need extra support with telling time to the minute. Explain the concept of anatomy as the study of the structure of human beings and animals, and talk about some anatomical features of people, such as the heart, brain and skin. You might also like to look at a labelled anatomical diagram of the human body for children.

Explain that today you'll be looking at the anatomy of a clock. Display a teaching clock or a real analogue clock and ask students what they can tell you about the parts they can see. Give students *BLM 12: Clock anatomy* and ask them to label its parts, drawing in any missing items such as the hands. Come back together as a group and encourage students to share their responses. If students haven't picked up on particular aspects of the clock make sure these are discussed. Also talk about which side of the clock shows "past" times and which side shows "to" times, and ask students how they could represent this on their diagram. Provide some extra time for students to add in any missing items or labels. Finish the session by modelling some times to the minute on your clock and asking students to identify what the time is. Make links to the parts of the clock to help students accurately tell the time.

Student Book with teacher support

Students to complete: Guided Practice activities, p. 85. Encourage students to articulate the calculations necessary for the conversions, and if needed, allow them to use a calculator to find the answers.

EXTENSION GROUP

Student Book

Students to complete: Guided and Independent Practice activities, pp. 85–86.

Activity sheet

Students to begin: *Activity sheet 21: Why do we have am and pm times?*

Session 3: Instruction and consolidation

WHOLE CLASS

Topic exploration: am or pm

As a springboard to discussing am and pm time, tell students that you're going to do the dishes at 9:30 today. Ask them how they might know if you're talking about 9:30 in the morning or 9:30 at night, and introduce the concept of am and pm time. Do students know what these terms stand for (*ante meridiem* and *post meridiem*) and what they mean? Put a card that says *am* on one side of the room and a card that says *pm* on the other side. Describe an activity, such as going to bed, and ask students to place themselves near the most appropriate card. Choose a few students to explain their choices. Continue describing other events, including some deliberately ambiguous ones that will spark discussion, such as reading a story or brushing your teeth.

AT-STANDARD GROUP

Teacher activity: Elapsed time

Time is a hugely important concept in our lives, and equipping students with the skills to manage time will help them as they become increasingly independent. To maintain students' interest as you explore the topic, use resources they can relate to,

such as TV guides. Provide pairs of students with a printed or online version of a TV guide and ask them to suggest which shows they could watch if they turned on the TV at five o' clock and turned it off at eight o'clock, linking the times with their knowledge of am and pm time. Pose a variety of problems to help students develop fluency with time calculations. For example, ask them if they started watching TV at 3:15 pm and finished at 5:40 pm, how long would they have watched for? Or if they finished watching at 8:30 pm and had watched for five and a half hours, when did they start watching? Challenge students to write their own problems using other examples from their lives for their peers to solve.

Student Book

Students to complete: Independent Practice activities, p. 87.

SUPPORT GROUP

Student Book with teacher support

Students to complete: Independent Practice activities, pp. 86–87, talking through the requirements of each problem to support students' understanding as needed.

EXTENSION GROUP

Student Book

Students to complete: Independent Practice activities, p. 87.

Activity sheet

Students to continue: *Activity sheet 21: Why do we have am and pm times?*

Session 4: Instruction and consolidation

WHOLE CLASS

Topic exploration: Constructing timetables

Show students an enlarged copy of your school or class timetable and analyse the structure of it together. How is the information organised? How does that help to interpret the times and events? Ask each student to construct their own individual weekly timetable showing the important activities that they regularly participate in, either on paper or on computer. Discuss appropriate time intervals to use and how students might lay the table out. When students have finished, pair them up and have them make five statements about each other's timetables to check if they have accurately represented their information.

AT-STANDARD GROUP

Student Book

Students to complete: Extended Practice activities, p. 88. Ask early finishers to construct a timetable showing what they would do on their ideal day.

Concept exploration and skill development: Working with elapsed time

Many students have difficulty with elapsed time calculations. Having to factor in the units and their conversions (such as how many minutes are in an hour) as well as the numerical calculation can be challenging. A number line can be a good support for this. Designate a specific colour for hours and a different colour for minutes. Pose a problem, e.g. "Owen went to the movies at 1:50 pm and came home at 4.30 pm. How long was he gone?" Model solving the problem on an empty number line, using the different colours to help students keep track of the different units in the calculations.

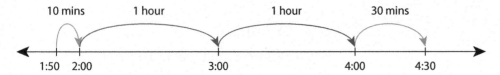

Invite students to suggest how much time has elapsed altogether, and discuss how they worked this out.

Pose similar problems to students to solve in pairs using an empty number line. If they are ready, challenge students with problems that move from am to pm time or vice versa, and talk through how to work out the elapsed time.

Student Book with teacher support

Students to complete: Extended Practice activities, p. 88, using empty number lines to support students with the elapsed time calculations as needed.

EXTENSION GROUP

Student Book

Students to complete: Extended Practice activities, p. 88.

Activity sheet

Students to complete: *Activity sheet 21: Why do we have am and pm times?*

Practice and Mastery Book

See page 4 for information about how to use the Practice and Mastery Book activities.

Session 5: Post-assessment

Students to complete: Post-test 14, Unit 5, Topic 6, p. 99.

Unit 5 Using units of measurement

Topic 7 Timelines

Student Book pages 89–92

Learning focus

Use knowledge of time to construct and interpret timelines in real-life situations

Materials

- blank cards
- markers of different colours
- a long piece of string
- access to relevant items such as figurines that relate to inquiry study
- online timeline maker

Potential difficulties: Scales

Students need a strong understanding of scale in order to be able to represent events that are not equally and accurately spaced on a timeline.

- Relate the concept of scale to students' other experiences with scales, such as on measuring instruments or maps, and explicitly discuss the scale for each timeline that you view together.

- Experiment using different scales with the same information on a timeline with students so that they can see the importance of choosing an appropriate scale. For example, plot the events in a school day on a timeline that has each half hour marked in and on a timeline that just has the morning and the afternoon blocks marked in, and discuss how easy or difficult it is to place events accurately on each.

Daily practice activity

Build a timeline together as you progress through the day, starting with marking the time that school begins and adding each major event as it occurs. Repeat on several days through the week to refine how to scale and represent the events accurately.

Session 1: Pre-assessment

Students to complete: Pre-test 15, Unit 5, Topic 7, p. 100.

Session 2: Topic introduction

WHOLE CLASS

Introductory activity: Constructing timelines

Discuss with students what a timeline is and when you might use one. Model a simple timeline of what you did on Saturday or Sunday, incorporating analogue and digital time as well as am and pm time. Explain how you decided where to place each event along your timeline to give an idea of the spacing of each event.

Review the different events with students, and ask them to suggest other pieces of information you could have included, such as a clock showing the finishing times, how long each event took, or even pictures to go with the events. In pairs, ask students to create their own timelines showing what they have done during the school day. Challenge them to include as much information as possible, and to make their timelines interesting to look at. When students have finished, display their timelines around the room for others to view.

Start times:

Walk the dog	Get ready for brunch	Brunch with friends	Relax with a book	Grocery shopping
8:45 am–9:30 am	9:30 am–10:00 am	10:00 am–12:10 pm	12:10 pm–3:00 pm	3:00 pm–4:05 pm

AT-STANDARD GROUP

Student Book

Students to complete: Guided and Independent Practice activities, pp. 89–91. Ask early finishers to research some other events in Australia's history and add them to the timeline on p. 91.

SUPPORT GROUP

Concept exploration and skill development: Conceptualising timelines

To consolidate students' understanding of timelines, give each student a set of about six blank cards and a different coloured marker. As a group, brainstorm events in students' lives that could be represented on a timeline, such as when they were born and when they learned to swim. Choose about six of the events, bearing in mind that students must know when they achieved each of the milestones, and ask students to record the events you decide on as a group on their individual cards.

Set out a long piece of string to represent a timeline and invite students to place their earliest event towards the left end of the string. What label might need to be included to show the timespan of the event? Add this on one of the spare cards in a different colour. Work through the remaining events, discussing the scale and placement for each one with the group. When everything is in place, work together to compare the timing of different events for each student. Are there any milestones that everyone reached at the same time? Leave the timeline in place and allow students to share their observations with the rest of the class, inviting questions about how the timeline was constructed from those who didn't participate.

Student Book with teacher support

Students to complete: Guided Practice activities, p. 89.

EXTENSION GROUP

Student Book

Students to complete: Guided and Independent Practice activities, pp. 89–91.

Session 3: Instruction and consolidation

WHOLE CLASS

Topic exploration: Experimenting with timelines

Choose a topic that you are currently studying in class that lends itself to timelines, such as history or an aspect of science that involves experiments or changes over time. In pairs or small groups, challenge students to choose the most important information that relates to the topic and use it to create a three-dimensional timeline display. The

timeline could include physical objects such as figurines as well as labels and additional information about the events or milestones on the timeline. Encourage students to be creative so that they produce a timeline that is visually interesting and informative, while still accurately representing the scale of the activities. Allow groups to view each other's completed timelines and to give each other feedback on how effective their timeline is in meeting its purpose.

AT-STANDARD GROUP

Teacher activity: Digital timelines

To extend students' experiences of timelines, challenge them to make a timeline using online software. Choose an area of interest to make a timeline as a group or allow students to select a topic of their own and identify the key events and related times. Students then put the information into the software to create the timeline and share it with the rest of the group. Discuss how the different events for the timeline were chosen, and encourage students to compare their experiences of using this method of constructing a timeline with their other experiences. Which method allowed for more accurate representation of the events? When might you choose to use each method?

Student Book

Students to complete: Extended Practice activities, p. 92.

SUPPORT GROUP

Student Book with teacher support

Students to complete: Independent and Extended Practice activities, pp. 90–92. Check in with students as they work through the Independent Practice activities, discussing any difficulties, before supporting them to complete the Extended Practice activities.

EXTENSION GROUP

Student Book

Students to complete: Extended Practice activities, p. 92.

Practice and Mastery Book

See page 4 for information about how to use the Practice and Mastery Book activities.

Session 4: Post-assessment

Students to complete: Post-test 15, Unit 5, Topic 7, p. 101.

OXFORD UNIVERSITY PRESS

Unit 6 Shape
Topic 1 2D shapes
Student Book pages 93–96

Learning focus

Understand and describe common properties of polygons. Investigate the effects of combining and splitting shapes

Materials

- pattern blocks
- attribute blocks (optional)
- digital camera or tablet
- *BLM 3: Splitting shapes*
- *Activity sheet 22: A world of patterns*

Activity sheet materials

- grid paper
- a pencil and ruler
- a geoboard with nine pins
- an elastic band

Potential difficulties: Language of geometry

The range and complexity of terms used when studying geometry can be overwhelming for some students.

- Offer simplified alternatives alongside technical language to ensure that students don't feel lost or confused. For example, talk about "polygons or many-sided shapes".
- Create and display visual references to support students as they work with 2D shapes, such as a chart that lists the names of common shapes, along with their properties, and a picture for students to refer to.

Daily practice activity

Draw a variety of shapes on the whiteboard each day and ask students to suggest different ways to group them. Encourage them to be creative using shape properties they're familiar with, such as parallel lines and right angles, as well as whether shapes are regular, irregular or congruent.

Session 1: Pre-assessment

Students to complete: Pre-test 16, Unit 6, Topic 1, p. 102.

Session 2: Topic introduction

WHOLE CLASS

Introductory activity: Triangle pictures

Choose students to draw different triangles on the board and compare them, reviewing the properties of each. How are they the same? How are they different? Encourage students to draw triangles in a variety of orientations to ensure they understand that they do not always have to sit on their base, and that changing the orientation does not change any of the other shape properties. Set students the task of drawing a picture using only triangles. They can combine the triangles any way they like to make new shapes, draw them in any orientation and at any size, but may not use any other shapes. Make resources such as pattern or attribute blocks available for students to trace or copy. Share and display students' pictures and discuss their findings about which 2D shapes can be made by combining triangles.

Introductory activity: Congruency

Show students two hexagons from a pattern block set and tell them that the shapes are congruent. Ask students to suggest what this might mean. Next, show them two of the diamonds and let them know that these are congruent, inviting students to refine their idea of what congruency is. Lastly, show students one large and one small square and let them know that although the two shapes are similar, they are not congruent. In pairs, ask students to write a short definition of what congruent means. Share responses as a class and record a final definition that you are all happy with.

In pairs, send students to go on a congruency hunt through the classroom. Have them either take photos of examples that they find, or to bring the examples out the front. As a class, review the items that were found, superimposing one on the other where possible, to check that they are congruent.

AT-STANDARD GROUP

Student Book

Students to complete: Guided and Independent Practice activities, pp. 93–95. Ask early finishers to make, draw and name as many shapes as they can by combining squares.

SUPPORT GROUP

Concept exploration and skill development: Comparing 2D shapes

To consolidate students' understanding of the names and properties of 2D shapes, create a polygon mind map as a group. The mind map could include elements such as the subsets of common shape types, such as quadrilaterals, and the number of corners and sides each shape has. (See below for example.) Add to or change the map as students' knowledge develops throughout the topic.

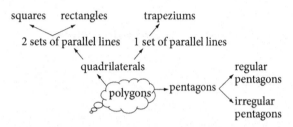

Student Book with teacher support

Students to complete: Guided Practice activities, p. 93. Encourage students to compare the table with their mind map, making adjustments or additions to the map as appropriate.

EXTENSION GROUP

Student Book

Students to complete: Guided and Independent Practice activities, pp. 93–95.

Activity sheet

Students to begin: *Activity sheet 22: A world of patterns*.

Session 3: Instruction and consolidation

WHOLE CLASS

Topic exploration: Combining shapes

Hands-on experience is the best way for students to understand the effect of combining different shapes. Using a whiteboard, demonstrate how combining common shapes can produce other shapes. For example, combine four small squares to make a large square or a long rectangle. Provide groups of students with pattern blocks and allow them to explore other combinations of shapes. Use a digital camera or tablet to take photos of the different shapes that students have made and present the photos in class displays or a slide presentation about 2D shapes. Encourage students to make observations of the properties of both the original and the new shapes they have made and record these in their presentations.

AT-STANDARD GROUP

Teacher activity: Splitting shapes

Many common and regular shapes can be split or divided into two or more equal parts, sometimes consisting of other shapes. Give students a copy of *BLM 3: Splitting shapes* and ask them to find a way to divide each shape into two or more equal parts. Challenge students to find more than one way to split each shape; for example, the star can be divided into five equal parts by making a mark at the mid-point and drawing lines out to each corner, or into two equal parts by drawing a line down the middle. Encourage students to share their findings about the shapes they split and which shapes they split them into. Also discuss whether both the original shapes and the shapes they were split into were regular or irregular.

Student Book

Students to complete: Extended Practice activities, p. 96.

SUPPORT GROUP

Student Book with teacher support

Students to complete: Independent and Extended Practice activities, pp. 94–96. Check in with students as they work through the Independent Practice activities, discussing any difficulties, before supporting them to complete the Extended Practice activities, giving them the opportunity to clarify any terms they aren't sure of as they work.

EXTENSION GROUP

Student Book

Students to complete: Extended Practice activities, p. 96.

Activity sheet

Students to complete: *Activity sheet 22: A world of patterns*.

Practice and Mastery Book

See page 4 for information about how to use the Practice and Mastery Book activities.

Session 4: Post-assessment

Students to complete: Post-test 16, Unit 6, Topic 1, p. 103.

OXFORD UNIVERSITY PRESS

Unit 6 Shape
Topic 2 3D shapes

Student Book pages 97–100

Learning focus

Analyse and describe 3D shapes using geometrical language. Sketch and name common 3D shapes

Materials

- plasticine
- matchsticks
- examples of prisms and pyramids, such as tissue boxes
- a shoe
- digital camera or tablet
- interlocking cubes
- *Activity sheet 23: Packaging*

Activity sheet materials

- an empty, rectangular-shaped tissue box

Potential difficulties: Spatial organisation

Students who have difficulty with visualisation can find 3D shape concepts challenging. These students may struggle to predict what a 3D shape will look like when it's rotated, or when it's cut to make a cross-section.

- Involve the class in creating a list of features to match pictures of 3D shapes, as a useful reference point to help students visualise changes.
- Allow students to see, feel, describe and draw objects from different perspectives to consolidate their understanding.

Daily practice activity

Each day, show students a different box or real-life 3D shape, such as a cereal box or an ice-cream cone, and ask them to name the corresponding 3D shape and describe it. Invite students to describe what they think the box or object would look like if you opened it out flat. Where possible, show them the result and discuss how the shapes visible on the flattened version relate to the 3D shape.

Session 1: Pre-assessment

Students to complete: Pre-test 16, Unit 6, Topic 2, p. 102.

Session 2: Topic introduction

WHOLE CLASS

Introductory activity: Constructing and naming 3D shapes

Revise the main features of 3D shapes, including faces, corners or vertices, and edges. In small groups, ask students to construct objects that meet set criteria using plasticine and matchsticks. For instance, ask students to make as many different 3D shapes as they can that have eight corners, or that have at least two triangular faces. Compare the results, discussing the relationships between the different attributes and allowing students to share the strategies they used for finding shapes with particular features.

AT-STANDARD GROUP

Student Book

Students to complete: Guided Practice activities, p. 97. Ask early finishers to practise sketching and labelling different objects.

SUPPORT GROUP

Concept exploration and skill development: Describing and classifying pyramids and prisms

Classifying 3D shapes is a good way to consolidate students' knowledge of their attributes. Spread a range of prisms and pyramids, including models and real-life examples, such as tissue boxes, in front of students. Ask for suggestions of ways to organise the objects, encouraging students to describe the reasons for their groupings. Separate the objects into prisms and pyramids. Can students identify the common features by which the objects have been grouped? Do they know the names of the 3D shapes in each collection? As a group, write definitions of prisms and pyramids based on students' observations.

Student Book with teacher support

Students to complete: Guided Practice activities, p. 97. Provide 3D examples of each object to help students with their sketching and identification as needed.

Student Book

Students to complete: Guided Practice activities, p. 97.

Activity sheet

Students to begin: *Activity sheet 23: Packaging.*

Session 3: Instruction and consolidation

WHOLE CLASS

Topic exploration: Top view, front view and side view

Introduce students to the idea that objects look different depending on where you view them from. Show students a shoe and ask them to describe what it looks like from the front. Rotate the shoe so that students can see the top. How is this different from the front view? What can they see that they couldn't before? Lastly, show students the side view of the shoe and ask them to describe it.

In pairs or small groups, ask students to use a digital camera or tablet to take pictures of the top, front and side views of three objects in the classroom. Students should then make a digital presentation, or print the photos to make a print version, labelling and describing the different views of their objects. Share students' presentations with the class. Are there any objects that look the same from two or more different views? When might you need to know what an object looks like from different perspectives?

AT-STANDARD GROUP

Teacher activity: Exploring 3D shape views

Draw four squares on the board in a 2 × 2 array as shown below.

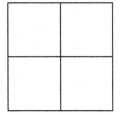

In pairs, give students a supply of interlocking cubes and ask them to make a 3D shape that has a front view that matches your drawing. Instruct students to check each other's shapes to make sure the front view is correct. Are all the students' shapes the same? Ask students to describe their 3D shapes using terms such as faces, edges and corners.

Repeat, drawing different combinations of squares and asking students to make a 3D shape with the same front, side or top view as you have drawn. Challenge students by asking them to make a 3D shape with both a front and a top view the same as your drawing.

Student Book

Students to complete: Independent and Extended Practice activities, pp. 98–100.

SUPPORT GROUP

Student Book with teacher support

Students to complete: Independent and Extended Practice activities, pp. 98–100. Check in with students as they work through the Independent Practice activities, discussing any difficulties, before supporting them to complete the Extended Practice activities, using 3D models and interlocking cubes to give them a visual reference point as needed.

EXTENSION GROUP

Student Book

Students to complete: Independent and Extended Practice activities, pp. 98–100.

Activity sheet

Students to complete: *Activity sheet 23: Packaging.*

Practice and Mastery Book

See page 4 for information about how to use the Practice and Mastery Book activities.

Session 4: Post-assessment

Students to complete: Post-test 16, Unit 6, Topic 2, p. 103.

Unit 7 Geometric reasoning

Topic 1 Angles

Student Book pages 101–104

Learning focus

Understand an angle as a measure of rotation and describe common angle types in relation to a right angle

Materials

- interlocking cubes
- digital cameras or tablets
- *Activity sheet 24: Angles in sport*

Potential difficulties: Spatial perception

Some students may have difficulty classifying angles in relation to a right angle without a physical reference point.

- Show students how to compare a right-angle finder with angles in the classroom, giving them visual confirmation of the size of an angle.
- To develop their ability to conceptualise angle sizes, encourage students to predict the relative size of an angle, then check this using an angle finder or a known right angle.

Daily practice activity

Focus on a different angle type each day and ask students to suggest examples of that angle within the classroom or in their daily lives. Record the examples in a list for display in the classroom.

Session 1: Pre-assessment

Students to complete: Pre-test 17, Unit 7, Topic 1, p. 104.

Session 2: Topic introduction

WHOLE CLASS

Introductory activity: Making different angles

Revise right angles with students, asking them to identify different examples of right angles around the room. Demonstrate how to make a right-angle finder using interlocking cubes connected to form an L-shape, and discuss how you can use this to check whether a particular angle is larger or smaller than

a right angle. In mixed-ability pairs, ask students to make their own right-angle finder from interlocking cubes. Students should then experiment with making angles that are bigger and smaller than a right angle with their bodies while doing sit-ups. One student can stop at a point during the sit-up, and their partner classifies the angle between their torso and their legs using their angle finder to help them. Test students' understanding by calling out a criterion, e.g. "Smaller than a right angle", and instructing them to form an angle of the designated size using their bodies.

AT-STANDARD GROUP

Student Book

Students to complete: Guided and Independent Practice activities, pp. 101–103. Ask early finishers to find examples of straight angles and revolutions, either in the classroom or online.

SUPPORT GROUP

Concept exploration and skill development: Comparing angles

Revise what an angle is and the main parts of an angle, such as the arms and the amount of turn. In pairs, ask students to make a right-angle finder with interlocking cubes in the same way they did for the whole class activity. Instruct students to find three things in the classroom that have a right angle, and to take a photo of each object with their angle finder to show that the angles are the same size. Repeat with identifying angles smaller than a right angle and larger than a right angle. Show students how to make a straight angle with interlocking cubes and ask them to locate and photograph three examples of straight angles in the classroom. Come back together as a group and share the photos, encouraging children to articulate how they compared each angle with their right-angle finder. You may also like to collate the students' responses and share them with the whole class.

Student Book with teacher support

Students to complete: Guided Practice activities, p. 101, using their right-angle finders to help them compare the angle sizes if needed.

EXTENSION GROUP

Student Book

Students to complete: Guided and Independent Practice activities, pp. 101–103.

Activity sheet

Students to begin: *Activity sheet 24: Angles in sport.*

Session 3: Instruction and consolidation

WHOLE CLASS

Topic exploration: Identifying and classifying angles

Students are surrounded by examples of different angles, so their immediate environment is a useful resource for the topic. Play a game of *Angle I Spy* as a class or in small groups. One student selects an angle and gives an I-Spy-type clue, e.g. "I spy with my little eye an angle that is smaller than a right angle". The other students must try and guess which angle the clue is referring to. After five guesses, a further clue may be required to narrow down the location of the angle, or to further refine its description, e.g. "My angle is smaller than the angle made by that book leaning against the wall". Discuss and compare the examples students find for each classification of angle.

Topic exploration: Angles and directions

Linking angles with directions is a good way to get across the concept of an angle as an amount of turn. Take students outside and divide them into two teams. Each team should choose one member to be the traveller. Have the traveller from one team start at one end of an area such as a basketball court while the traveller from the other team starts at the other end. Each team also needs three direction givers. The other students need to arrange themselves on the basketball court in a way that makes it difficult for the opponent to make it from one end to the other in a straight line. The traveller from team 1 starts walking until they encounter another player on the court. The direction givers must then suggest in which direction the traveller needs to turn and by how much – for example, a right-angle turn counter clockwise. After the turn is complete, it is team 2's turn. Each turn consists of the traveller moving until they reach another student or the edge of the court and are instructed to make a turn ready for their next move. The winning team is the first to get their traveller to the other end of the court. After students have played the game once, switch roles and encourage students to think about how to place themselves to make it more difficult for the opposition to get past without many turns.

AT-STANDARD GROUP

Teacher activity: Angles in shapes

Computers are a good tool through which to investigate angles, as you can create and manipulate a variety of shapes relatively easily. Ask students to devise a poster for printing or online presentation showing how angles in different shapes compare with right angles. Students should include shapes that only have right angles, shapes that have at least one right angle, and shapes that have no right angles. To get them started, you could model one or two shapes on the board, writing descriptions of the number of right angles and the number of angles bigger and smaller than right angles for each one. Encourage students to present their work to the whole class to consolidate their learning.

Student Book

Students to complete: Extended Practice activities, p. 104.

SUPPORT GROUP

Student Book with teacher support

Students to complete: Independent and Extended Practice activities, pp. 102–104. Check in with students as they work through the Independent Practice activities, discussing any difficulties, before supporting them to complete the Extended Practice activities. Help them visualise invisible angle arms such as the base of the doorway that makes an angle with the open door, and, if necessary, using a straight object such as a ruler to trace the invisible arm.

EXTENSION GROUP

Student Book

Students to complete: Extended Practice activities, p. 104.

Activity sheet

Students to complete: *Activity sheet 24: Angles in sport.*

Practice and Mastery Book

See page 4 for information about how to use the Practice and Mastery Book activities.

Session 4: Post-assessment

Students to complete: Post-test 17, Unit 7, Topic 1, p. 105.

OXFORD UNIVERSITY PRESS

Unit 8 Location and transformation
Topic 1 Symmetry

Student Book pages 105–108

Learning focus

Use transformations to investigate and create symmetrical patterns

Materials

- mirror
- square tiles
- grid paper
- cookie cutters
- scissors
- modelling clay or plasticine (optional)
- pattern blocks (optional)
- computers or tablets
- digital cameras or tablets
- graphics program or app such as KidPix or Pattern Shapes (optional)
- *Activity sheet 25: Line and rotational symmetry*

Potential difficulties: Visualising symmetry

As with many concepts in mathematics, symmetry needs to be exact. Students need to understand that although some patterns or pictures may look symmetrical, small discrepancies make them asymmetrical.

- Ask students to look at their faces in a mirror, or at each other's faces. Are they symmetrical? How can they tell they are not?
- Show students how to match elements in a pattern or picture point to point to check if they are exactly symmetrical.

Daily practice activity

On the first day, present an equilateral triangle and ask students to predict and then test how many lines of symmetry it has. Record the number of sides and the number of lines of symmetry on a chart. Each day, present a different regular shape (square, pentagon, hexagon, octagon, etc.) and complete the same activity, recording the results on

the chart. On the final day, invite students to share their observations about regular shapes and lines of symmetry.

Session 1: Pre-assessment

Students to complete: Pre-test 18, Unit 8, Topic 1, p. 106.

Session 2: Topic introduction

WHOLE CLASS

Introductory activity: Exploring line symmetry

Revise the definition of symmetry, and ask students to suggest some examples they can see in the classroom. Explain that a pentomino is a geometric figure made by joining five squares together so that the edges of adjacent tiles align. In mixed-ability pairs, give students five square tiles, and explain that they are going to make different pentominoes and find out whether each has line symmetry. Students should record each pentomino they make on grid paper and note their findings about symmetry next to each one. Share the results, classifying the pentominoes according to their symmetrical properties.

AT-STANDARD GROUP

Student Book

Students to complete: Guided and Independent Practice activities, pp. 105–107. Ask early finishers to write their first name and then try to write it three times beneath, reflecting it vertically each time. Students can then repeat the exercise, this time reflecting their names horizontally.

SUPPORT GROUP

Concept exploration and skill development: Consolidating line symmetry

Manipulating shapes is a good way for students to develop an understanding of line symmetry. Present students with a collection of cookie cutters of different shapes and sizes. Ask them to trace inside the shapes onto paper and cut them out, or press them into modelling clay or plasticine. Guide students to close their eyes and visualise whether each shape has any lines of symmetry, and to describe what they are picturing. Encourage students to fold their paper or clay shapes to check if their assessment is correct and to find additional lines of symmetry. Discuss their findings as a group, allowing students to explain and demonstrate how they reached their conclusions.

Student Book with teacher support

Students to complete: Guided Practice activities, p. 105. Model the patterns with pattern blocks or shape cut-outs to support students' understanding as needed.

EXTENSION GROUP

Student Book

Students to complete: Guided and Independent Practice activities, pp. 105–107.

Activity sheet

Students to begin: *Activity sheet 25: A world of symmetry.*

Session 3: Instruction and consolidation

WHOLE CLASS

Topic exploration: Multiple lines of symmetry

Students can often readily identify that an object has one line of symmetry, but may struggle to understand that some shapes have multiple lines of symmetry. On an interactive whiteboard, or using a computer and data projector, draw a square and ask students whether it's symmetrical. Invite students to close their eyes and visualise the different lines of symmetry that the shape has. Choose a student to draw a line of symmetry on the square, then ask if anyone can find a second line. Inform students that a square actually has four lines of symmetry and see if they can visualise and then find them all. Are students aware that lines of symmetry can be horizontal, vertical or diagonal? Have pairs of students conduct their own symmetry investigations on a computer or tablet, creating shapes, visualising the lines of symmetry and drawing in lines to test their predictions. Share and record their findings as a class.

Topic exploration: Symmetrical patterns in the environment

There are many examples of symmetry in nature and the broader environment. Brainstorm with students where they have seen symmetry in the schoolyard, such as in playground equipment or a spider web. Give pairs of students a digital camera or tablet and allow them time to find and photograph as many examples of symmetry as they can. When they return, have the students put together a slide presentation or other digital presentation including their pictures and a description of the patterns that they found. Ask students to also include whether or not the pattern shows tessellation, and any transformations of shapes that are evident in the pattern. Share the completed presentation with the class or at a school assembly.

AT-STANDARD GROUP

Teacher activity: Making symmetrical patterns and pictures

Allowing students to create their own symmetrical patterns and pictures can help consolidate the concept of symmetry. Use a graphics program or app such as KidPix or Pattern Shapes to demonstrate how to make a symmetrical pattern using shapes and stamps. Set students the task of making a pattern with only one line of symmetry and making a second pattern with two or more lines of symmetry. Invite students to present their work to the class, explaining how each pattern is symmetrical. How can students check if the patterns are symmetrical? Do they understand how multiple lines of symmetry work? This activity could also be completed using pattern blocks if you do not have access to an appropriate computer program.

Student Book

Students to complete: Extended Practice activities, p. 108.

SUPPORT GROUP

Student Book with teacher support

Students to complete: Independent and Extended Practice activities, pp. 106–108. Check in with students as they work through the Independent Practice activities, discussing any difficulties, before supporting them to complete the Extended Practice activities, using pattern blocks to test whether shapes tessellate as needed.

EXTENSION GROUP

Student Book

Students to complete: Extended Practice activities, p. 108.

Activity sheet

Students to complete: *Activity sheet 25: A world of symmetry.*

Practice and Mastery Book

See page 4 for information about how to use the Practice and Mastery Book activities.

Session 4: Post-assessment

Students to complete: Post-test 18, Unit 8, Topic 1, p. 107.

OXFORD UNIVERSITY PRESS

Unit 8 Location and transformation

Topic 2 Scales and maps

Student Book pages 109–112

Learning focus

Use scales, legends and grid references to locate features on a grid, and follow directions involving compass points

Materials

- 30 cm rulers
- a range of maps such road maps, street directories and maps from tourist attractions
- directional compasses
- metre rulers or tape measures
- BLM 41: Scale drawings
- BLM 42: Grid map
- Activity sheet 26: Using grid references

Potential difficulties: Digital maps

As maps are increasingly being accessed through digital technology such as Global Positioning System (GPS) devices, it's important that students also experience maps in digital form.

- Compare paper and digital maps to see which features they have in common and which are unique to each.
- Familiarise students with the conventions of online maps, such as zooming in to see features and areas in more detail.

Daily practice activity

Display a different map on the whiteboard each day and ask students to describe as many features as they can.

Session 1: Pre-assessment

Students to complete: Pre-test 19, Unit 8, Topic 2, p. 108.

Session 2: Topic introduction

WHOLE CLASS

Introductory activity: Scales

Scales can be difficult for students to understand, so it's useful to present simpler representations of scale while they are mastering the concept. In pairs, give students BLM 41: Scale drawings and ask them to use a ruler to measure the height and width of the smallest square. Explain that it has been reduced in size and drawn to a scale of 1 cm = 2 cm, then ask them which of the other three squares shows how large it would be in real life. Guide students to measure the three larger squares and choose the shape that shows the actual size of the smallest square. Ask students to complete the other examples to experience different scales, then encourage pairs to team up and compare their answers. If students are coping well, challenge them to create an example of their own for other students to complete.

AT-STANDARD GROUP

Student Book

Students to complete: Guided and Independent Practice activities, pp. 109–111. Ask early finishers to work with a partner to measure the classroom and try to make a scale drawing of it, using a scale such as 1 cm to equal 1 m.

SUPPORT GROUP

Concept exploration and skill development: Investigating map features

Provide a variety of different maps for students to look at, such as road maps, street directories and maps from tourist attractions. Ask each pair to choose a map and write a list of at least five things that their map shows. The list may include general things, such as the fact that the map has mountains on it, or specific observations, such as the fact that there is a kiosk at B4 on the map. Discuss students' findings as a group and have them identify whether features that other students have noted are also on their maps.

Student Book with teacher support

Students to complete: Guided Practice activities, p. 109. Work with students to ensure that they can accurately interpret the scale and find the distances on the map.

EXTENSION GROUP

Student Book

Students to complete: Guided and Independent Practice activities, pp. 109–111.

Activity sheet

Students to begin: Activity sheet 26: Using grid references.

Session 3: Instruction and consolidation

WHOLE CLASS

Topic exploration: Compass points

Students are likely to be aware of the main points on a compass, but may not have had experience relating these to actual directions and locations in real life. Ask students if they know which way north is. Do they point upwards, or do they have a general idea of the correct direction? Distribute compasses to pairs of students and show them how to identify where north is. Can they locate the other cardinal points using this information? Have pairs of students write simple directions from one point in the classroom or school to another, using compass points as a guide. Swap the instructions around and see if students can accurately follow the directions to reach the correct end point.

AT-STANDARD GROUP

Teacher activity: Legends

Constructing their own maps can help consolidate students' understanding of key features. Give students, individually or in pairs, *BLM 42: Grid map* and ask them to design a map of their ideal theme park. Brainstorm essential elements, such as toilets and food outlets, as well as a list of other possible attractions, to get students started. Each map must have a legend that visitors could use to find their way around. Remind students of the importance of choosing appropriate symbols to represent places on the map and legend. When the maps are completed, ask students to share their work with other students.

Student Book

Students to complete: Extended Practice activities, p. 112.

SUPPORT GROUP

Student Book with teacher support

Students to complete: Independent and Extended Practice activities, pp. 110–112. Check in with students as they work through the Independent Practice activities, discussing any difficulties, before supporting them to complete the Extended Practice activities, assisting students with using grid references and compass directions as needed.

EXTENSION GROUP

Student Book

Students to complete: Extended Practice activities, p. 112.

Activity sheet

Students to complete: *Activity sheet 26: Using grid references*.

Practice and Mastery Book

See page 4 for information about how to use the Practice and Mastery Book activities.

Session 4: Post-assessment

Students to complete: Post-test 19, Unit 8, Topic 2, p. 109.

OXFORD UNIVERSITY PRESS

Unit 9 Data representation and interpretation
Topic 1 Collecting data

Student Book pages 113–116

Learning focus

Collect, organise and display data using surveys and simple graphs

Materials

- adhesive
- *Activity sheet 27: The words we use*

Potential difficulties: Questioning skills

Some students find it difficult to phrase appropriate questions to gather the information they need.

- Revise the basics of questioning, including question words, to help students generate a range of questions for different situations.
- Conduct activities, such as challenging students to write 20 different questions about a single topic, to further develop their skills. Question-and-answer matching activities can also help students develop an understanding of the kinds of answers that particular questions may elicit.

Daily practice activity

Give students an answer, such as "a book", and ask them to suggest questions that could elicit that response. Discuss students' suggestions, and ask them to suggest which questions are the most effective and why.

Session 1: Pre-assessment
Students to complete: Pre-test 20, Unit 9, Topic 1, p. 110.

Session 2: Topic introduction
WHOLE CLASS

Introductory activity: Data collection methods

When planning and conducting data investigations, make sure students have some background knowledge about their options. Brainstorm different methods of collecting data, such as asking questions, observing situations or outcomes, or classifying and counting items. Have students think of investigations that each method would be appropriate for. For instance, observation of the number of bikes in the bike rack might be a good way of finding out how many students rode to school that day, whereas survey questions would be a better way to find out how each student got to school. Discuss the most effective way to record the data for each method. What sort of information would best be recorded on a list? When would a table be more appropriate? Encourage students to use this knowledge as they complete data collection exercises.

AT-STANDARD GROUP

Student Book

Students to complete: Guided and Independent Practice activities, pp. 113–115. Ask early finishers to choose an appropriate survey topic for their classmates and write a question to ask them. Have them survey 10 students and record their results.

SUPPORT GROUP

Concept exploration and skill development: Open and closed questions

Students need to be familiar with different question types and the kinds of answers they are likely to elicit. This will help them choose appropriate questions when gathering data. Explain that questions that elicit a "Yes" or "No" response are known as closed questions, while questions that need longer answers are open questions. Have students suggest examples of both question types. Ask each student to write a question on a piece of paper, then put them in pairs and give each pair two of the questions. Students should review their questions and decide if they are open or closed. Allocate an area for each question type on the board or a blank area of wall and ask students to place their questions in the correct category using adhesive. Do students agree with the classification of each question? Discuss when you might use each question type, linking this to data collection situations, such as surveys.

Student Book with teacher support

Students to complete: Guided Practice activities, p. 113. Link the questions with students' knowledge of open and closed questions, referring them to the question displays as required.

EXTENSION GROUP

Student Book

Students to complete: Guided and Independent Practice activities, pp. 113–115.

Activity sheet

Students to begin: *Activity sheet 27: The words we use.*

Session 3: Instruction and consolidation

WHOLE CLASS

Topic exploration: Designing and executing a survey

Find a genuine reason for students to conduct a survey, such as finding out how much brain food is eaten in the school as part of a unit on healthy eating. In small mixed-ability groups, students should design their survey question, then work out how they're going to gather their information and record their data. Give groups time to follow through on their investigations and construct a pictograph or bar graph to display the results. As a class, compare the data and discuss whether students' questions elicited the information they wanted. Which questions were the most effective? Why?

AT-STANDARD GROUP

Teacher activity: Organising data

Students need to be able to make lists and tables so they can keep data in an organised manner, ensuring it can be easily used for analysis or to make graphs. Using a program such as Microsoft Excel lays the foundations for using digital technologies to construct data displays. Present relevant tables to students, such as school sports results, to allow them to connect their learning with real life. Revise the major parts of a table, such as headings and where the collected data is recorded, and ask students to identify the parts in your sample table. Discuss what a database is and model how to set up a table in Excel or Word. Give students a simple data investigation to conduct, such as finding the favourite colours of students in the group, then have them record the information in a simple tabular database they have created on the computer. Compare students' tables to see if they are organised in the same way, and if they all contain the same data. Did anyone divide the information up according to a second variable, such as gender? Invite students to suggest questions that could be answered by the information in the database. When could tables be used to help organise data that students have collected?

Student Book

Students to complete: Extended Practice activities, p. 116.

SUPPORT GROUP

Student Book with teacher support

Students to complete: Independent and Extended Practice activities, pp. 114–116. Check in with students as they work through the Independent Practice activities, discussing any difficulties, before supporting them to complete the Extended Practice activities, reminding them of the key parts of a graph as needed.

EXTENSION GROUP

Student Book

Students to complete: Extended Practice activities, p. 116.

Activity sheet

Students to complete: *Activity sheet 27: The words we use.*

Practice and Mastery Book

See page 4 for information about how to use the Practice and Mastery Book activities.

Session 4: Post-assessment

Students to complete: Post-test 20, Unit 9, Topic 1, p. 111.

OXFORD UNIVERSITY PRESS

Unit 9 Data representation and interpretation

Topic 2 Displaying and interpreting data

Student Book pages 117–120

Learning focus

Collect, display and interpret data using simple graphs. Identify and read the range and scale on graphs

Materials

- adhesive
- scissors
- Unifix cubes (optional)
- *BLM 26: Pictograph pictures*
- *BLM 27: Weather in Dataland*
- *Activity sheet 28: What's in a name?*

Potential difficulties: Making fair comparisons

When students are constructing data displays, it's important that they understand how to use scales correctly, so that represented data can be compared directly.

- Make sure students know that all the pictures on a picture graph should represent the same value, e.g. 1 picture = 2 responses
- When comparing class bar graphs, ensure that students set them up with the same scales, so they can be fairly compared. Use data displays in books or the media as examples of graphing comparable data.

Daily practice activity

Each day, count students' responses to a simple question, such as which colour house they are in. Organise students into a human bar graph to represent the data and discuss the results.

Session 1: Pre-assessment

Students to complete: Pre-test 20, Unit 9, Topic 2, p. 110.

Session 2: Topic introduction

WHOLE CLASS

Introductory activity: Pictographs

Students may be accustomed to creating and interpreting simple pictographs but may not have seen graphs where one picture represents many data values. Conduct a quick survey about students' pets under the categories *Dog, Cat, Fish, Bird* and *Other*. Record the actual number of each pet that the students have, e.g. if a student has three dogs, record this as 3. Using *BLM 26: Pictograph pictures* and Blu-Tack, construct a pictograph to display the data. Discuss with students what the range and the scale of the graph is. Ask students what changes you'd need to make if each picture represented two animals. Invite volunteers to come up and alter the graph to meet this new requirement. Can students suggest what to do for an odd number in the data? Model including a legend that shows what number each picture represents. Discuss the similarities and differences between the two graphs, focusing on the range and the scale, and discuss situations where you might want to have a picture representing more than one data value.

In mixed-ability pairs, give students BLM 26. Ask each pair to construct a graph displaying your class pet data. For some groups, one picture represents 3 data values, for others one represents 4 and for some, each picture represents 5. Compare the graphs when they are finished and discuss the similarities and differences. Would it be a good idea to have one picture representing 10 values and another representing 2 on the same graph? Why or why not?

AT-STANDARD GROUP

Student Book

Students to complete: Guided and Independent Practice activities, pp. 117–119. Ask early finishers to rewrite the data displayed on the graph on p. 119 in a table and as a pictograph.

SUPPORT GROUP

Concept exploration and skill development: Statements of finding

Graphs often immediately convey particular pieces of information, but you have to look at them in more detail to understand them fully. Enlarge a copy of *BLM 27: Weather in Dataland*, or give a copy to each pair of students. Ask students what they can tell at first glance, without looking at the numbers on the graph, and model how to phrase these observations as statements of finding, e.g. "There were fewer snowy days than overcast days". Repeat with some statements of finding that relate to the numbers on the graph, such as "The weather in Dataland was cloudy for 10 days", ensuring that students understand how to read and interpret the data values.

Challenge pairs of students to come up with as many statements of finding from the graph as they can. Encourage them to make comparative observations between different categories, and to combine categories to compare them, e.g. "It was sunny on more days than snowy and cloudy days combined". Make a list of all the students' statements, asking other members of the group to check that they are correct.

Student Book with teacher support

Students to complete: Guided Practice activities, p. 117. Use concrete materials such as Unifix cubes to model the bar graph as needed.

EXTENSION GROUP

Student Book

Students to complete: Guided and Independent Practice activities, pp. 117–119.

Activity sheet

Students to begin: *Activity sheet 28: What's in a name?*

Session 3: Instruction and consolidation

WHOLE CLASS

Topic exploration: Comparing data displays

Provide students with a simple data set in list or tally form, such as the number of students in each class, or conduct a quick survey with students to collect data. In small mixed-ability groups, students should represent the data in a table, a pictograph and a bar graph. Ask each group to write a short report explaining what information each display provides. Share this information as a class and work out some guidelines about the data that is best suited to each form of data display.

Topic exploration: Selecting appropriate data displays

Following on from the previous activity, identify a source of data that is either relevant to students' current areas of study or that can easily be collected, such as the number of students in each class in the school. In pairs, have students discuss why you might want to display the data and who the audience would be. Each group then constructs an appropriate data display based on their aims. Arrange the completed graphs so that students can view them and discuss as a class which ones are the most effective and why.

AT-STANDARD GROUP

Teacher activity: Using digital technologies

The graph function in a program such as Excel is a good way for students to learn to record and display data without having to choose and represent an accurate scale. Conduct a quick survey with the group on a single variable, such as favourite football teams, and set up a simple database in an Excel spreadsheet to record the results. Highlight the data and choose the **Bar graph** option from the **Charts** menu. Select **Clustered column** and the graph will automatically be created. Discuss the different parts of the graph, ensuring students understand the role of the x- and y-axes and the data labels. Students can set up their own simple databases and use the same data to create their own graphs. Encourage them to experiment with different graph types within the Charts menu and share any discoveries with the group.

Student Book

Students to complete: Extended Practice activities, p. 120.

SUPPORT GROUP

Student Book with teacher support

Students to complete: Independent and Extended Practice activities, pp. 118–120. Check in with students as they work through the Independent Practice activities, discussing any difficulties, before supporting them to complete the Extended Practice activities, allowing students to talk through their responses as a group.

EXTENSION GROUP

Student Book

Students to complete: Extended Practice activities, p. 120.

Activity sheet

Students to complete: *Activity sheet 28: What's in a name?*

Practice and Mastery Book

See page 4 for information about how to use the Practice and Mastery Book activities.

Session 4: Post-assessment

Students to complete: Post-test 20, Unit 9, Topic 2, p. 111.

Unit 10 Chance

Topic 1 Chance events

Student Book pages 121–124

Compare, rank and evaluate the probability of common events

Materials

- sticky notes
- long piece of paper
- board game, card game or computer game (optional)
- *BLM 34: Chance continuum*
- *Activity sheet 29: What are the chances?*

Potential difficulties: Media representations of probability

The media focus on particular events can lead students to wrongly believe that those events are more likely to happen than others. For example, media coverage of a natural disaster may cause students to be concerned that another disaster is more likely to occur.

- Count the number of reports about a current event in a newspaper, comparing the coverage with earlier or later editions to show students that the amount of coverage does not influence the probability of the event.
- Discuss the probability of the event occurring and place it on a probability scale, along with other uncommon events that may be more likely to occur, such as twin elephants being born at the zoo.

Daily practice activity

Place the label *very unlikely* at one end of the room or an outdoor space and *very likely* at the other end. Make a variety of statements, such as, "You will have a sandwich for lunch", or "You will wear a dress to school tomorrow", and ask students to place themselves along the continuum according to their responses. Discuss the results for each statement.

Session 1: Pre-assessment

Students to complete: Pre-test 21, Unit 10, Topic 1, p. 112.

Session 2: Topic introduction

WHOLE CLASS

Introductory activity: Ordering chance

As a class, brainstorm a list of events that might happen during the school year, recording them on the board. In pairs, give students an enlarged copy of *BLM 34: Chance continuum* and ask them to write the events in, ranking them from least likely to most likely. Display the continuum on the board, then select a student to write their least likely event on a sticky note and place it where they think it belongs on the chart. Did other students place this in a different position? Why? Repeat with other events, discussing the relative probability of them occurring and identifying reasons why the likelihood might vary from person to person.

AT-STANDARD GROUP

Student Book

Students to complete: Guided and Independent Practice activities, pp. 121–123. Ask early finishers to think of and record an event to match each of the terms on the likelihood scale on p. 122.

SUPPORT GROUP

Concept exploration and skill development: Chance language

There are many different words that can be used when discussing probability. Take some time to consolidate and extend students' thinking by exploring a range of appropriate words. Provide some sticky notes and ask students to write down any words or phrases they can think of that describe how likely something is to happen, putting each term on a separate sticky note. Once you have a good selection, bring out a long piece of paper and draw a line to act as a probability continuum along the middle of it. Ask students to identify which words might go at the ends, such as "impossible" or "certain", and have them put them in the correct place. If none of the students wrote these words, prompt them to suggest appropriate terms. Work through the rest of the students' words or phrases, discussing where to place them on the scale. Are there any pairs or groups of words that are harder to distinguish from one another on the scale? Encourage students to think of events from their own lives that could be matched to different points on the scale.

Student Book with teacher support

Students to complete: Guided Practice activities, p. 121. Link the activities with the words and events on the continuum that students have just created with you.

EXTENSION GROUP

Student Book

Students to complete: Guided and Independent Practice activities, pp. 121–123.

Activity sheet

Students to begin: *Activity sheet 29: What are the chances?*

Session 3: Instruction and consolidation

WHOLE CLASS

Topic exploration: Influences on chance

Some events have a fixed chance, such as the likelihood of spinning a 5 on a 6-sided dice, while the chance of other events occurring can change depending on the circumstances. Tell students a chance story, such as the following, or use an existing story that you're familiar with.

Yesterday, the weather started out rainy. I got soaked as I walked to school, and I was late. By the time I got home, it was sunny again. I had my favourite snack for afternoon tea, but when I went to turn on the television, the remote control was broken. I could have turned the television on at the switch, but instead I went to the garage to check on my dog, who was expecting puppies. To my surprise, there was already one puppy there, a boy with white fur and brown ears. I wondered if the other puppies would all be boys as well. After a few hours, three more puppies had been born. All of them were white with brown ears except the last one, which was black.

My baby sister slept through the whole thing and was amazed to wake up and find that there were four new puppies to play with.

Read the story a second time, this time asking students to note down all the chance events that are represented. Classify the events according to whether or not it's possible for each event to occur when another related event is occurring. For example, your sister cannot be asleep at the same time as she is awake. Can students think of other events that cannot happen simultaneously?

Reclassify the events depending on whether or not the outcome of the event affects the outcome of subsequent events. For example, the first puppy's gender and colour will not affect the characteristics of the second puppy, whereas being late for school might affect the events that follow. Ask students to talk to a partner about one event in their lives that will affect what happens after, and one that will not.

AT-STANDARD GROUP

Teacher activity: Chance in games

Many, although not all, games have an element of chance. In small groups, ask students to choose a game they are familiar with. It might be a board game, card game, physical game or even a computer game. Students should work together to identify events in the game that rely on chance and use a probability scale, either in words or fractions, to rank the probability of each occurring. Are there events that do not depend on chance? Students should share their findings in any form that they feel appropriate. Encourage students to make a judgement about the fairness of the game, giving reasons for their opinions.

Student Book

Students to complete: Extended Practice activities, p. 124.

SUPPORT GROUP

Student Book with teacher support

Students to complete: Independent and Extended Practice activities, pp. 122–124. Check in with students as they work through the Independent Practice activities, discussing any difficulties, before supporting them to complete the Extended Practice activities, discussing the possible perspectives of people in question 1 as needed.

EXTENSION GROUP

Student Book

Students to complete: Extended Practice activities, p. 124.

Activity sheet

Students to complete: *Activity sheet 29: What are the chances?*

Practice and Mastery Book

See page 4 for information about how to use the Practice and Mastery Book activities.

Session 4: Post-assessment

Students to complete: Post-test 21, Unit 10, Topic 1, p. 113.

Unit 10 Chance

Topic 2 Chance experiments

Student Book pages 125–128

Learning focus

Predict and explore probability based on experimental events and evaluate the effects of one event on another

Materials

- 10-sided dice (two per pair of students)
- playing cards (one deck per pair of students)
- 6-sided dice (two per pair of students)
- bag of counters
- *BLM 35: 0–99 chart*
- *BLM 36: Dice roll table*
- *BLM 37: Snakes and ladders board*
- *Activity sheet 30: It's not fair!*

Potential difficulties: Sample sizes

Students may not understand that if too few trials have been performed during a probability experiment, the results may not be reliable. For example, if a coin is tossed three times and comes up heads each time, this may suggest that the probability of landing on heads is higher than it really is.

- Give students the opportunity to compare the results of small trials with larger trials of the same experiment to compare the results.
- When students are designing their own experiments, explicitly ask them how many trials they are conducting and why.

Daily practice activity

Introduce chance elements into each day. For instance, ask students to choose *heads* or *tails*, then flip a coin. The students whose side lands face-up get to go to their seats first. Compare how often students are in the "lucky" group.

Session 1: Pre-assessment

Students to complete: Pre-test 21, Unit 10, Topic 2, p. 112.

Session 2: Topic introduction

WHOLE CLASS

Introductory activity: Predicting chance outcomes

In pairs, give students two 10-sided dice. Each student should predict which 2-digit number will be made when the two dice are rolled, reading the numbers from left to right as they land. The pairs should record both their predictions and the results of each roll. Repeat for 20 trials, then discuss the results as a class. Did anyone make an accurate prediction? Were there any numbers that came up more often than others? Display an enlarged copy of *BLM 35: 0–99 chart* and discuss the fact that it represents all the possible outcomes of rolling the two dice. Invite each pair of students to come up and tick the numbers they rolled. What can students conclude from the results? What is the likelihood of any particular combination of two numbers being rolled?

AT-STANDARD GROUP

Student Book

Students to complete: Guided and Independent Practice activities, pp. 125–127. Ask early finishers to predict the outcome if they tried the experiment described in question 2 on p. 126, and performed it 20 times. Students should conduct the experiment, then compare the results with their prediction.

SUPPORT GROUP

Concept exploration and skill development: Experimenting with cards

Many students these days are unfamiliar with the composition of a standard deck of cards. Allow small groups of students some time to investigate what makes up a pack of cards, then share their observations to build the idea that there are 52 cards, with 26 of each colour, 13 of each suit and 4 of each particular card type. Invite students to suggest what the outcomes could be if you draw out a card to look at its colour. How likely is it that you will draw out a black card from a full deck? In their groups, ask students to draw out 10 cards and record the colour of each one, then consolidate their answers. What result are the students expecting? What is the actual result? Try some different experiments based on suits or particular cards, discussing all the possible results and then conducting some trials to see what is drawn out.

Student Book with teacher support

Students to complete: Guided Practice activities, p. 125. Discuss the probability terms and how they relate to the spinners as students work.

EXTENSION GROUP

Student Book

Students to complete: Guided and Independent Practice activities, pp. 125–127.

Activity sheet

Students to begin: *Activity sheet 30: It's not fair!*

Session 3: Instruction and consolidation

WHOLE CLASS

Topic exploration: Chance and fairness

Many chance games, especially those that are associated with gambling, are organised so that some outcomes are a lot more probable than others. In pairs, give students *BLM 36: Dice roll table* and have them complete it by adding the different combinations possible if you roll two 6-sided dice. When they are finished, ask students to suggest which totals are most likely to be rolled and which are least likely.

In pairs, give students *BLM 37: Snakes and ladders board*, two 6-sided dice and a counter each. Tell students that they are going to play the game with different rules. Player A moves the corresponding number of spaces if a 2, 3, 4, 10, 11 or 12 is rolled, while player B moves if a 5, 6, 7, 8 or 9 is rolled. Instruct students to decide who will be player A and who will be player B, then play the game. When they have finished, discuss the rules. Were they fair? Why or why not? Allow students to experiment with other rules for the game to see if they can come up with other fair or unfair ways of playing.

AT-STANDARD GROUP

Teacher activity: Tree diagrams and chance

A tree diagram is an effective tool to help students explore possible outcomes of a chance experiment and also demonstrate that the chance of a particular outcome is not affected by the result of any previous experiments. Demonstrate a simple tree diagram to students using two coins:

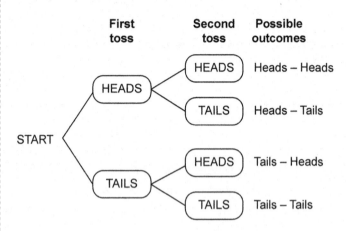

For the first toss, there are two options: heads or tails. For the second toss, each of the first two options has another two options, for a total of four possible outcomes. Ask students to use the tree diagram to suggest the four combinations possible. How many options would there be if you conducted a third toss? Erase the current possible outcomes and invite students to extend the tree diagram to show the possibilities if another toss is undertaken.

Challenge pairs of students to create their own tree diagram for a chance experiment where you draw one of three different coloured counters out of a bag, assuming the counters are returned to the bag each time. How many possibilities are there after one draw? What about after two or three? If students are coping with the concept, encourage them to explore how many possible outcomes there would be after four or even five draws. Discuss as a group when you might use this method.

Student Book

Students to complete: Extended Practice activities, p. 128.

SUPPORT GROUP

Student Book with teacher support

Students to complete: Independent and Extended Practice activities, pp. 126–128. Check in with students as they work through the Independent Practice activities, discussing any difficulties, before supporting them to complete the Extended Practice activities, using counters to model and identify the possible outcomes as needed.

EXTENSION GROUP

Student Book

Students to complete: Extended Practice activities, p. 128.

Activity sheet

Students to complete: *Activity sheet 30: It's not fair!*

Practice and Mastery Book

See page 4 for information about how to use the Practice and Mastery Book activities.

Session 4: Post-assessment

Students to complete: Post-test 21, Unit 10, Topic 2, p. 113.

1 How many?

○ 1443   ○ 1344

○ 1433   ○ 1434

2 2145 can be re-named as:

○ 21 tens and 4 ones

○ 214 tens and 5 ones

○ 214 hundreds and 5 ones

○ 2 tens and 14 ones

3 Write 7340 in words.

_____

_____

4 Write these numbers in order from smallest to largest.

2435   2543   2453   2534

_____   _____   _____   _____

UNIT 1: TOPIC 2

5 Which is the even number?

○ 547

○ 457

○ 574

○ 475

6 Fill in the gaps in this even number pattern.

88	90					

7 What digits can odd numbers end in?

_____

8 Underline the even numbers. Circle the odd numbers.

5438   6329   5286

4500   7387   5381

1 What is the value of the underlined digit?

26 538

○ 60 000

○ 6000

○ 600

○ 60

2 63 509 can be re-named as:

○ 635 tens and 9 ones

○ 6359 tens and 0 ones

○ 635 hundreds and 9 ones

○ 635 hundreds and 9 tens

3 Write 60 704 in words.

_____

_____

4 Write these numbers in order from smallest to largest.

63 087   63 807   63 078   63 780

_____ _____ _____ _____

UNIT 1: TOPIC 2

5 Which is the even number?

○ 68 483

○ 52 465

○ 24 687

○ 73 592

6 Use these digits to write the largest possible odd number.

| 5 | 6 | 4 | 8 | 9 |

_____

7 Use these digits to write the smallest possible even number with 1 in the thousands place.

| 4 | 1 | 5 | 2 | 3 |

_____

8 Odd number + odd number = even number. Fill in the blanks for the following.

a odd + even = _____

b even − even = _____

c odd × even = _____

d odd × odd = _____

1 $29 + 15 =$

- ○ 34
- ○ 44
- ○ 54
- ○ 64

2 $3 + 12 + 17 =$

- ○ 30
- ○ 31
- ○ 32
- ○ 33

3 Split into 10s and 1s to add.

$43 + 36 =$

_____ + _____ + _____ + _____

= _____ + _____

= _____

4 Rearrange the numbers to make it easier to add.

$32 + 6 + 18 + 4 =$

_____ + _____ + _____ + _____

= _____

5 Use the open number line to solve.

$37 + 36 =$ _____

⟵——————————————⟶

6 Complete the addition problem.

T	O
4	3
5	5

$+$

7 Complete the addition problem.

H	T	O
3	5	5
2	4	5

$+$

8 Solve $1459 + 365$ by writing as vertical addition.

Th	H	T	O

$+$

1 3 + 17 + 25 =

○ 40   ○ 50

○ 45   ○ 55

2 Rearrange the numbers to add in your head.

a 48 + 37 + 2 = _____

b 16 + 17 + 4 + 3 = _____

3 Use an empty number line to add.

a 47 + 38 = _____

←————————————————→

b 156 + 147 = _____

←————————————————→

4 Use mental strategies to add.

a 347 + 635

_____

b 2438 + 1782

_____

5 Split the numbers to add 534 + 265. Start with the ones.

= (___ + ___ + ___) + (___ + ___ + ___)

= ___ + ___ + ___ + ___ + ___ + ___

= _____ + _____ + _____

= _____

6 Solve using trading.

H	T	O
	7	9
+	4	5

7 Complete the addition problem.

Th	H	T	O
3	6	2	8
+ 2	4	7	7

8 Solve 34 843 + 7087 by writing as a vertical algorithm.

Ten Th	H	T	O
+			

1 $19 - 7 =$

- ◯ 14
- ◯ 13
- ◯ 12
- ◯ 11

2 77 – 33 is the same as:

- ◯ 77 – 30 – 3
- ◯ 77 – 3 – 3
- ◯ 77 – 30 – 30

3 Complete the subtraction problem.

$54 - 19 =$ _____

4 Complete the subtraction problem.

$175 - 26 =$ _____

UNIT 1: TOPIC 6

5 Complete the subtraction problem.

$74 - 22 =$ _____

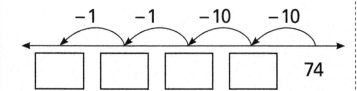

74

6 Complete the subtraction problem.

$85 - 34 =$ _____

7 What is 427 take away 214?

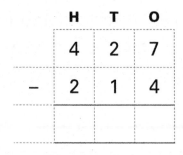

H	T	O
4	2	7
– 2	1	4

8 Rewrite 785 – 324 as a vertical algorithm and solve.

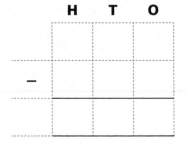

H	T	O
–		

UNIT 1: TOPIC 5

1 54 – 19 is the same as:

◯ 54 – 20

◯ 54 – 20 then add 1

◯ 54 – 20 then take away 1

2 Circle one word for each.

a 745 – 198 = 647 | Correct | Incorrect

b 833 – 299 = 534 | Correct | Incorrect

3 Solve the subtraction problems.

a 734 – 728 = ________

b 1953 – 1946 = ________

4 Solve the subtraction problems.

a 734 – 199 = ________

b 865 – 202 = ________

c 1477 – 298 = ________

UNIT 1: TOPIC 6

5 Solve using the split strategy.

786 – 454 =

786 – ______ – ______ – ______

= ________

6 Solve 43 – 25 as a vertical algorithm.

	T	O
	4	3
–	2	5

7 Solve 3625 – 2427 as a vertical algorithm.

	Th	H	T	O
	3	6	2	5
–	2	4	7	7

8 Solve 45 313 – 5578 as a vertical algorithm.

	Ten Th	Th	H	T	O
–					

1 Use the multiplication fact to write the division fact.

3 groups of 5 = 15

_____ shared between 5 is _____ .

2 Use the division fact to write the multiplication fact.

20 shared between 4 is 5.

_____ groups of 4 = _____ .

---

3 Make a turnaround multiplication fact to match the array.

_____ × _____ = _____

_____ × _____ = _____

4 Make a turnaround division fact to match the array.

_____ ÷ _____ = _____

_____ ÷ _____ = _____

---

5 Complete the fact family.

3 × 7 = 21

_____ × _____ = 21

21 ÷ _____ = _____

21 ÷ _____ = _____

6 Complete the fact family.

30 ÷ 5 = 6

30 ÷ _____ = _____

_____ × _____ = 30

_____ × _____ = 30

---

7 **a** Complete the multiplication fact.

8 × 3 = _____

b Write a matching division fact.

_____ ÷ _____ = _____

8 **a** Complete the division fact.

24 ÷ 4 = _____

b Write a matching multiplication fact.

_____ × _____ = _____

1 This array shows that 6 × 4 = 24. It also shows that:

○ 4 × 5 = 20 ○ 4 × 6 = 24
○ 5 × 5 = 25 ○ 5 × 6 = 30

2 This array shows that 21 ÷ 3 = 7. It also shows that:

○ 21 ÷ 7 = 3 ○ 28 ÷ 4 = 7
○ 20 ÷ 4 = 5 ○ 24 ÷ 6 = 4

3 Write a multiplication fact and a division fact for this array.

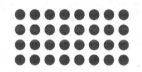

_____ × _____ = _____

_____ ÷ _____ = _____

4 Write a multiplication fact and a division fact for this array.

_____ × _____ = _____

_____ ÷ _____ = _____

5 Which is true about the 6 times table facts?

○ The last digit is always 6.

○ The last digit is always odd.

○ The last digit is always even.

6 Which is true about the 9 times table facts?

○ The last digit is always 9.

○ The digits in the number always add up to 9.

○ The last digit is never even.

7 Use the numbers 7 and 9 in 2 multiplication and 2 division sentences.

_____ × _____ = _____

_____ × _____ = _____

_____ ÷ _____ = _____

_____ ÷ _____ = _____

8 Use the numbers 6 and 8 in 2 multiplication and 2 division sentences.

_____ × _____ = _____

_____ × _____ = _____

_____ ÷ _____ = _____

_____ ÷ _____ = _____

1 3 × 14 is the same as:

○ 3 × 1 + 3 × 4

○ 3 × 10 + 3 × 4

○ 3 × 10 + 2 × 40

2 2 × 35 is the same as:

○ 2 × 30 + 2 × 5

○ 2 × 30 + 2 × 50

○ 2 × 3 + 2 × 5

3 Solve using the grid method.

×	20	4
3		

3 × 24 = [ ]

4 Use your choice of written strategy to solve 5 × 37.

5 Solve the division problem.

12 ÷ 4 = ____

6 Divide the array into groups of 5 and solve the division problem.

20 ÷ 5 = ____

7 Draw an array to solve 28 ÷ 7.

28 ÷ 7 = ____

8 Solve the division problem.

42 ÷ 6 = ____

Show how you got the answer.

1 Solve 3 × 32 using extended multiplication.

	T	O
	3	2
×		3
			← 3 × 2
			← 3 × 30

2 Solve 4 × 58 using extended multiplication.

	H	T	O
		5	8
×			4

3 Solve 6 × 74 using contracted multiplication.

	H	T	O
		7	4
×			6

4 Rewrite 5 × 93 as contracted multiplication and solve.

	H	T	O
×			

5 Solve 84 ÷ 2.

$$2\overline{)84}$$

6 Solve 72 ÷ 3.

$$3\overline{)72}$$

7 Rewrite and solve 96 ÷ 6.

8 Solve and rewrite.

$$7\overline{)91}$$

_____ ÷ _____ = _____

1 The shaded part is:

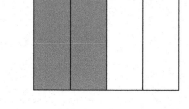

○ $\frac{1}{4}$

○ $\frac{1}{3}$

○ $\frac{2}{4}$

○ $\frac{2}{3}$

2 Look at the rectangle in question 1. True or false?

The fraction of the rectangle that is white is $\frac{1}{2}$.

_____

3 Shade $\frac{1}{4}$ of the rectangle.

4 Shade $\frac{1}{5}$ of the rectangle.

5 Write the missing fraction on the number line.

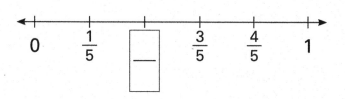

6 How far past 1 is the triangle?

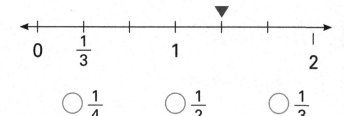

○ $\frac{1}{4}$ ○ $\frac{1}{2}$ ○ $\frac{1}{3}$

7 Draw a triangle $\frac{4}{4}$ of the way along the number line.

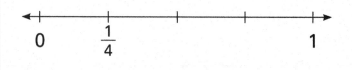

8 How far along the line is the triangle?

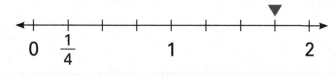

○ $\frac{4}{7}$ ○ $\frac{3}{4}$ ○ $\frac{7}{4}$

1 Which fraction is equivalent to $\frac{3}{4}$?

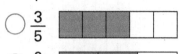

○ $\frac{3}{5}$

○ $\frac{2}{3}$

○ $\frac{6}{8}$

2 Label this pair of equivalent fractions.

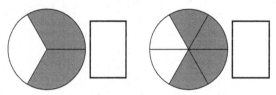

3 Colour $\frac{4}{5}$ of the first rectangle. Colour and label an equivalent fraction of the second rectangle.

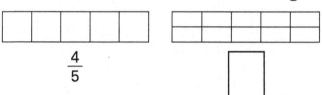

$\frac{4}{5}$

4 Which list has fractions that are all equivalent?

○ $\frac{1}{2}, \frac{2}{5}, \frac{3}{6}, \frac{4}{8}$ ○ $\frac{2}{4}, \frac{3}{6}, \frac{4}{8}, \frac{5}{10}$

○ $\frac{3}{6}, \frac{6}{12}, \frac{4}{8}, \frac{4}{9}$ ○ $\frac{1}{2}, \frac{2}{4}, \frac{5}{8}, \frac{6}{12}$

5 How far along the number line is the triangle?

○ $\frac{5}{8}$ ○ $\frac{6}{4}$ ○ $\frac{5}{4}$ ○ $\frac{6}{8}$

6 Which pair describes the position of the triangle?

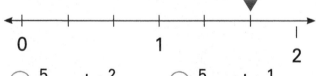

○ $\frac{5}{6}$ and $1\frac{2}{3}$ ○ $\frac{5}{3}$ and $1\frac{1}{3}$

○ $\frac{4}{3}$ and $1\frac{1}{3}$ ○ $\frac{5}{3}$ and $1\frac{2}{3}$

7 Write the position of the diamond as:

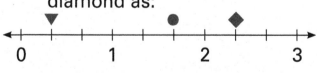

a an improper fraction. _____

b a mixed number. _____

8 Look at question 7.

a How much further along is the diamond than the triangle? _____

b Write the position of the circle as a mixed number. _____

1 The fraction shaded is:

○ $\frac{1}{10}$

○ $\frac{2}{10}$

○ $\frac{3}{10}$

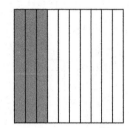

2 The fraction shaded is:

○ $\frac{9}{10}$

○ $\frac{8}{10}$

○ $\frac{7}{10}$

3 Shade 4 columns and write as a fraction.

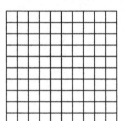 _____

4 Shade 7 columns and write as a fraction.

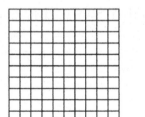 _____

5 There are 100 small squares. Write the shaded amount as a fraction.

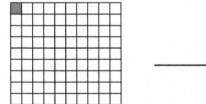 _____

6 There are 100 small squares. Write the shaded amount as a fraction.

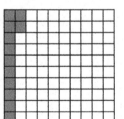 _____

7 Shade $\frac{15}{100}$ of the square.

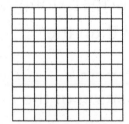

8 Shade $\frac{50}{100}$ of the square.

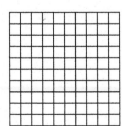

1 The amount shaded is:

○ $\frac{1}{10}$

○ $\frac{10}{10}$

○ $\frac{1}{100}$

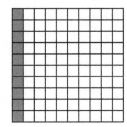

2 As a decimal, $\frac{2}{100}$ is written as:

○ 0.05

○ 0.2

○ 0.02

○ 0.20

---

3 Shade $\frac{3}{10}$ of the grid and write as a decimal.

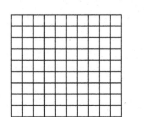

_____

4 Shade $\frac{7}{100}$ of the grid and write as a decimal.

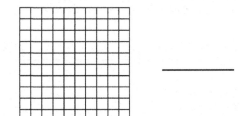

_____

---

5 Write the shaded amount as a common fraction and as a decimal.

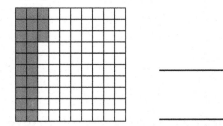

_____

_____

6 Shade 0.09 of the grid and write as a common fraction.

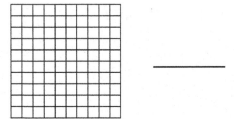

_____

---

7 Complete the number line.

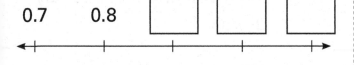

0.7   0.8   [ ]   [ ]   [ ]

8 Complete the number line.

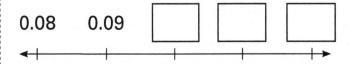

0.08   0.09   [ ]   [ ]   [ ]

1 Draw four coins that make 70c.

2 Draw three coins that make 20c.

3 How could you give the exact money for a 90c drink using the least number of coins?

_____

4 How could you give the exact money for a $1.80 item using the least number of coins?

_____

5 How much change from $1 would you get for something that costs 65c?

_____

6 How much change from $5 would you get for something that costs $3.85?

_____

7 Imagine that a drink costs 99c.

  a What is the lowest value coin you could use to pay for it?

  _____

  b How much change would you get? _____

8 Imagine that a snack costs $1.92.

  a What is the lowest value coin you could use to pay for it?

  _____

  b How much change would you get? _____

1 Round $1.67 to the nearest 5c.

_____

2 Round $1.68 to the nearest 5c.

_____

3 How much change would you get from $2 for a drink that costs $1.49?

_____

4 How much change would you get from $5 for a game that costs $3.97?

_____

5 How much change would you get from $5 for three toys at 99c each?

_____

6 How much change would you get from $10 for three pens at $2.02 each?

_____

7 How much change would you get from $50 for four items at $8.99 each?

_____

8 How much change would you get from $100 for six items at $9.89 each?

_____

1 Follow the rule to finish the pattern.

Rule: Add 4.

6	10	14					

2 Write the rule for this number pattern.

105	95	85	75	65	55	45	35

Rule: _____

3 Fill in the numbers and write the rule.

Rule:

_____

Number Machine	
In	Out
5	13
9	17
84	
77	

4 Fill in the numbers and write the rule.

Rule:

_____

Number Machine	
In	Out
47	35
59	47
36	
45	

5 Write the missing number.

$6 + \boxed{} = 14$

6 Make the equation balance.

$9 + 3 = 5 + \boxed{}$

7 Use +, −, × or ÷

a $10 \boxed{} 7 = 70$

b $19 \boxed{} 7 = 12$

c $90 \boxed{} 3 = 30$

8 Eva has $48. Emma has $37. How much more does Eva have? Write a number sentence to solve the word problem.

_____

1 Complete the pattern.

Rule: Add 5.

1	2	3	4	5
4	9			

2 Write the rule and find the 10th term.

1	2	3	4	5	10
70	67	64	61	58	

Rule: _____

3 Write the rule for the function machine.

50 → 65
42 → 57
84 → 99

Rule: _____

4 **a** Write the first 10 multiples of 2.

_____

b Circle the multiples of 4.

c Which multiples of 2 and 4 are also multiples of 8? _____

5 Jack has 37 marbles. He loses 8. Which number sentence shows how many he has left?

○ 37 + 8 = 45   ○ 37 − 8 = 29

○ 8 + 37 = 45   ○ 37 × 8 = 296

6 What number added to 36 gives the same answer as 4 × 10? Complete the equation to show the answer.

4 × 10 = _____

7 Fill in the gaps.

a $85 - \boxed{} = 71$

b $\boxed{} \times 9 = 72$

8 Fill in the gaps.

a $115 - \boxed{} = 76 + 24$

b $\boxed{} \times 4 = 64 \div 2$

c $55 \boxed{} 5 = 99 - 88$

1 How long is the line?

_____ cm

2 Use a ruler to find the length of the line.

_____ cm

3 How long is the line?

- ○ $1\frac{1}{2}$ cm
- ○ $2\frac{1}{2}$ cm
- ○ 2 cm
- ○ 3 cm

4 Use a ruler to draw a line that is $4\frac{1}{2}$ cm long.

UNIT 5: TOPIC 2

5 The shape is drawn on centimetre squares. What is the area?

- ○ 8 cm²
- ○ 8 cm
- ○ cm 8
- ○ 2 cm 8

6 The shape is made of centimetres squares. What is the area? _____ cm²

7 The shape is made of centimetres squares. What is the area?

_____

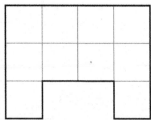

8 Use the cm² grid to draw a shape with an area of 20 cm².

1 Write the length of the line in centimetres and in millimetres.

_____ cm   _____ mm

2 Write the length of the line in millimetres.

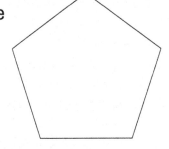

_____ mm

3 How many:

a millimetres in 4.2 cm?

_____

b centimetres in $4\frac{1}{2}$ m?

_____

4 Write the perimeter of this shape in mm.

_____

5 What is the most likely area for a netball court?

○ 4 cm²   ○ 4 m²

○ 400 cm²   ○ 400 m²

6 What is likely to have an area of 90 cm²?

○ a classroom

○ a smart phone

○ a desk top

○ a fingernail

7 The shape is drawn on centimetre squares. What is the area in cm²? _____

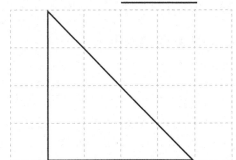

8 Use the cm² grid to draw 2 different shapes, each with an area of 6 cm².

1 The model is made from centimetre cubes.

The volume is _____ cm³.

2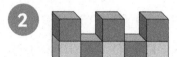

The volume of this centimetre cube model is _____.

3 Which sentence is true?

A   **B**

○ A has a bigger volume than B.

○ A has the same volume as B.

○ A has a smaller volume than B.

4 Look at the centimetre cube model.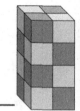

a How many layers? _____

b How many cubes on each layer? _____

c What is the volume of the model? _____

5 A bucket holds:

○ about 6 litres.

○ more than 6 litres.

○ less than 6 litres.

6 A teaspoon holds:

○ about 5 mL.

○ about 50 mL.

○ about 5 L.

7

250 millilitres   1 litre   600 millilitres

A   **B**   **C**

Order the drink containers from smallest capacity to largest capacity.

_____

8 Look at the drink containers in question 7.

a Which container holds $\frac{1}{4}$ of a litre? _____

b What is the total capacity of the 3 containers? _____

1 The model is made from centimetre cubes.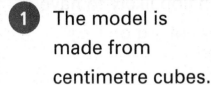

The volume is _____ cm³.

2 Which is true?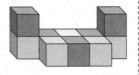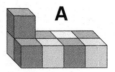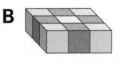

A   B

○ Model A has a larger volume.

○ Model B has a larger volume.

○ They have the same volume.

3 a How many layers?

____

b How many cm³ on each layer? ____

c What is the volume? _____

4 This box can fit 2 identical layers of centimetre cubes. What is the volume? _____

UNIT 5: TOPIC 3 CAPACITY

5 Which is true?

550 mL
A

½ L
B

○ A holds the same as B.

○ A holds more than B.

○ A holds less than B.

6 Shade the jug to show the level after the 2 drink containers have been poured into it.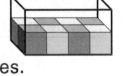

200 mL   200 mL

1 L
½ L

7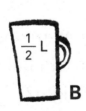

1150 mL   ¾ L   950 mL   1L 100 mL

A   B   C   D

Which of the jugs holds closest to 1 L? ____

8 a Order the jugs in question 7 from smallest to largest capacities. _____

b If 200 mL is poured out of jug B, how much is left?

_____

1 How many grams in 2 kg?

○ 20

○ 200

○ 2000

2 **a** Is a melon likely to have a mass of 1 g or 1 kg?

_____

b Is a feather likely to have a mass of 1 g or 1 kg?

_____

3 How heavy is a teddy likely to be?

○ 5 g

○ 500 g

○ 50 kg

4 The cat has a mass of 1 kg. Write the same mass in a different way.

_____

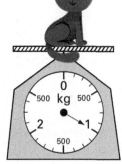

5 How many 5 g weights would balance a 50 g weight?

_____

6 How many 20 g weights would balance a 100 g weight? ____

7 Two identical books have a mass of 1 kg 500 g. What is the mass of one book?

_____

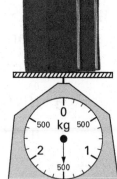

8 What is the mass of one pencil sharpener?

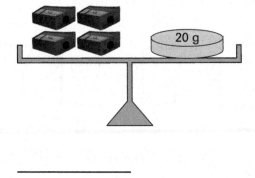

20 g

_____

1 The box has a mass of 1 kg 500 g. This can also be written as:

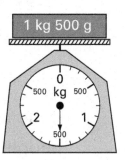

○ 15 kg

○ 1.5 kg

○ 1 kg 5 g

2 Another way of writing $\frac{1}{4}$ kg is:

○ 2500 g

○ 25 g

○ 250 g

3 The box has a mass of 2.75 kg. This can also be written as:

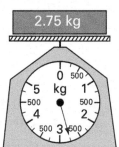

○ 275 g

○ 2 kg 75 g

○ 2 kg 750 g

4 How many grams in $3\frac{1}{2}$ kg?

_____

5 Write the mass in 2 ways.

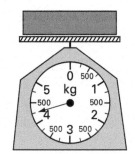

_____

_____

6 Write the mass in 2 ways.

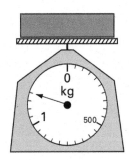

_____

_____

7 The box has a mass of 0 kg 650 g. Draw the pointer on the scale.

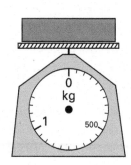

8 Draw the pointer on the scale.

0.25 kg

800 g

1 Which word describes the water in a bath?

○ warm　　○ cold

○ boiling　○ freezing

2 Which word describes a winter's day?

○ boiling　○ cool

○ warm　　○ hot

3 If the temperature is 28°C, people are likely to wear:

○ a T-shirt.

○ a thick coat.

○ a scarf and gloves.

○ a woollen jumper.

4 If the temperature is 7°C, people are likely to wear:

○ a singlet.

○ a T-shirt.

○ a thick coat.

○ swimmers.

5 What temperature is the grey shading on this thermometer showing?

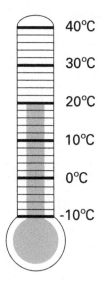

_____°C

6 **a** Shade the thermometer so that it shows a temperature 6°C lower than the one in question 5.

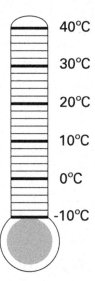

b Write the temperature.

_____

1 Which word describes the temperature of a cup of tea?

○ cool   ○ cold

○ hot   ○ freezing

2 Which word describes the temperature of a drink of water?

○ boiling   ○ cold

○ hot   ○ freezing

3 If a pool temperature is 1°C, people are likely to say that the water is:

○ just right.   ○ too cold.

○ too warm.   ○ frozen.

4 Which temperature is more likely for a winter's day in Melbourne?

○ 45°C   ○ 28°C

○ 33°C   ○ 11°C

5 What temperature does this thermometer show?

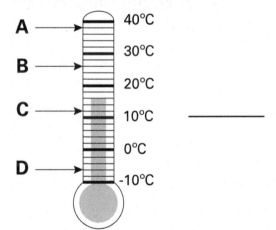

_____

6 a Shade to show a temperature on a warm day.

b Write the temperature.

_____

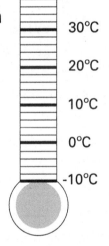

7 Look at question 5.

a Which letter shows the temperature inside a freezer? ____

b Which letter shows the temperature 18°C above the temperature of D? ____

8 What is the difference between the temperatures shown at:

a B and C? _____

b A and C? _____

c A and D? _____

1 What time does the clock show?

_____ past _____

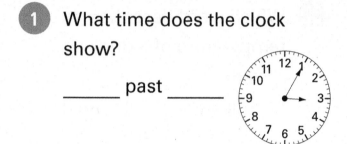

2 What time does the clock show?

_____ to _____

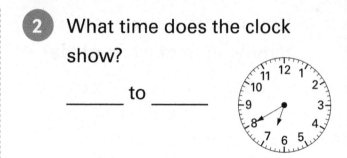

3 Write the time in question 1 on the digital clock.

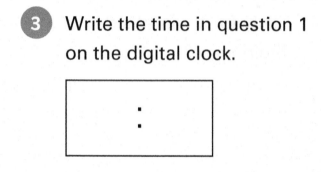

4 Write the time in question 2 on the digital clock.

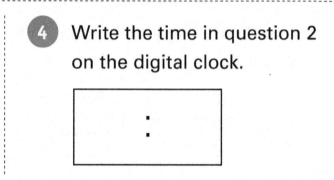

5 What time does the clock show?

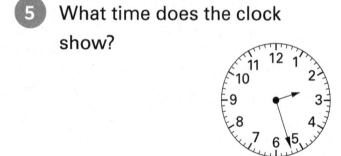

_____

6 Draw 26 minutes to 4 on the clock face.

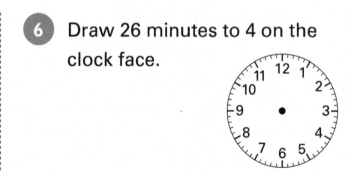

7 Show 11 minutes past 10 on the analogue and digital clocks.

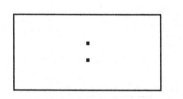

8 Look at the time in question 5. Show the time after 15 minutes have passed.

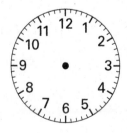

1 How many seconds in 2 minutes?

- ⚪ 20
- ⚪ 120
- ⚪ 60
- ⚪ 160

2 How many hours in 2 days?

- ⚪ 24
- ⚪ 50
- ⚪ 48
- ⚪ 72

3 Circle the longer time in each pair.

a 2 hours or 124 minutes

b 10 days or 220 hours

4 Arrange the periods of time from shortest to longest by writing the letters in order.

A: $1\frac{1}{2}$ minutes

B: 115 seconds

C: 1 minute 20 seconds

D: 75 seconds

_____

5 Write the time as **am** or **pm** time.

Eating breakfast

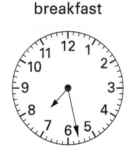

_____

6 Write the time as **am** or **pm** time.

Asleep in bed

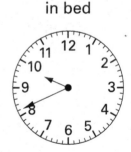

_____

7 Draw the time that school finishes. Write the time using am or pm.

_____

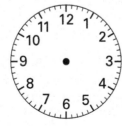

8 Draw the time that you usually get up. Write the time using am or pm.

_____

1 Another way to write 11 am is:

○ 11 pm.

○ 11 m.

○ 11 o'clock in the evening.

○ 11 o'clock in the morning.

2 An hour after midnight, the time is:

○ 11 pm. ○ 1 pm.

○ 1 am. ○ 11 am.

3 These are some special times from Tom's birthday.

5:30 am 11:30 am 7 am 4:30 pm

Which time came first?

○ 4:30 pm ○ 5:30 am

○ 7 am ○ 11:30 am

4 Write the times from question 3 in order from earliest to latest.

_____

5 At which of the times from question 3 do you think Tom went shopping?

_____

6 At which of the times from question 3 do you think Tom's party started?

_____

7 Below are some events from the morning of Tom's birthday.

Breakfast: 8 o'clock

Opened presents: $\frac{1}{2}$ past 7

School starts: $\frac{1}{4}$ to 9

Birthday snack: $\frac{1}{2}$ past 9

Put the times in order from earliest to latest.

_____

8 Write the times, arrows and events from question 7 on the timeline.

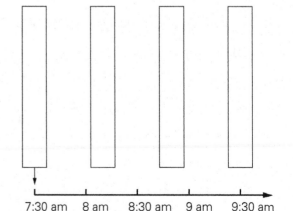

7:30 am 8 am 8:30 am 9 am 9:30 am

1 This is a timeline for Eva's party.

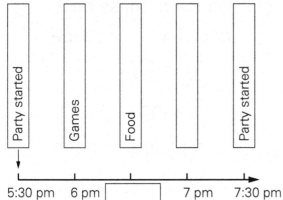

Party started   Games   Food   Party started

5:30 pm   6 pm   [ ]   7 pm   7:30 pm

Write the missing time on the timeline.

3 The party games started at 6 pm. Draw an arrow to the correct place on the timeline.

5 Everyone started eating 45 minutes after the games started. Draw an arrow to the correct place on the timeline.

7 At 7:45 pm, Eva and her family tidied up. It took half an hour. They washed the dishes for 15 minutes and chatted for a quarter of an hour. Then they watched TV for three-quarters of an hour before bedtime. Write the times these things started.

Washed dishes _____

Chatted _____

Watched TV _____

Bedtime _____

2 At what time did the party start?

◯ 5:30 pm   ◯ 7 pm

◯ 6 pm   ◯ 7:30 pm

4 There was dancing after the party food. Write "Dancing" in the correct box on the timeline.

6 The dancing started a few minutes after 7 pm and lasted for 30 minutes. Draw arrows to the timeline to show when the dancing started and when the party ended.

8 Use the information in question 7 to complete the timeline for after the party.

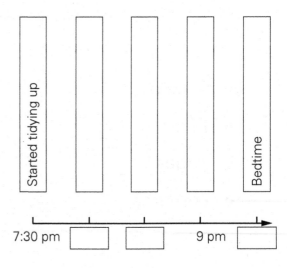

Started tidying up   Bedtime

7:30 pm   [ ]   [ ]   9 pm   [ ]

1 This shape is a: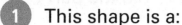

○ trapezium.

○ rectangle.

○ parallelogram.

2 Which of these best describes this shape?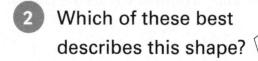

○ pentagon

○ hexagon

○ regular pentagon

3 What shape will be made if the two triangles are joined?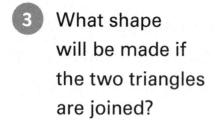

_____

4 What shapes can you see?

_____

_____

5 Circle the pyramid.

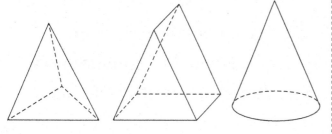

6 Circle the shape that has all flat faces.

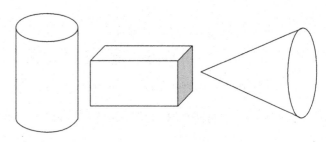

7 How many:

a faces? _____

b edges? _____

c corners? _____

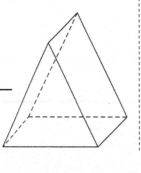

8 How do you know that this is a pyramid?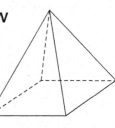

_____

_____

1 If a shape has 6 sides and 6 angles, it is a:

○ triangle. ○ square.

○ hexagon. ○ octagon.

2 a Name this shape.

_____

b Draw a line that splits the shape into 2 triangles.

3 a This shape is a

_____.

b Draw a line to split it into a rectangle and a triangle.

4 a Draw an 8-sided shape that can be made from these shapes.

b Name the new shape. _____

5 This shape is:

○ a rectangular pyramid.

○ a cube.

○ a rectangular prism.

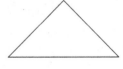

6 a Join the base corners to the dot.

b Name the shape.

_____

7 a Name the shape.

_____

b The 2D shape from the side view is a _____.

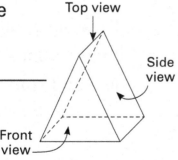

8 Draw the top, front and side views of this shape.

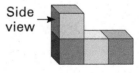

Top view	**Front view**	**Side view**

1 This angle is: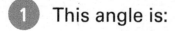

- ○ smaller than a right angle.
- ○ a right angle.
- ○ larger than a right angle.

2 This angle is:

- ○ smaller than a right angle.
- ○ a right angle.
- ○ larger than a right angle.

---

3 Circle the angle that is smaller than a right angle.

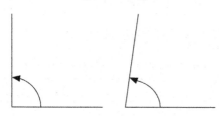

4 Circle the right angle.

---

5 What sort of angle do the hands make at 2 o'clock?

_____

_____

6 What sort of angle do the hands make at 4 o'clock?

_____

_____

---

7 Draw an angle that is smaller than a right angle. Use the base line and start from the dot.

●_____

8 Draw an angle that is larger than a right angle. Use the base line and start from the dot.

●_____

1 This angle is smaller than a right angle. It is:

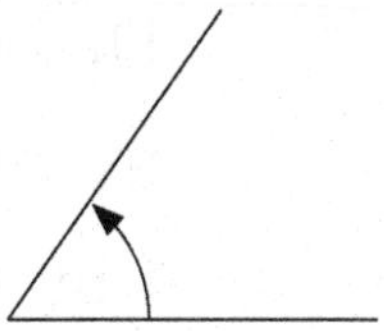

○ an acute angle.

○ an obtuse angle.

○ a reflex angle.

2 This angle is larger than a straight angle. It is:

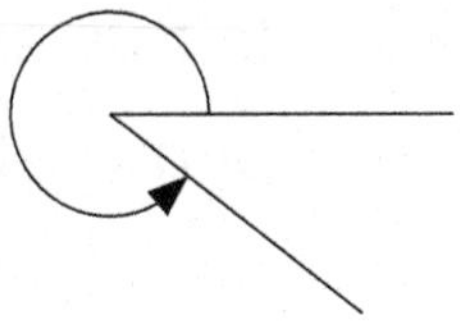

○ an acute angle.

○ an obtuse angle.

○ a reflex angle.

3 Write the angle name.

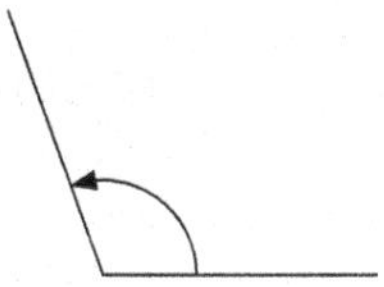

_____

4 Write the angle name.

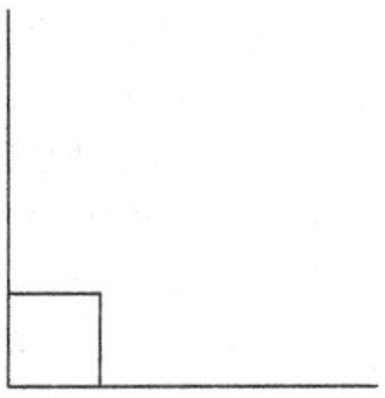

_____

5 Use a pencil and a ruler to draw an acute angle. Use the base line and start from the dot.

6 Use a pencil and ruler to draw an obtuse angle. Use the base line and start from the dot.

7 Draw a 2D shape that has a right angle and 2 acute angles.

8 Name the angle types.

A: _____

B: _____

C: _____

D: _____

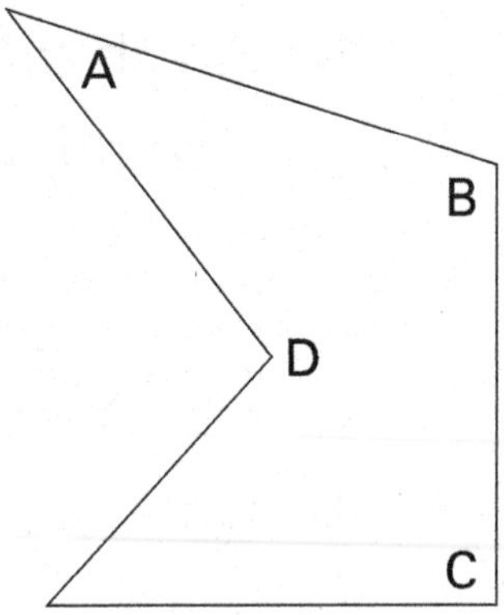

1 Is this shape symmetrical?

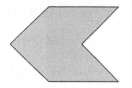

_____

2 Draw a line of symmetry on this shape.

3 Draw 2 lines of symmetry on this shape.

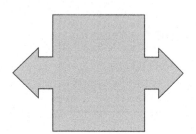

4 Finish this drawing of a symmetrical shape. The dotted line shows the line of symmetry.

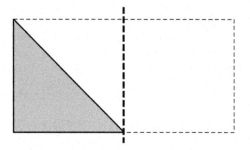

5 Flip, slide or turn?

_____

6 Flip, slide or turn?

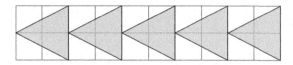

_____

7 **a** Finish the pattern by flipping the triangle.

b Is the pattern symmetrical?

_____

8 **a** Finish the pattern by sliding the triangle.

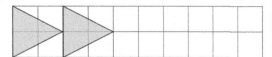

b Is the pattern symmetrical?

_____

1 This pattern has been made by:

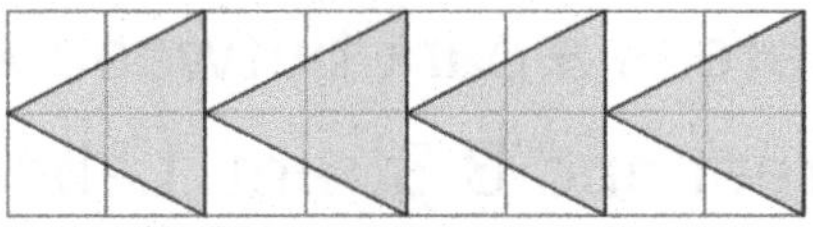

- ◯ reflecting the triangle.
- ◯ translating the triangle.
- ◯ rotating the triangle.

2 This pattern has been made by:

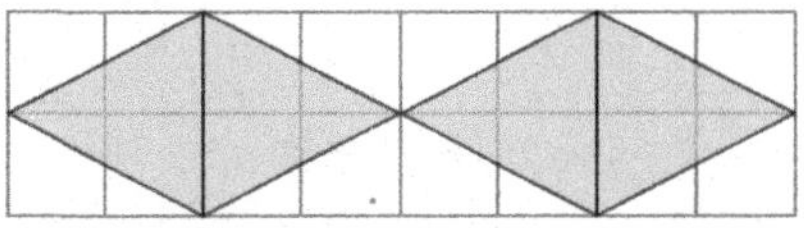

- ◯ reflecting the triangle.
- ◯ translating the triangle.
- ◯ rotating the triangle.

3 Make a pattern by reflecting the triangle.

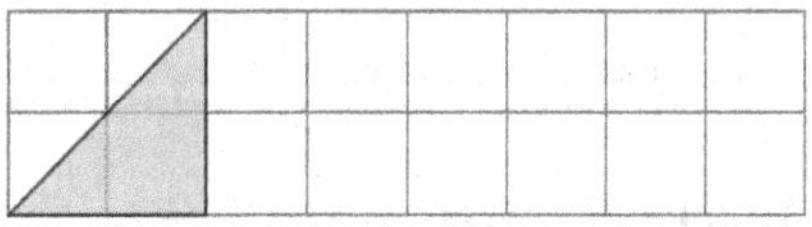

4 Make a pattern by rotating the triangle a $\frac{1}{4}$ turn clockwise.

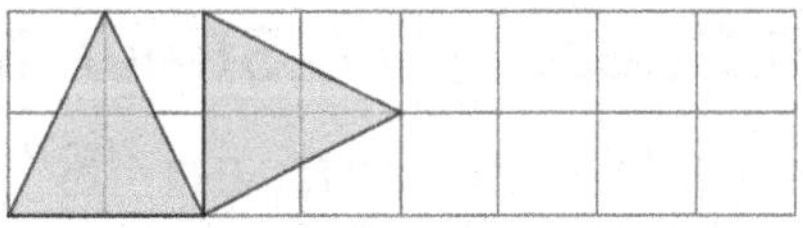

5 **a** Draw a line of symmetry on this pattern.

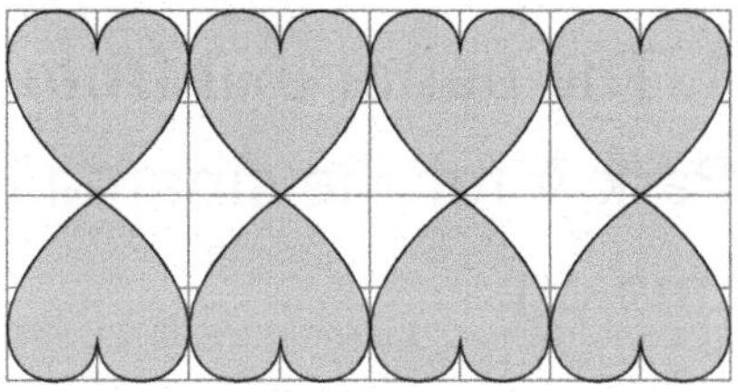

b Finish this sentence. The pattern has been made by reflection and _____.

6 **a** Draw a line of symmetry on each arrow head.

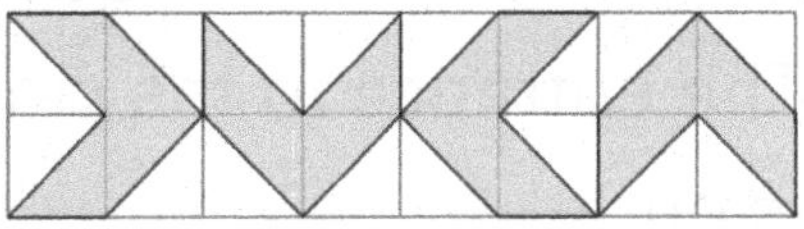

b True or false? The pattern is symmetrical.

_____

7 **a** Draw a symmetrical pattern by reflecting the shape across and down.

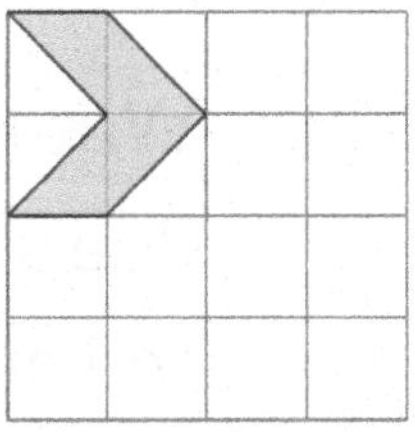

b Draw the lines of symmetry that show the pattern is symmetrical.

8 **a** Make a symmetrical pattern using this shape.

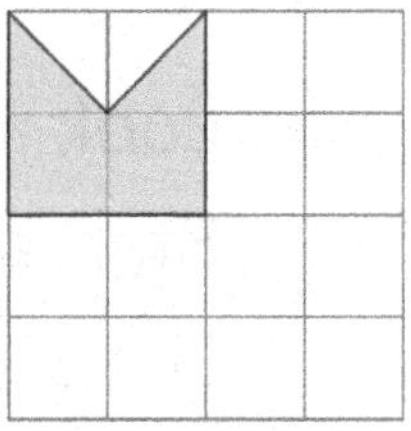

b Describe the way you made the pattern.

_____

_____

1 This is where Joe lives.

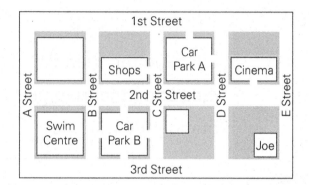

Sam lives on the corner of 2nd Street and C Street. Mark Sam's house with an "S" for Sam in the box on the map.

2 Look at the map in question 1. There is a park between A Street and B Street. Label the park on the map.

3 Look at the map in question 1. Is the Swim Centre closer to Sam's house or Joe's house?

_____

4 Look at the map in question 1. Which car park has 4 entrances? _____

5 Look at the map in question 1. The entrance to the cinema is on:

○ 1st Street.

○ 2nd Street.

○ D Street.

○ E Street.

6 Look at the map in question 1. The better exit from Car Park A for the cinema is the one on:

○ 1st Street.

○ 2nd Street.

○ C Street.

○ D Street.

7 Look at the map in question 1. Start at Joe's house. Go along 3rd Street and turn right at C Street. Go along C Street until you pass 2nd Street. What is on your left? _____

8 Write directions to get from Joe's house on 3rd Street to the cinema.

_____

_____

_____

1 The legend on a map tells us what:

Legend
🚲 Bikes
🍴 Cafe
🚻 Toilet

○ the symbols mean.

○ the map costs.　　○ to do first.

2 This symbol tells us where to:

○ buy a table.　　○ meet a friend.

○ find a picnic area.

---

3 This is a map for a bike track.

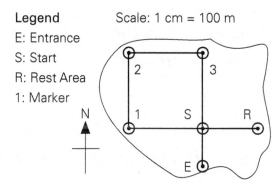

Legend
E: Entrance
S: Start
R: Rest Area
1: Marker

Scale: 1 cm = 100 m

Write S (South), E (East) and W (West) on the compass rose.

4 Look at the map in question 3. The 4th marker is also the start of the track. Write '4' by the 4th marker.

---

6 Use the map in question 3.

a In real life, how far is it from Marker 3, past Marker 4 and to the Rest Area? _____

b In real life, how far is it from the Start to the Rest Area and back again? _____

---

5 Use the map in question 3.

a In real life, how far is it from the Entrance to the start of the track? _____

b If you went from the start to Marker 1, in which direction would you be going? _____

8 Use the map in question 3.

a There is a cafe 150 metres north of the Rest Area. Mark the cafe with a C and a dot at the correct place.

b Draw a line to show the track from the Rest Area to the Café.

---

7 Use the map in question 3. How far would you travel if you cycled from the Entrance to the Start, you did 4 laps, went to the Rest Area and then went back to the Entrance again?

_____

1 Choose the best question to find out how often people watch TV.

○ Do you like watching TV?

○ How many hours a day do you watch TV?

○ What is your favourite program?

2 Evie made a tally of the number of pages she read each day. Write the totals.

Day	Tally	Total
Monday	ЖЖ ЖЖ II	
Tuesday	ЖЖ IIII	
Wednesday	ЖЖ III	
Thursday	ЖЖ ЖЖ I	
Friday	ЖЖ IIII	

3 The graph shows how many stickers Evie received. On Friday, she got 12. Finish the graph.

The number of stickers Evie got

☺ = 2 stickers

Weds	Thurs	Fri

4 Look at the graph in question 3. On which day did Evie get 9 stickers? _____

6 Look at the graph in question 3. What was the total number of stickers for the 3 days? ____

5 Look at the graph in question 3. What is the difference between the number of stickers on Friday and Wednesday? ____

8 Draw a bar graph using the data in questions 3 and 7.

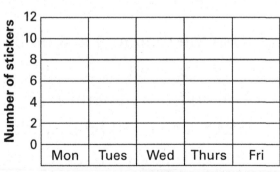

Number of stickers Evie got in a week

Number of stickers / Day

7 On Monday, Evie got 11 stickers. On Tuesday, she got 10. What was her total for the week? _____

UNIT 9: TOPIC 1

1 Choose the best survey question to find out people's favourite sport.

○ Do you like to play sport?

○ Do you like to watch sport?

○ What is the best sport?

2 Write a survey question about books for which the responses could range from "really dislike" to "really like".

_____

_____

3 Tally the number of times you find each vowel used in this group of words.

a	e	i	o	u

4 Use the data in question 3 to complete a bar graph.

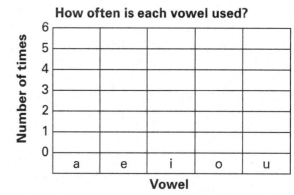

How often is each vowel used?

UNIT 9: TOPIC 2

5 Look at the graph in question 4.

a Which vowel was used the least? ____

b What was the total number of vowels used? ____

6 Look at the sentence in question 3. True or false? More than half the letters used were vowels. _____

7 The survey in question 3 showed that "a" is the least used vowel. Is that always true? Repeat the survey by tallying the vowels in this sentence: An apple is always an ideal food.

a	e	i	o	u

8 **a** Compare the data in questions 3 and 7.

b What would be a good way to find out which vowels are used most and least?

UNIT 10: TOPIC 1

1 If you choose one bead without looking, how likely is it that you will choose black?

○ Impossible
○ Likely
○ Unlikely

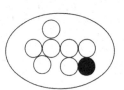

2 If you choose one bead without looking, how likely is it that you will choose white?

○ Impossible
○ Certain
○ Unlikely

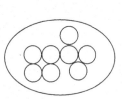

3 Imagine you pick a sock without looking. Describe the chance of taking a grey sock.

_____

4 Look at the socks in question 3. Show the possible outcomes when you take 2 socks without looking.

UNIT 10: TOPIC 2

5 Imagine you have 3 pieces of paper turned over. "Yes" is written on 2 of them and "No" is on the 3rd. Is it **impossible** or **possible** that you will choose 2 with "Yes" written on them without looking? _____

6 What are all the possible outcomes when you choose 2 of the papers in question 5 without looking? Draw or write your answer.

7 Colour the spinner red, yellow, blue and green so that each colour has the same chance.

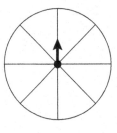

8 Follow these rules to colour the spinner red, blue, yellow and green. Half of the spinner is red. Blue and yellow have the same chance. Green has a better chance than blue.

1 Which describes the chance of a 6-sided dice landing on 5?

◯ Unlikely   ◯ Likely

◯ Certain   ◯ Impossible

2 Which describes the chance of you being asleep at midnight?

◯ Unlikely   ◯ Very likely

◯ Certain   ◯ Very unlikely

3 Imagine you take a bead without looking. Describe the chance of choosing a black bead.

_____

4 Write a likelihood term for this spinner landing on each number.

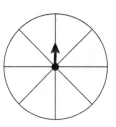

3: _____

2: _____

1: _____

5 Follow the rules to write the numbers 1, 2, 3 and 4 on this spinner.

- 4 has very little chance.
- 3 has the same chance as 2.
- 1 has the best chance.

6 You need 4 small squares of paper that are the same size. Write "N" on 2 of them and "A" on 2 of them. What are the possible outcomes if you choose 2 without looking? Draw or write your answer.

7 Turn over the papers from question 6. Shuffle them. Choose 2. Write the result in the table (e.g. A, N or A, A). Carry out the experiment 6 times.

Turn	1st	2nd	3rd	4th	5th	6th
Result						

8 **a** Which outcome happened most often?

_____

b Would it be the same if you repeated the experiment? Why?

_____

BLM 1

Place value cards

10 365	**539**	**3817**
91 453	**74 680**	**28 104**
9721	**82 946**	**36 072**

BLM 2

Australian births in 2009 and 2014

State/Territory	2009	2014
Australian Capital Territory	4858	5552
Victoria	70 920	74 224
Queensland	66 097	63 066
South Australia	19 734	20 384
New South Wales	92 783	91 074
Tasmania	6626	5935
Northern Territory	3819	4026
Western Australia	30 878	35 403
Total in Australia (including other territories)	**295 715**	**299 664**

4

BLM 3

Splitting shapes

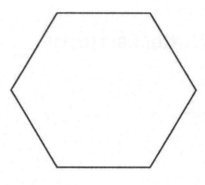
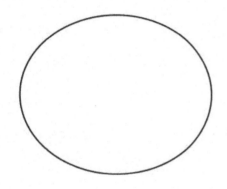
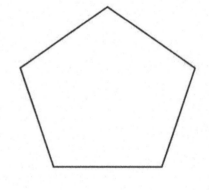

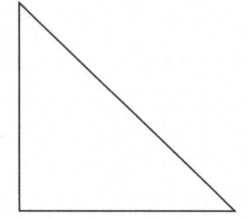

Name:

Class:

BLM 4

Splitting sums

$$142 + 537 =$$

$$635 + 348 =$$

$$2813 + 1126 =$$

BLM 5

Find the answers

Game board 1

90987	534	8388
64489	921	87378
136739	7791	13977

Game board 2

560	48169	13576
110067	7659	96987
7879	931	84877

BLM 5

Find the answers

Game cards

107 + 453	4652 + 3139	9214 + 4362
15648 + 32521	23435 + 41054	50230 + 86509
60005 + 50062	2379 + 5280	71842 + 25145
428 + 106	3827 + 4561	8243 + 5734
634 + 287	476 + 455	4284 + 3595
39754 + 51233	82506 + 4872	76341 + 8536

4

BLM 6

Addition place value chart

Thousands	Hundreds	Tens	Ones

+

Name:

Class:

BLM 7

Blank fraction wall

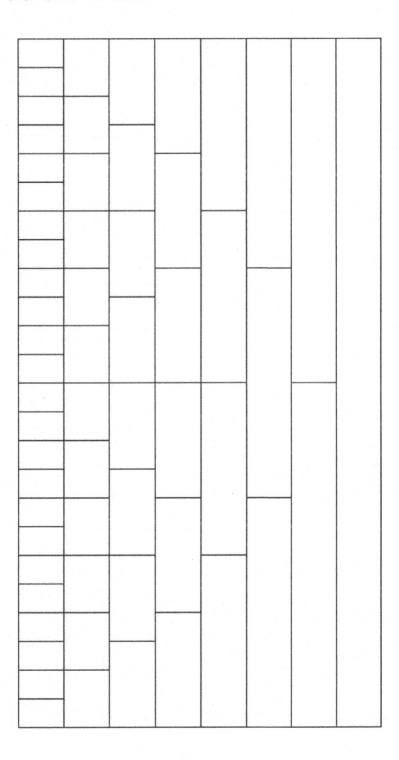

Name:

Class:

BLM 8

Make mine equivalent

a

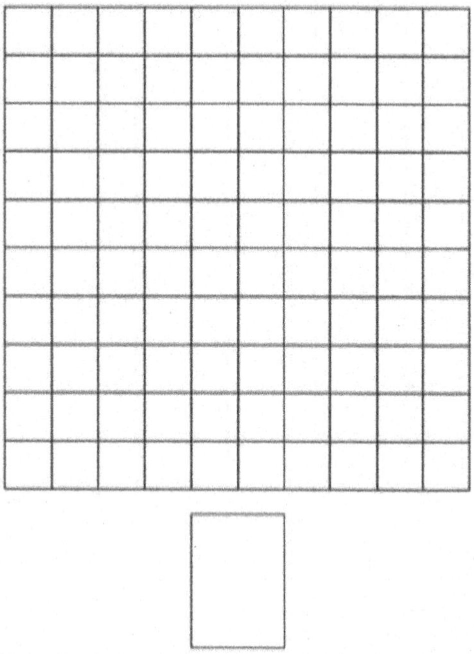

b

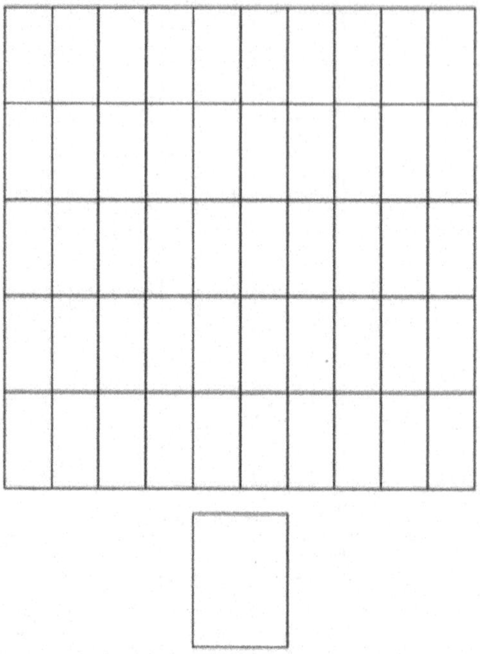

c

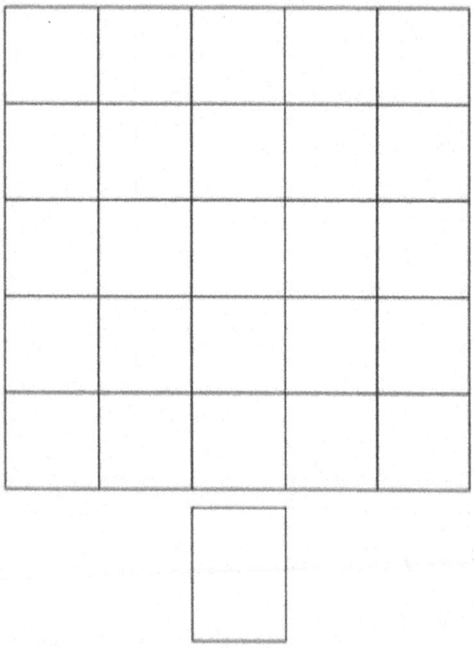

d

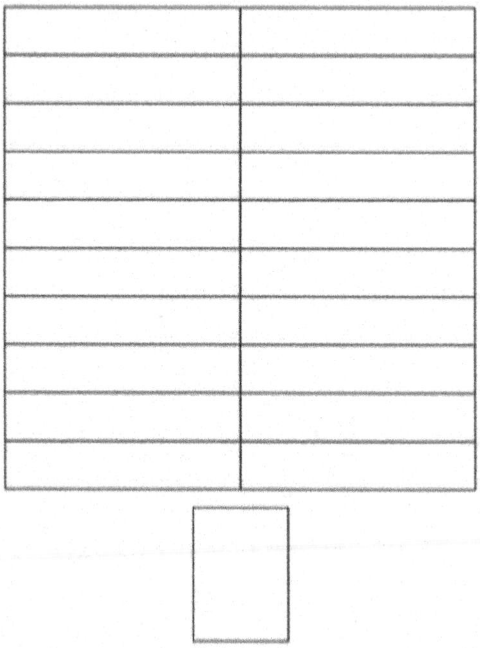

BLM 9

Scone recipe

Ingredients

$2\frac{2}{3}$ cups self-raising flour

$\frac{1}{3}$ cup butter

$1\frac{1}{4}$ cups milk

$\frac{3}{4}$ cup whipped cream

$\frac{1}{4}$ cup jam

Method

1   Preheat the oven to 200°C.

2   Sift the flour into a bowl.

3   Rub the butter into the flour with your fingers until it resembles fine breadcrumbs.

4   Make a well in the centre and add half the milk, mixing until a dough forms. Add more

milk as required to make a soft dough.

5   Knead the dough on a floured surface until smooth.

6   Roll out the dough to 2 cm thick and use a 5 cm cutter to make the scones.

7   Put the scones on a greased baking tray 3 cm apart. Bake for 20–25 minutes.

8   Serve with cream and jam.

BLM 10

Think board

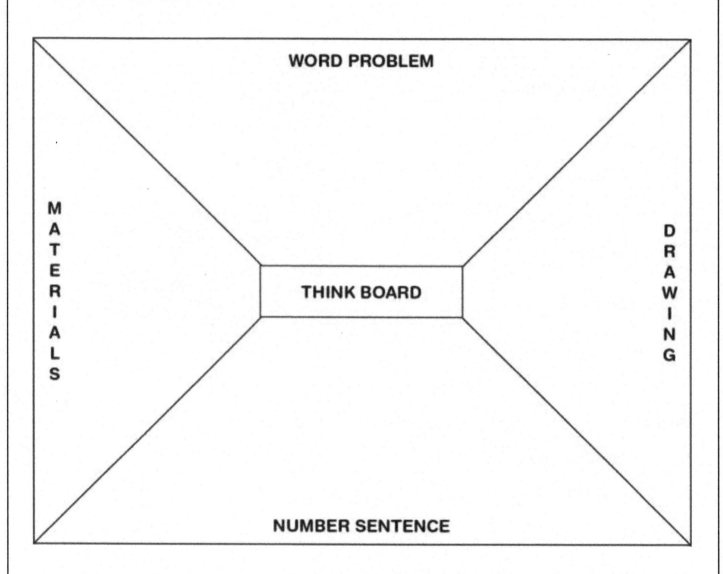

Name:

Class:

BLM 11

Race to two minutes

Time tally

10 seconds _____

20 seconds _____

30 seconds _____

40 seconds _____

50 seconds _____

60 seconds _____

70 seconds _____

80 seconds _____

90 seconds _____

100 seconds _____

110 seconds _____

120 seconds _____

Name:

Class:

BLM 12

Clock anatomy

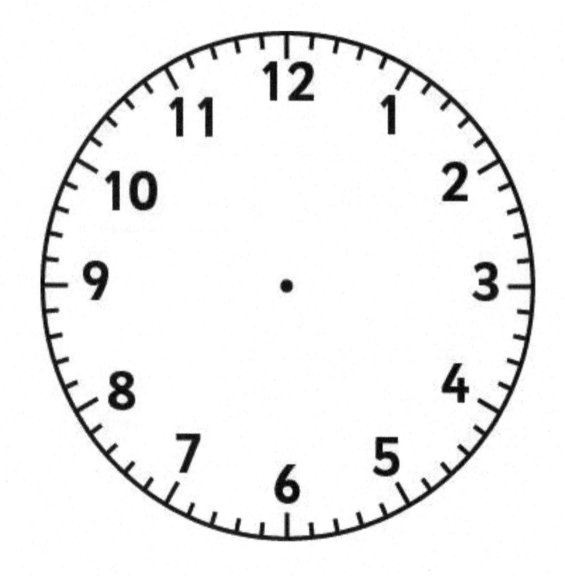

BLM 13

Digit cards

0	1	2	3	4
5	6	7	8	9

0	1	2	3	4
5	6	7	8	9

Name:

Class:

BLM 14

Subtraction ladders

2-digit subtraction

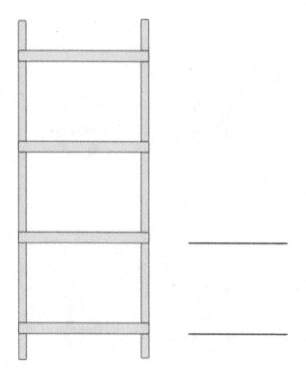

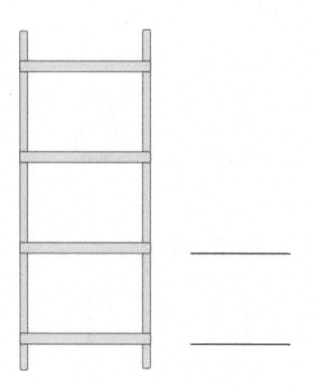

Name:

Class:

3-digit subtraction

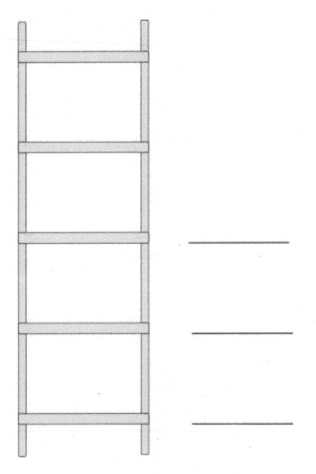

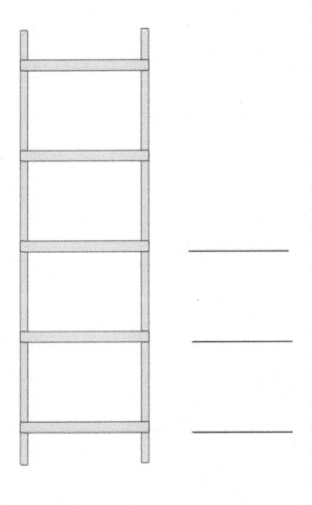

BLM 15

Subtraction place value chart

Thousands	Hundreds	Tens	Ones

Name:

Class:

BLM 16

Odd and even conditions

Write …		Answer	Are they correct?
a number sentence with two 3-digit numbers that will add up to an *odd* number.			
a subtraction problem involving two 3-digit numbers that will result in an *even* answer.			
a 2-digit by 2-digit multiplication problem that will result in an *odd* answer.			
an addition problem involving two 5-digit numbers that will add up to an *even* number.			
an addition problem involving three 4-digit numbers that will result in an *even* answer.			
a subtraction problem involving two 4-digit numbers that will result in an *odd* answer.			
a division problem involving two 3-digit numbers that will result in an *even* answer.			
a 3-digit by 3-digit multiplication problem that will result in an *even* answer.			

BLM 17

Investigating area

Estimate the area of this shape in base-10 tens.   _____

Check the area of this shape using base-10 tens.   _____

What is the area of the shape in square centimetres?   _____

How do you know?

_____

_____

_____

Name:

Class:

Estimate the area of this shape in base-10 tens. _____

Check the area of this shape using base-10 tens. _____

What is the area of the shape in square centimetres? _____

How do you know?

_____

_____

_____

BLM 18

Exploring number patterns

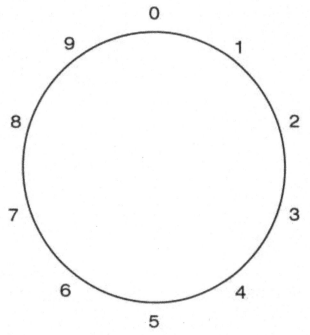

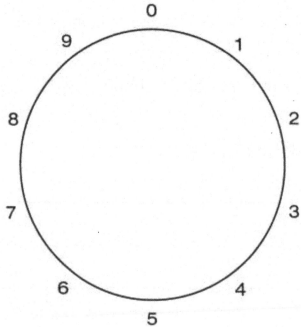

4

BLM 19

Number pattern record sheet

Counting on number	Counting pattern shape	Counting pattern (final digit)
2	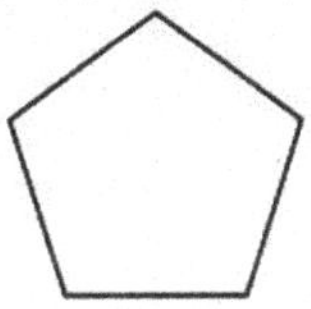 ⬠	0, 2, 4, 6, 8 1, 3, 5, 7, 9
3		0, 3, 6, 9, 2, 5, 8, 1, 4, 7
4		
5		
6		
7		
8		
9		

Name:

Class:

BLM 20

10-frames

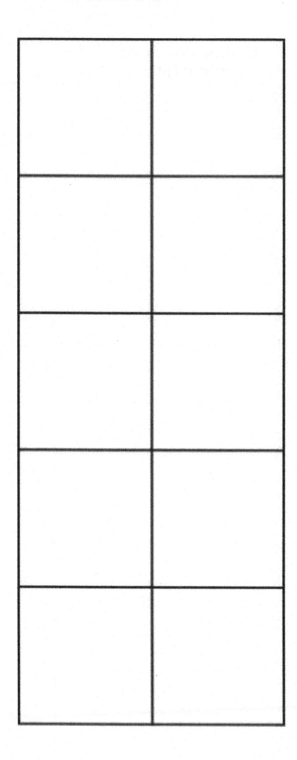

Oxford Mathematics Primary Years Programme Year 4 © Oxford University Press 2019. This sheet may be photocopied for non-commercial classroom use

Name:

Class:

4

BLM 21

Decimal place value chart

Hundreds	Tens	Ones	.	Tenths	Hundredths

BLM 22

Decimal number expanders

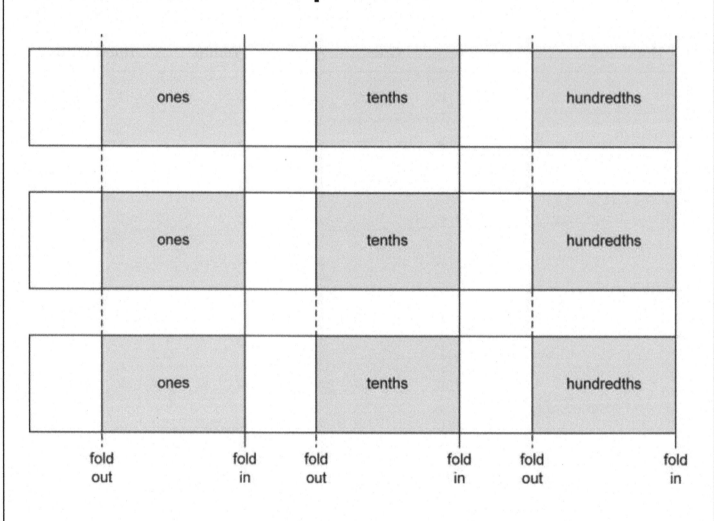

| ones | tenths | hundredths |

fold out   fold in   fold out   fold in   fold out   fold in

BLM 23

Decimal fraction snap cards

$\dfrac{5}{10}$	$\dfrac{5}{100}$	$\dfrac{67}{10}$	$\dfrac{67}{100}$
$\dfrac{14}{10}$	$\dfrac{4}{10}$	$\dfrac{99}{100}$	$\dfrac{9}{100}$
$\dfrac{33}{10}$	$\dfrac{3}{100}$	$\dfrac{6}{10}$	$\dfrac{30}{100}$
0.5	0.05	6.7	0.67
1.4	0.4	0.99	0.09
3.3	0.03	0.6	0.3

BLM 24

Tens cards

10	**20**	**30**
40	**50**	**60**
70	**80**	**90**

4

BLM 25

Contracted multiplication game

Game 1

H	T	O
x		

Game 2

H	T	O
x		

Game 3

H	T	O
x		

Game 4

H	T	O
x		

Name:

Class:

Game 5

H   T   O

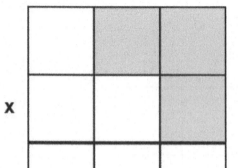

x

Game 6

H   T   O

x

BLM 26

Pictograph pictures

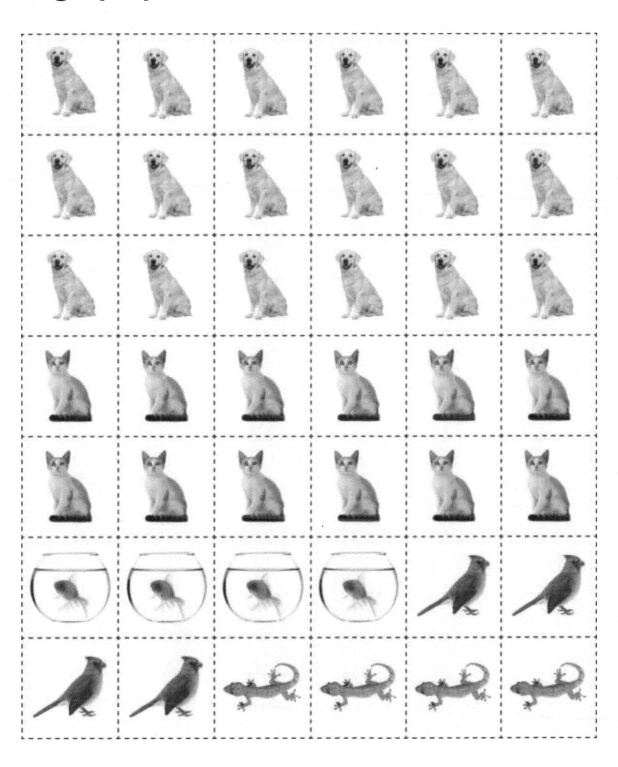

4

BLM 27

Weather in Dataland

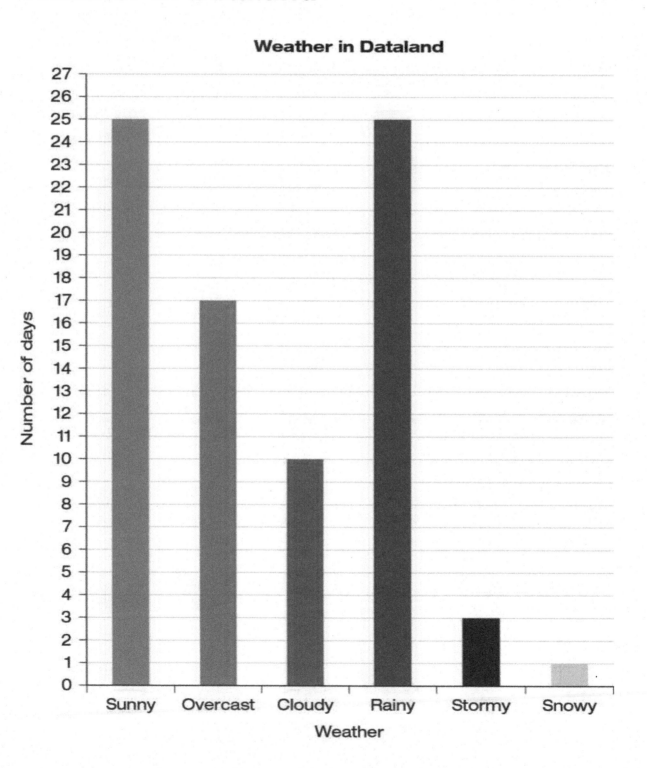

Weather in Dataland

4

BLM 28

Comparing capacity

Containers to be filled	Estimated number of yoghurt containers full of water	Actual number of yoghurt containers	Difference between your estimation and the actual number
 Sour cream			
 Cream			
 Water			
 Juice			

4

BLM 29

Long word problems

Problem 1

The other day, I walked to the shops to buy some donuts and apples for the staffroom. The weather was terrible! On my way to the bakery, a big truck with 10 wheels drove past and splashed me with water. I bought 17 donuts from the bakery that cost $2 each. Then I walked to the greengrocer. There were three small dogs sitting outside. One barked at me, but I managed to get inside without getting bitten. Apples were on special for $1 each, so I bought 20. When I got back, the principal asked me how much I spent. Help me work it out.

Problem 2

It was harvest time at Spring Orchard. Farmer Sam counted 343 peaches on his trees. He decided it was time they were picked. Sam had two fruit pickers working for him. Wendy had been picking peaches for 20 years and was very fast at it. It was Lenny's very first season as a fruit picker and he worked much more slowly. By lunchtime, Wendy had managed to pick 128 peaches; Lenny had only picked 57. Sam asked the fruit pickers how many peaches were still on the trees. What is the answer?

4

BLM 30

Division and multiplication Venn diagram

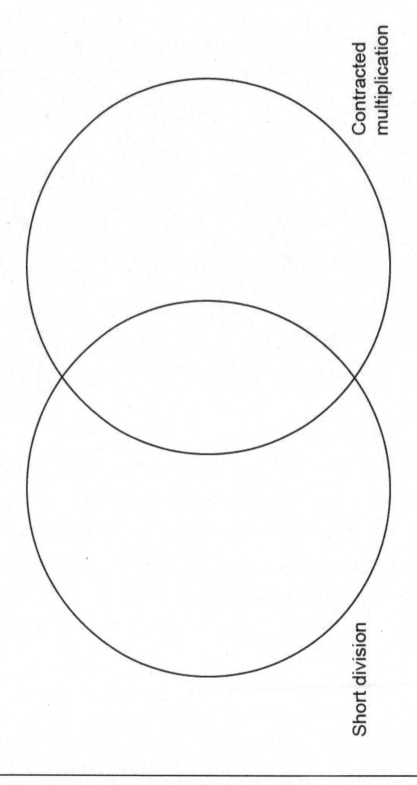

Contracted multiplication

Short division

4

BLM 31

Missing number division

1

$$2 \overline{) \begin{array}{cc} 3 & 4 \\ \square & \square \end{array}}$$

2

$$5 \overline{) \begin{array}{cc} 1 & 7 \\ \square & \square \end{array}}$$

3

$$\square \overline{) \begin{array}{cc} 3 & 2 \\ 6 & 4 \end{array}}$$

4

$$\square \overline{) \begin{array}{cc} 2 & 9 \\ 8 & 7 \end{array}}$$

5

$$2 \overline{) \begin{array}{cc} 2 & \square \\ \square & 8 \end{array}}$$

6

$$4 \overline{) \begin{array}{cc} 2 & \square \\ \square & 2 \end{array}}$$

Name:

Class:

BLM 32

Division think board

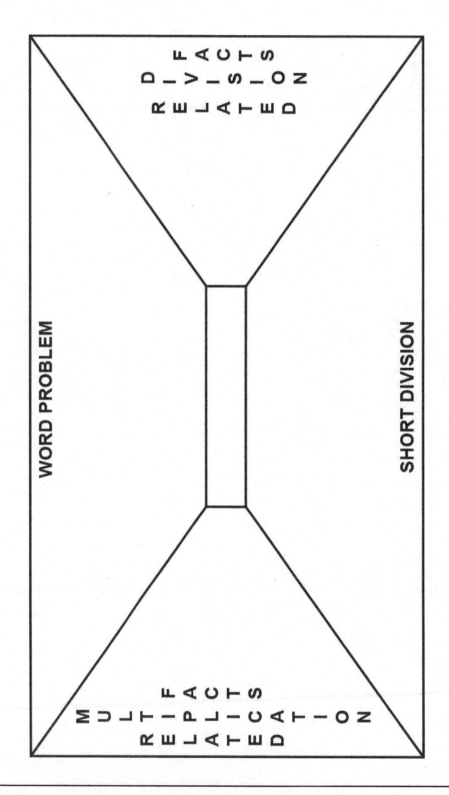

DIVISION FACTS RELATED

WORD PROBLEM

SHORT DIVISION

MULTIPLICATION FACTS RELATED

BLM 33

Sequencing division

Divide the divisor into the ones.

Divide the divisor into the largest place value column.

Trade any leftover tens for ones and record them in the ones column.

Write the answer above the tens of the dividend, on top of the division bracket.

Write the dividend inside the division bracket and the divisor outside.

Write the answer above the ones in the dividend, on top of the division bracket.

BLM 34

Chance continuum

most likely

least likely

Oxford Mathematics Primary Years Programme Year 4 © Oxford University Press 2019. This sheet may be photocopied for non-commercial classroom use

Name:

Class:

BLM 35

0–99 chart

0	1	2	3	4	5	6	7	8	9
10	11	12	13	14	15	16	17	18	19
20	21	22	23	24	25	26	27	28	29
30	31	32	33	34	35	36	37	38	39
40	41	42	43	44	45	46	47	48	49
50	51	52	53	54	55	56	57	58	59
60	61	62	63	64	65	66	67	68	69
70	71	72	73	74	75	76	77	78	79
80	81	82	83	84	85	86	87	88	89
90	91	92	93	94	95	96	97	98	99

BLM 36

Dice roll table

	1	2	3	4	5	6
6						
5						
4						
3						
2						
1						

Oxford Mathematics Primary Years Programme Year 4 © Oxford University Press 2019. This sheet may be photocopied for non-commercial classroom use

4

BLM 37

Snakes and ladders board

0	1	2	3	4	5	6	7	8	9
10	11	12	13	14	15	16	17	18	19
20	21	22	23	24	25	26	27	28	29
30	31	32	33	34	35	36	37	38	39
40	41	42	43	44	45	46	47	48	49
50	51	52	53	54	55	56	57	58	59
60	61	62	63	64	65	66	67	68	69
70	71	72	73	74	75	76	77	78	79
80	81	82	83	84	85	86	87	88	89
90	91	92	93	94	95	96	97	98	99

BLM 38

Change scenarios

1   Selena buys a sandwich for $5.95 and pays for it with three $2 coins. How much change does she receive?

2   Mrs Lu's grocery bill is $156.41. She pays for it with a $100 note, a $50 note and a $20 note. How much change does she receive?

3   Lino buys a pack of mints for 55 cents, but he only has a $20 note. How much change does he receive?

4   The total of Mitchell's shopping is $53.39. If he started with a $100 note, how much does he have left?

BLM 39

Money pathways

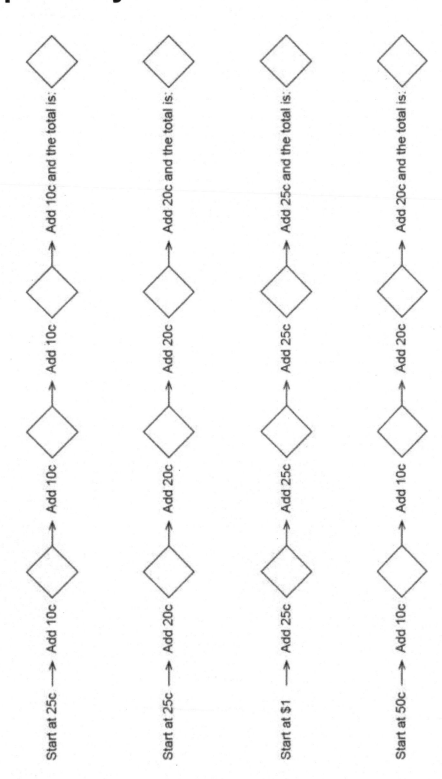

Start at 25c → Add 10c → Add 10c → Add 10c → Add 10c and the total is:

Start at 25c → Add 20c → Add 20c → Add 20c → Add 20c and the total is:

Start at $1 → Add 25c → Add 25c → Add 25c → Add 25c and the total is:

Start at 50c → Add 10c → Add 10c → Add 20c → Add 20c and the total is:

Name:

Class:

BLM 40

Rupees and yen

Indian rupees

4

Japanese yen

Name:

Class:

BLM 41

Scale drawings

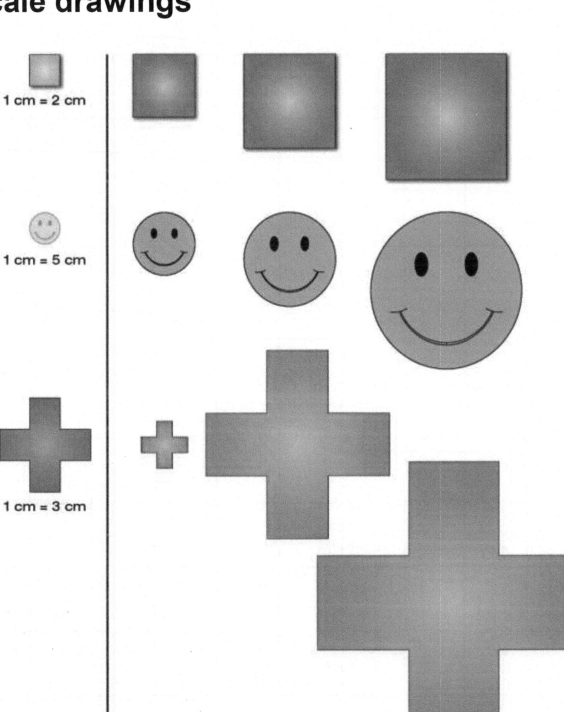

1 cm = 2 cm

1 cm = 5 cm

1 cm = 3 cm

BLM 42

Grid map

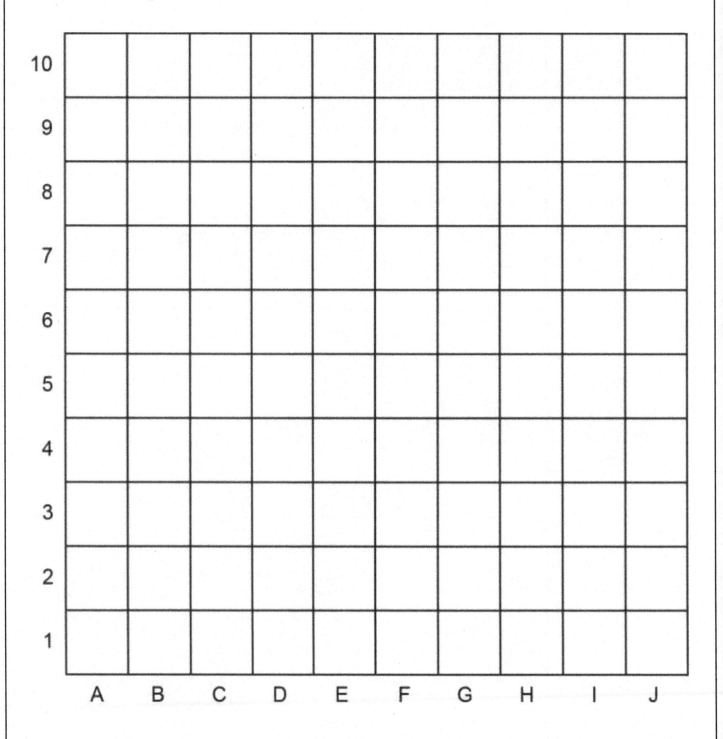

Name:

Class:

BLM 43

Thermometer template

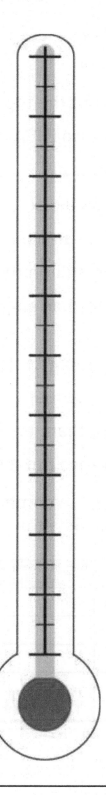

Number facts and fun

1. The following numbers relate to eight of the top 10 cat-owning countries. They are listed in random order.

| 8 895 000 | 8 050 000 | 8 583 100 | 10 450 000 |
| 17 800 000 | 11 300 000 | 10 550 000 | 10 726 000 |

Read these clues and then put the top 10 countries in the correct order.

- The United States of America (USA) is number one with 79 695 000 cats.

- Brazil has 17 262 000 cats.

- Germany has the lowest number.

- Russia has more cats than Brazil.

- Canada has about half a million more than Germany.

- The United Kingdom (UK) has slightly less than ten and a half million cats.

- Japan has about six million less than Brazil.

- Ukraine has the closest number to nine million.

- France has slightly more than ten and a half million cats.

- China has more than France but less than Japan.

2. As the following data shows, in some countries dogs are even more popular than cats. This table lists the top 10 dog-owning countries.

	Country	Number of pet dogs	Rounded number
1	USA		
2	Brazil		
3	China		
4	Mexico		
5	Japan		

(continued)

	Country	Number of pet dogs	Rounded number
6	Russia		
7	Philippines		
8	Ukraine		
9	France		
10	South Africa		

a The figures for each of the top 10 dog-owning countries are listed below, in random order. Complete the third column of the table using these numbers.

12 270 000   9 651 500   27 034 000

65 791 000   8 495 000   33 745 000

    7 449 000   13 618 000   8 517 000   17 859 000

b All of these numbers have been rounded to the nearest thousand, except for one. Which country's number has not been rounded?

c Round the number identified in question 2b to the nearest thousand.

d Complete the fourth column of the table, rounding the numbers to the nearest million.

e How many more pet dogs would South Africa need in order to have the same number (rounded to the nearest million) as France?

3 If you took a 2 and a 3 from a deck of playing cards, you could arrange them to make two different numbers: 23 or 32. If you took three cards, such as 2, 3 and 4, you could make more than three different numbers – in fact, you could arrange them in six different ways!

a Find out how many ways you could arrange four playing cards – 2, 3, 4 and 5 – to make as many different numbers as you can. (You will need a large sheet of paper – there are more than twenty ways!)

b Write down the numbers in order, from the smallest to the largest.

That's odd!

Starting from the number 1, half of all numbers are odd and half are even, but what about zero? Is it odd or even? Even mathematicians can't agree about that!

1 **a** Fill in the second column of this table to remind yourself of the result when working with odd and even numbers.

Number operation	Is the answer odd or even?	Proof
even + even =		
odd + even =		
odd + odd =		
even − even =		
even − odd =		
odd − odd =		
even × even =		
even × odd =		
odd × odd =		

b In the third column, prove that each statement is true by writing equations with 2-digit numbers.

(continued)

2 We already know that if a number ends in zero, it's an even number, but what about zero itself?

a Do you think zero is even, odd or neither?

b This table lists some ways to check if a number is even. Test each method using an even number, then by using zero itself.

A number is even if …	Test with an even number	Test with zero
the answer is even when it's added to an even number.		
there is no remainder when it's divided by 2.		
the numbers either side of it are odd.		
the answer is even when it's added to itself.		
there is no remainder when the number is halved.		
the answer is odd when the number is added to an odd number.		
the answer is odd when the number is taken away from an odd number.		

c Now that you have tested each method, do you think zero is an even number? Give a reason for your answer.

3 Discover some interesting facts about odd and even numbers.

a There is only one number that is both prime and even. What is it? (Note: Zero is *not* a prime number because it can be "divided" by more than just 1 and itself.)

b Is the difference between any square number and the next square number always odd, always even, or sometimes odd and sometimes even?

c Write the first 10 square numbers. What do you notice about the way the list of numbers grows?

(continued)

4 Is there such a thing as an even–odd number? The Greek mathematician and philosopher Pythagoras believed that there is. Here's the explanation:

- The numbers 2, 4, 6, 8 and 10 are all even.

- The number 4 is even because $4 = 2 \times 2$.

- The number 6 can also be called an even–odd number because it's the product of an even number multiplied by an odd number ($6 = 2 \times 3$).

a Show why 10 can also be called an even–odd number.

b Find some other even–odd numbers between 2 and 20.

c Which of the even numbers between 2 and 20 are not even–odd?

5 Certain numbers are considered special or lucky. Two of these are odd numbers: 3 and 7.

a Conduct some research and then make a list of special things about the numbers 3 and 7. The list has been started for you.

Special things about ...	
3	**7**
There are three primary colours.	There are seven colours of the rainbow.

b Can you think of any other numbers that are considered special or lucky?

Rounding, estimating and calculating

You will need

- a calculator

1

a If someone used a calculator to work out 1003 + 2005 and wrote the answer as 1208, how would you know that the answer was wrong?

b What is 1003 + 2005?

c Which calculator keys is the person likely to have pressed to get 1208 as the answer?

2 In question 1, you could have checked the answer by rounding and estimating. For example: 1003 + 2005 rounds to 1000 + 2000 = 3000. So the actual answer must be close to 3000.

Round to an easy number, then estimate the answer for each of the following. Underline the answer that's likely to be correct. An example has been done for you.

The problem	Round the numbers	Estimate the answer	Underline the likely answer
3050 + 4969	3000 + 5000	8000	9019 or <u>8019</u>
697 + 208			805 or 905
1925 + 3064			4989 or 5989
4195 + 4827			9022 or 10 022
19 882 + 9968			29 850 or 39 850
29 021 + 60 889			89 910 or 99 910
103 465 + 99 332			102 797 or 202 797

3 A few years ago, the top three makes of stolen cars were Toyota, Volkswagen and Ford. The numbers of cars stolen were:

Toyota – 404 217   Volkswagen – 307 680   Ford – 264 017

Is the closest estimate for the total number of cars stolen 925 000, 950 000 or 975 000?

(continued)

4 Round to an easy number and estimate the answer. Then find the answer on a calculator; if it's not close to your estimate, check again! An example has been done for you.

The problem	Round the numbers	Estimate the answer	Calculator answer
419 + 189	400 + 200	600	608
317 + 586			
1214 + 827			
7835 + 4098			
21 235 + 30 638			
68 131 + 29 427			
101 323 + 98 472			
415 328 + 298 520			
253 729 + 47 395			

5 American football games draw in huge crowds. An average of 68 776 people attend each game. Normally, we round off a number like that.

a Round the figure of 68 776 people.

b Complete the following.

- Choose a sports league and find the attendance for each team in a particular week.

- Round the attendance figure for each team.

- Use mental strategies to find the total number of people who attended games that week.

- Work out the average number of spectators per game by dividing the total by the number of teams.

Working with large numbers

Once you have learned how to do a 4-digit addition algorithm, it's easy to work with numbers of any size. The only difference is that large number additions take longer than short number additions.

1 The Australian Football League (AFL) and international football attract big sports crowds at the Melbourne Cricket Ground. The table below shows the size of some of the largest crowds this century.

Year	Sport	Event	Crowd
2006	AFL	Grand Final: West Coast v Sydney Swans	97 431
2006	International football	Socceroos v Greece	95 103
2007	AFL	Geelong v Collingwood	98 002
2007	AFL	Grand Final: Geelong v Port Adelaide	97 302
2008	AFL	Grand Final: Geelong v Hawthorn	100 012
2009	AFL	Grand Final: St Kilda v Geelong	99 251
2010	AFL	Finals: Collingwood v Geelong	95 241
2010	AFL	Grand Final: Collingwood v St Kilda	100 016
2011	AFL	Grand Final: Collingwood v Geelong	99 537
2012	AFL	Grand Final: Hawthorn v Sydney	99 683
2013	International football	Melbourne Victory v Liverpool	95 446
2013	AFL	Grand Final: Hawthorn v Fremantle	100 007
2014	AFL	Grand Final: Sydney Swans v Hawthorn	99 454
2015	International football	Manchester City v Real Madrid	99 382
2015	AFL	Grand Final: Hawthorn v West Coast	98 633

(continued)

Use the information in the table on the previous page to answer the following questions.

a Which game had the biggest crowd?

b Round the size of the two 2006 crowds to the nearest 10 000, and calculate the approximate total.

c What was the exact total of the crowds at the two 2006 games?

d Round the size of the crowds at the three international football games to the nearest 10 000, and write the approximate total.

e What was the total number of people who watched the international football games?

f Round the size of the crowds at the five games that Hawthorn played in to the nearest 10 000, and write the approximate total.

g How many people watched the five games that Hawthorn played in?

h Rounding the totals of each game to the nearest 10 000, is the approximate total number of spectators at the 15 games more or less than one million?

i What is the exact total number of spectators for the 15 games?

2 In Sydney, the Roosters rugby league club attracts large numbers of National Rugby League (NRL) supporters. More than 200 000 people watched their 12 home games in a recent season. The statistics are listed below.

- Total attendance: 211 116

- Average attendance: 17 593

However, these figures don't tell us the size of the crowd at each game. Using the figures above, make a list of possible attendances for the 12 games. Note: the crowds were *not* the same size each week.

3 The answer to an addition problem is 11 110. Use the digits 3, 5 and 7 to write the addition problem. Each digit can be used more than once.

4 If you add 30 622 + 84 264 + 8570, you will see that the answer makes a number pattern. Make up some addition problems that continue this pattern.

Unlocking your subtraction skills

It's good to have several subtraction strategies to choose from. That way, you can use the one that works best for you!

If two people worked out 98 – 37 in their heads, one person might get the answer this way: "First, I split 37 into 30 and 7. Next, 98 – 30 is 68. Then I took away 7. So, 98 – 37 = 61."

The other person might use the compensation strategy to get the answer: "The number 37 is nearly 40, so I worked out 98 – 40. That makes 58. Then I added 3 back on because I took away 3 too many. That makes 61."

1 Choose a mental strategy to answer the following equations as quickly as you can. Explain how you got each answer.

    a 1500 – 600   **b** 174 – 39   **c** 2387 – 2004

    d 1577 – 1122   **e** 2950 – 1960

2 If you were using a calculator for 19 008 – 9006 and the answer came up as 2, would you trust the answer? If you used your rounding skills, you would know that the answer must be about 10 000 because 19 000 take away 9000 is 10 000.

Use your rounding skills to complete the following table. The first one has been done for you.

Subtraction	Calculator answer	Rounding	Can we trust the calculator answer?
1507 – 998	509	1500 – 1000 = 500	yes
173 – 141	32		
412 – 195	317		
3103 – 1104	1999		
1997 – 1490	507		
2008 – 397	1711		
2985 – 1030 – 874	2081		

(continued)

3 Eva wants a new TV. She finds the same model in two shops.

Shop 1 is advertising the TV for $3999, with a saving of $1100.

Shop 2 is offering the TV for $4099, with a discount of $1299.

Which shop is offering the better deal? Use mental strategies to find the answer.

4 In the days before electronic cash registers, shopkeepers used the counting-up strategy to work out change for customers. This strategy also works for normal subtraction.

Finn bought a pencil set for $3.85. He paid using a $5 note. Instead of doing a subtraction algorithm, the shopkeeper started at $3.85 and counted up to $5.

- $3.85 up to $3.90 is 5c.
- $3.90 up to $4 is another 10c.
- $4 up to $5 is $1.
- The change is 5c + 10c + $1 = $1.15.
- That's another way of saying $5 − $3.85 = $1.15.

Use the counting-up strategy to work out the change if you paid for each of the following items using a $10 note.

a a game for $8.50

b a book that costs $7.75

c a pack of stickers for $2.50

d a calculator priced at $4.15

5 Listed below are the five least-populated countries in the world.

Country	Population
Vatican City	932
Tuvalu	11 636
Nauru	12 809
Palau	20 016
San Marino	28 503

(continued)

a   How far off 1000 is the population of the Vatican City?

b   What is the difference between the largest and smallest populations in the list?

c   Find out the population of a town near you. Which country in the list has the closest population figure to the population of your chosen town?

d   Find out the difference between the population of one of the countries and the town where you live.

Using your subtraction skills

There's an easy way to make sure your subtraction work is correct.

	4	2	6	3			1	2	7	5
−	1	2	7	5		+	2	9	8	8
	2	9	8	8			4	2	6	3

Add the subtraction answer to the number on the second line of the equation. If the result is the same as the number on the top line of the equation, your answer is correct.

1 Complete the following subtractions and use the addition method to check that they are correct.

a

	3	1	4	5			1	1	8	6
−	1	1	8	6		+				

b

	5	4	8	6						
−	3	7	9	8		+				

(continued)

c

	2	7	3	9	4								
−	1	4	6	3	7		+						

d

	4	3	3	0	5								
−	2	7	4	2	7		+						

2 Australia has no land border with any other country. Its border is coastline, which is 34 218 km long. The table below shows how Australia compares to the countries with the longest land borders.

Country	Border length (km)	Country	Border length (km)
China	22 117	Kazakhstan	12 012
Russia	20 017	Democratic Republic of the Congo	10 730
Brazil	14 691	Argentina	9665
India	14 103	Canada	8893
USA	12 034	Mongolia	8220

Use the information in the table to answer the following questions.

a What is the difference between the length of Australia's coastline and the country with the longest border?

b Which two countries have the least difference in border length?

c Which two countries have the greatest difference in border length?

d Which two countries have a difference that is closest to 2000 km?

e Which two countries have a difference that is closest to 8000 km?

f Which two countries have a difference that is closest to 10 000 km?

(continued)

3   Fill in the gaps.

a

	5	8	4	7	9
−	☐	2	5	7	☐
	4	5	9	0	1

b

	4	5	1	3	☐
−	2	☐	☐	2	9
	2	2	0	0	9

c

	5	0	9	☐	9
−	2	4	☐	5	9
	☐	6	7	8	0

d

	☐	5	0	0	☐
−	1	3	☐	2	1
	7	1	7	8	3

4   An Indian mathematician, D. R. Kaprekar, discovered something very interesting about the number 6174.

  a   Use the digits to make the largest number. What is it?

  b   Make the smallest number with the same digits. What is it?

  c   Find the difference between the two numbers. What is it?

This is called *Kaprekar's constant.* D. R. Kaprekar also found out something even more amazing – it doesn't matter which digits you use. As long as at least two of the digits are different, you'll eventually end up with the magic number of 6174, even if you have to repeat the process a few times.

  d   Try Kaprekar's constant with the digits 9, 8, 7 and 1.

Getting organised

You will need

- a large piece of paper

Many people use their knowledge of multiplication and division facts to help them get organised.

1 In Class 4F there are 30 students. The teacher wants to organise them into groups.

    a Draw arrays to show all the possible ways of organising the groups.

    b If you were the teacher, which way would you organise the groups? Give a reason for your answer.

2 People who display items in shops use multiplication and division facts. Items are often displayed in arrays. For example, if there are nine items, they can be displayed in three ways: one row of nine, nine rows of one or three rows of three.

But what if there are 24 items? How many different ways could 24 apples be arranged? Draw the arrays on your large piece of paper. Write the multiplication fact next to each array. Can you find more than six ways of arranging the apples?

3 How many different ways can you fill these boxes so that the answer is always four?

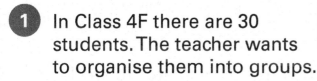

$$\boxed{}\boxed{} \div \boxed{} = 4$$

4 There are 96 students in Year 4. The students need to be divided into equal groups for sport.

    a How would you group the students? Give a reason for your answer.

    b If one more student joined Year 4, how would that affect the grouping of the students?

(continued)

5 Write the multiples on the correct boards. Some numbers may go on more than one board.

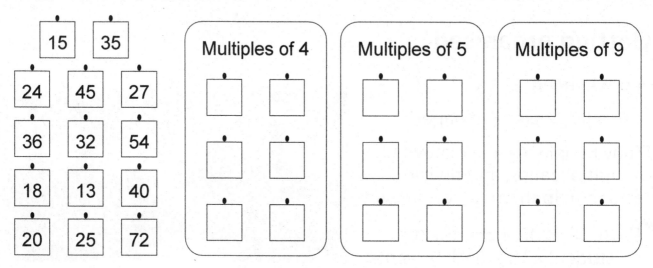

6 Amy, Ava and Eve have $16 to share. They use a calculator to work out how much they should each get. They enter 16 ÷ 3 and the calculator shows:

Ava says they should round $5.33 to $5.35, but Eve says that won't work. Eve is right.

a Explain why.

b How should they split $16 between the three of them?

Using your multiplication skills

You will need

- a calculator (optional)

A multiple is the number you get when you multiply a number by another whole number. Using your multiplication skills saves time.

1 Look at these numbers: 2, 5, 8, 9

Which three of these numbers can be arranged to form a multiplication that gives a product of:

a 200? **b** 252? **c** 416?

d 490? **e** 472? **f** 522?

2 Lin is reading a book. She wants to know how many words are on a page.

"I know a way to find out," says her friend, Ben. "We can count how many words are on one line, then multiply that by the number of lines."

a There are nine words on a line and 67 lines on a page. About how many words are on a page?

b Why do you think question 2a asks "*About* how many words" and not "*Exactly* how many words"?

c Choose a reading book. Write a multiplication algorithm to work out how many words there might be on a page.

3 Fill in the boxes in three different ways.

$$\begin{array}{cccc} & \square & \square & \square \\ \times & & & \square \\ \hline 1 & 4 & 0 & 8 \end{array}$$
$$\begin{array}{cccc} & \square & \square & \square \\ \times & & & \square \\ \hline 1 & 4 & 0 & 8 \end{array}$$
$$\begin{array}{cccc} & \square & \square & \square \\ \times & & & \square \\ \hline 1 & 4 & 0 & 8 \end{array}$$

(continued)

4 Here are some amazing facts about the human body.

- We take a breath about 12 times per minute.
- We lose about 257 g of skin per year.
- Our eyes move about 4100 times every hour.
- We lose about 80 hairs every day.
- We have about 59 200 km of tiny blood tubes, called capillaries.

a How many hairs have you lost in the last week?

b How many breaths do you normally take in a quarter of an hour?

c How much skin did you lose up to your seventh birthday? Write your answer in kilograms and grams.

d About how many times do your eyes move in a normal school day?

e How long are the capillaries in a group of four students?

f Find out something interesting about the human body and turn it into a multiplication fact. For example, how many times does your heart beat in one hour?

5 This table shows how much water goes over six of the world's biggest waterfalls (measured in megalitres per second).

Name	Location	Megalitres (ML) per second
Inga Falls	Democratic Republic of the Congo	42
Livingstone Falls	Democratic Republic of the Congo	35
Boyoma Falls	Democratic Republic of the Congo	17
Guaira Falls	Brazil/Paraguay	14
Khone Falls	Laos	11
Niagara Falls	Canada/USA	6

a How many megalitres go over the Inga Falls in the time it takes you to write your full name?

b How many megalitres go over the three falls in the Democratic Republic of the Congo in eight seconds?

c Write some facts about one or two of the waterfalls, referring to the amount of water that goes over in a minute, an hour and so on. You may need a calculator.

Share and share alike

1 The factors of a number tell us the ways the number can be divided without leaving a remainder. What are the factors of 21?

2 Not every number can be divided equally by other numbers. For example, the answer to 11 ÷ 3 is 3 r2.

Write algorithms for these. Use remainders where necessary in the answers.

a 97 ÷ 5   **b** 72 ÷ 3   **c** 145 ÷ 6   **d** 386 ÷ 7

3 In real life, we have to work out what to do with remainders. Provide answers to these real-life situations.

a How can two girls share seven doughnuts?

b Two children are given nine marbles. How many can each child have?

c Two sisters share $13. How much do they each get?

4 Poppins Public School has 161 children in the senior classes.

a What is the mean (average) number of students in each class?

b Complete the table to show the actual number that could be in each class. Two rows have been filled in for you. Apart from those already filled in, no two classes have the same number of students.

Class	Number of students
3W	
3/4D	26
4M	26
5S	
5/6H	
6T	

c Looking at your completed table, what are the median (the number that is "in the middle") and mode (most common) numbers?

5 At Charlie's Chicken Farm they pack 3000 eggs per day. Each box holds eight dozen eggs. How many boxes are needed for 3000 eggs?

(continued)

6 An American man named Donald Gorsk ate 18 350 Big Macs in a 30-year period. That's an average of 611.6 Big Macs a year! If you work out the average number of Big Macs Donald ate in a week (or in a day), you will see that he was not a healthy eater!

Conduct some research and find out about someone who did something interesting like Donald Gorsk. When you have the information, average the number into smaller lengths of time. Do your research, calculate the averages and present your information in an interesting way.

Half of a half

You will need

- two pieces of coloured paper
- a sheet of poster paper
- scissors   • glue   • a piece of A4 paper

When a whole object is split into two equal pieces, two halves are formed. Sometimes, when an object has been split into two unequal pieces, someone may ask for the "bigger half".

1 The number of pieces a whole object is split into becomes the denominator in a fraction. So if a pie is split into two equal pieces, the denominator is two and each piece is called one half ($\frac{1}{2}$). If one pie is split into eighths and another identical pie is split into tenths, which pie has the smaller pieces?

2 Arrange these fractions from the smallest to the largest.

$\frac{1}{5}$ $\frac{1}{10}$ $\frac{1}{8}$ $\frac{1}{12}$ $\frac{1}{3}$ $\frac{1}{100}$

3 Show that $\frac{1}{4}$ is bigger than $\frac{1}{8}$ by drawing and dividing two "pies" and shading the appropriate fractions.

4 Compare yourself to some record-breakers!

a In 2010, Australian man Damien Kerley threw 46 custard pies in his friend's face in one minute. If you threw half that number, how many would you have thrown?

b In 2009, another Australian, Grahame Cellodoni, snapped 96 bananas in half with his hands in one minute. If you could snap a quarter of that number, how many bananas would you have snapped?

c American Zachery George can hold 24 eggs in one hand without dropping them. If you could hold one-sixth of that number, how many would you hold?

(continued)

5 In 2007 an Australian, Nick Moraitis, paid $35 000 for the first box of cherries of the season.

   a If Nick gave you one-seventh of the cherries, and he gave one-fifth to your friend, who would have more cherries?

   b How much would your cherries be worth?

   c How much would your friend's cherries be worth?

6 In a fraction, the bigger the number in the denominator, the smaller each part becomes. To demonstrate this, start with two pieces of coloured paper that are the same size.

   a Glue one of the pieces onto a sheet of poster paper and label it *one whole*.

   b Fold the other piece in half. Cut out one half, glue it on your poster paper and label it as $\frac{1}{2}$.

   c Fold and cut the remaining piece into two again. Take one of the pieces and decide what fraction of the whole it is. Glue it on your poster paper and label it.

   d Repeat step c. How small can you go?

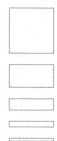

7 Many mathematicians believe that it's impossible to fold a piece of paper more than eight times. Some people claim to have disproven this theory. How many times can you fold a piece of A4 paper in half? When you can't fold the paper any more, write down the number of folds, open the paper out and find the fraction the folds have made.

More than a whole one

If you have more than one whole, you can show the amount as either a mixed number or an improper fraction. In the picture below, we can see that the amount of pizza left is $\frac{12}{8}$. We can also write this as $1\frac{4}{8}$, or $1\frac{1}{2}$.

  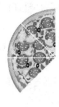

1 Write the amount of pizza as an improper fraction and as a whole number.

a

b

2 a Shade $1\frac{5}{8}$. Write the amount as an improper fraction.

b Shade $\frac{8}{3}$. Write the amount as a mixed number.

3 Draw lines and shade the amount shown for each.

a $1\frac{3}{4}$ 　　　　　　**b** $\frac{17}{8}$

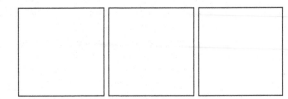

(continued)

c $\frac{7}{2}$

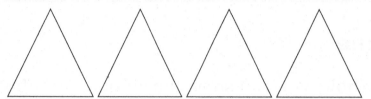

4 **a** Draw a diagram to show $3\frac{1}{4}$.

b How many quarters did you shade on your diagram?

5 Write a fraction or mixed number that is:

a bigger than 1 but less than $1\frac{1}{4}$.

b less than 2 but larger than $1\frac{1}{2}$.

c the same as $2\frac{3}{4}$.

6 Organise this list into two groups. Explain how you chose the two groups.

$1\frac{1}{4}$ $\qquad$ $\frac{5}{4}$ $\qquad$ $2\frac{1}{2}$ $\qquad$ $\frac{15}{6}$ $\qquad$ $\frac{10}{8}$ $\qquad$ $2\frac{4}{8}$ $\qquad$ $1\frac{2}{8}$ $\qquad$ $\frac{10}{4}$

7 Put these fractions in the correct places on the number line.

$\frac{5}{4}$ $\qquad$ $\frac{1}{8}$ $\qquad$ $\frac{2}{3}$ $\qquad$ $\frac{23}{12}$ $\qquad$ $\frac{13}{8}$ $\qquad$ $\frac{11}{10}$ $\qquad$ $\frac{4}{8}$

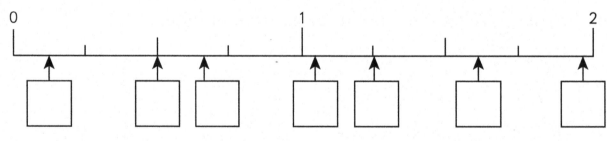

8 Find combinations of fractions that can be added together to make one and a half, such as adding two halves and one half. Find as many combinations as possible, then compare your list to someone else's.

Working with decimals

You will need

• a digital stopwatch

If a whole is split into 100 equal parts, each part is a hundredth. We can write this as a decimal: 0.01

1 **a** Shade nine-hundredths of the first square. Shade 0.11 of the second square.

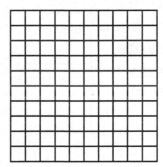 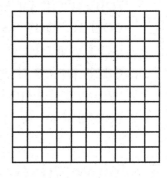

b Which is larger – nine-hundredths or 0.11?

c Write the unshaded part of the first square as a decimal.

2 Shade the square in the colours listed below.

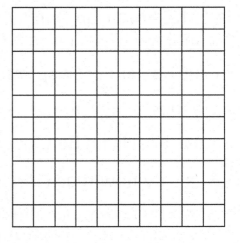

a Red: 0.1 **b** Blue: 0.25

c Green: $\frac{27}{100}$ **d** Yellow: 0.05

e Purple: 0.18

f Choose a colour to shade the rest. Write that part as a fraction and a decimal.

g Write all the decimals and fractions from questions 2a–f in order, from the largest to the smallest.

3 Write each letter at the correct place to read the message.

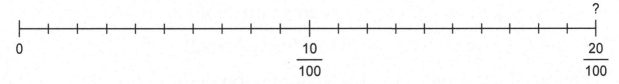

0          $\frac{10}{100}$ $\frac{20}{100}$?

a Put a letter *H* at 0.01.

b Put a letter *O* at 0.03 and at $\frac{17}{100}$.

(continued)

c Put a letter *Y* at 0.15.

d Put a letter *E* at 0.12.

e Put a letter *W* at $\frac{5}{100}$.

f Put a letter *A* at 0.08.

g Put a letter *U* at 0.19.

h Put a letter *R* at 0.1.

4 We can think of $1 as one whole and the cents as the tenths and hundredths. The following prices are correct but have been oddly written. Write each price the way we would normally represent it.

Item	Oddly written price	Normal representation
muffin	$1.7	
bottle of water	1\frac{1}{4}$	
eraser	$1 and five-hundredths of $1	
sharpener	$\frac{9}{10}$ of $1	
pen set	$2.9	

Timing world records

The first ever world record in the 100 m sprint was set in 1912. American Don Lippincott ran it in 10.6 seconds. Today, we use technology to split a second into tenths and hundredths.

In 2007 a Jamaican sprinter, Asafa Powell, ran 100 m in 9.74 seconds.

He knocked $\frac{3}{100}$ of a second off his previous record. In 2009, another

Jamaican, Usain Bolt, beat the world record with a time of 9.58 seconds.

5 **a** By how much did Usain Bolt beat Asafa Powell's time?

b By how much did Asafa Powell's time of 9.74 seconds beat Don Lippincott's time?

c What was Asafa Powell's previous record time?

d Try timing some world records in your class using a digital stopwatch. Below are some events you could time.

- writing the alphabet with the "wrong hand"

- spelling the name of your school backwards

- writing out the seven times table

- tying a shoelace

Money then, now and around the world

Dollars and cents were introduced in some countries a long time ago. Before then, some countries used pounds, shillings and pence. The abbreviations come from the Latin words *librae* (for pounds – £), *solidi* (for shillings – s) and *denarii* (for pence – d).

1 There are 100 cents in $1 which makes counting money quite easy. Previously, counting money was very complicated.

- If you had 12d, it was worth 1s.
- If you had 20s, it was worth £1.

a How many pounds did you have if you had 40s?

b If you had 2s, how many pence could you change it for?

c You needed a lot of pence to make one pound. How many d = £1?

2 Students had to add and subtract using pounds, shillings and pence.

a How many shillings did you have if you had 2s and 6d in one pocket and 1s and 6d in another?

b How many shillings did you have if you had 3s and 10d in one piggy bank and 2s and 2d in another?

c If you had 5s and spent 4s and 6d, how much did you have left?

3 The UK was the last English-speaking country to change to decimal currency. Today, most countries use decimal currency because it is much easier. Some countries even have their own dollar, e.g. the Australian dollar. List two other countries that use their own type of dollar.

4 Many countries in Europe use euros and cents.

a Find the symbol that is used for a euro.

b Write the names of two countries that use the euro.

5 What currency is used in:

a South Africa? **b** Japan? **c** Thailand?

6 Are there any countries that do not use decimal currency?

Patterns with numbers

You will need

- a calculator
- a pencil and ruler

Every number in the world is based on just *ten* digits!

1 Using your calculator, try the following.

a Press **2 × 3 =**. Then press = again. What is the answer? What did the calculator do?

b Press = a third time. What is the answer? What did the calculator do?

c What pattern is the calculator following?

d What will the calculator show if you press = a fourth time?

e Now try **3 × 2 =**. The answer will be 6. What do you think will happen if you press = again? Try it. What happened? Press = again, and a fourth time, and a fifth. How has the pattern changed?

2 Let's see what will happen if you ask the calculator to perform two operations.

a What answer do you think the calculator will give if you press **3 × 2 + 2 =**?

b Now try it. Were you right?

c What happens if you continue to press =, just as you did in question 1?

3 Now let's try reversing the operations from question 4 – first add and then multiply.

a What answer do you think the calculator will give if you press **3 + 2 × 2 =**?

b Now try it. Were you right?

c What happens if you continue to press =, just as you did in question 1?

(continued)

4 You can make artwork using multiples.

a Start at 0. Use a pencil and ruler to draw a straight line from the dot at 0 to the dot at 2. Then count on 2 more and draw another line between the two dots. Keep counting in multiples of 2 and drawing lines until you get back to 0. What shape did you draw?

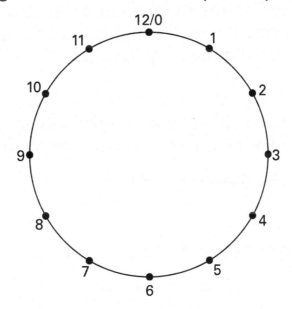

b Now start at 0 and count on by 5. Use a pencil and ruler to draw a straight line from the dot at 0 to the dot at 5. Then count on 5 more and draw another line between the two dots. Keep counting in multiples of 5 and drawing lines until you get back to 0. What shape did you draw? Write a sentence or two about the difference between the patterns.

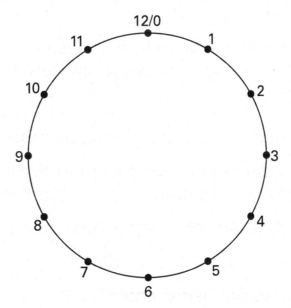

c Try using other multiples, such as 9 or 11, to make different patterns. You could also use a 24-point circle to make a pattern of multiples.

Mystery numbers

Sometimes we need to find the mystery number to complete a number sentence. One way to solve this problem is to use *opposites*. In this number sentence, a star replaces the mystery number.

$\star + 3 = 20$

If we put the 3 on the other side of the number sentence, we do the opposite operation. So instead of adding three, we take away three.

Now the number sentence says $\star = 20 - 3$.

So the mystery number = 17.

1 Solve these problems by using opposites.

    a $\star + 5 = 18$ **b** $\star - 4 = 10$ **c** $\star \times 4 = 28$

          $\star = 18 -$ $\star = 10 +$ $\star = 28 \div$

          $\star =$ $\star =$ $\star =$

    d $\star \div 3 = 9$ **e** $\star - 10 = 25$ **f** $\star \times 7 = 42$

          $\star = 9 \times$ $\star =$ $\star =$

          $\star =$

Some word problems also ask us to find a mystery number. One way to solve a word problem is to make it less complicated.

For example:

I'm thinking of a number. If you double it and add three, the answer is eleven.

It sounds complicated, but let's make it simpler. We'll use $\star$ for the mystery number and change the word sentence into a number sentence, like this:

-   $\star \times 2 + 3 = 11$. That looks simpler already! Now we can use *opposites*.

-   $\star \times 2 = 11 - 3$

-   $\star \times 2 = 8$. Use opposites again.

(continued)

- $\star = 8 \div 2$
- $\star = 4$

2 Solve these word problems by making them simpler.

a I'm thinking of a number. If you halve it and then add two, the answer is five. What is the number?

$\star \div 2 + 2 = 5$

$\star \div 2 = 5 - 2$

$\star =$

b I'm thinking of a number. If you multiply it by three and subtract four, the answer is eight. What is the number?

$\star \times 3 - 4 = 8$

c I'm thinking of a number. If you multiply it by three and take away half of six, the answer is 18. What is the number?

$\star =$

d I'm thinking of a number. If you multiply it by 10 and add six, the answer is 36. What is the number?

$\star =$

e I'm thinking of a number. If you multiply it by itself and then add 10, the answer is 35. What is the number?

$\star =$

3 You already know that the sign = means *is equal to*. You might be able to guess that ≠ means **not** *equal to*. Put the correct sign in the gap to make these number sentences correct.

For example: $4 \times 2 \neq 2 \times 3$

a $3 + 6 \boxed{} 6 + 3$

b $2 \times 4 \boxed{} 4 \times 2$

c $3 \times 4 \boxed{} 6 \times 2$

d $5 \times 4 \boxed{} 7 \times 3$

e $6 \times 4 \boxed{} 5 \times 5$

f $6 \times 6 \boxed{} 8 \times 4 + 4$

(continued)

4 You've been asked to get the tables ready for a class party. The tables are square. If there is just one table, this is how people will be seated.

If two tables are joined together, this is how people will be seated.

You could show the number of tables (and the number of people that could sit at them) like this:

Number of tables	1	2	3	4	5	6
Number of people	4	6				

a Fill in the gaps in the table above.

b How many people could sit at 10 tables joined together?

c How many tables would be needed for a class of 28 students?

d How many tables would be needed for your class?

5 Here are the items needed for the class party:

- glow sticks – two for each student

- sausage rolls – three for each student

- party favours – four for each student, plus eight spares

- cake – one cake serves eight students

For this activity, let ★ equal the number of students in a class. The number of glow sticks needed for a class of any size is ★ × 2.

a Write number sentences for each of the other items listed above. Solve the number sentences using the number of students in your class.

b Make a number sentence to show how many sausage rolls would be needed for a class with four vegetarians.

The importance of accuracy

If a family travelled 299 km and 900 m to go on a holiday, you could probably say their journey was 300 km long. However, sometimes it's necessary to be accurate.

1 If you measured the following items, which lengths would you accept as being OK?

   a A new 20 cm pencil: 20 cm and 1 mm, 15 cm, 18 cm, 19 cm and 9 mm

   b A 60 cm bike wheel: 59 cm, 60 cm, 60 cm and 5 mm, 61 cm

   c A 21 cm shoe: 209 mm, 210 mm, 211 mm, 212 mm

2 **a** If a football field is 100 m long and 50 m wide, how far would a person have run after one lap?

   b Your answer to question 2a will only be accurate if the person ran exactly along the rectangle edge of the field. Do you think the actual distance the person ran would be more or less than the perimeter of the field? Give a reason for your answer.

3 If a football club asked someone to mark out a 100 m × 50 m field, it would be difficult to get the dimensions absolutely correct.

   Which of the following sizes do you think would be acceptable? Why?

   a 100 m and 1 cm long, 50 m wide

   b 120 m long, 60 m wide

   c 99 m and 50 cm long, 50 m and 5 cm wide

   d 100 m and 10 cm long, 41 m wide

4 Calculate the exact perimeters of the football fields in questions 3a–d.

5 What shortcut do you know for finding the perimeter of a rectangle?

An even shorter shortcut

We have already looked at the following shortcut to find the area of a rectangle:

area = length × width

Now we will look at an even shorter shortcut – programming a computer to calculate area!

4 cm

2 cm

1 Why will multiplying the length of this rectangle by the width give its area?

2 Use the formula to find the areas of these rectangles. (Note: These shapes are not drawn to scale.)

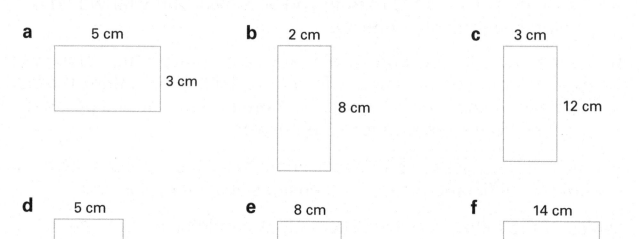

a 5 cm   3 cm

b 2 cm   8 cm

c 3 cm   12 cm

d 5 cm   6 cm

e 8 cm   10 cm

f 14 cm   10 cm

3 You can use a computer program such as Microsoft Excel to calculate area. Try it using the first rectangle in question 2.

- Open a new Excel workbook.
- Enter the following information in cells A2, A3, A4, B1, B2 and B3 by clicking on each cell in turn.

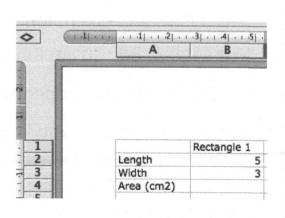

	A	B
1		Rectangle 1
2	Length	5
3	Width	3
4	Area (cm2)	

(continued)

Now you need to tell the computer to multiply the length by the width. Since you want it to calculate the area of any rectangle, not just this one, you need to enter a *formula* (calculation).

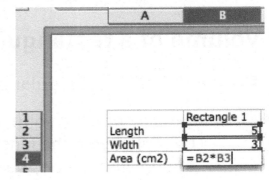

- Click on cell B4 and type (with no spaces) = *B2*B3*. (Excel uses * for a multiplication sign.)

- Press *Enter*. You should see *15* appear in cell B4. (If you don't see this, ask your teacher for help.)

Excel can calculate complicated dimensions just as quickly. Try changing the length to 5.29 and see how the area changes automatically. This formula will calculate the area of any rectangle, no matter how long or short the sides are. Try entering different lengths and widths.

4 You can also calculate the areas of many rectangles at once. To do this, just drag the information from one cell to other cells.

- Click on cell B1 (This is the cell that says *Rectangle 1*.)

- Hover the mouse over the bottom right-hand corner of the cell until the icon changes to a + sign.

	Rectangle 1	R
Length	5	
Width	3	
Area (cm2)	15	

- Click and hold the mouse on the + sign and drag the cursor to the right, across seven columns. This will stretch the cell.

Rectangle 1

- After seven columns, let go of the mouse. The columns will now be named *Rectangle 2, Rectangle 3*, and so on.

- Click on cell B4. (This is the cell you typed in the formula.)

- Drag the information across by repeating the steps above.

- Now just enter the lengths and widths of other rectangles and Excel will calculate the areas for you.

Volume of a rectangular prism

The volume of a rectangular prism = length × width × height.

1 **a** Explain why the volume of this box can be found by multiplying the length by the width and then multiplying the answer by the height. (Please note: The box is not drawn to its true size.)

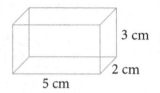
3 cm
2 cm
5 cm

b What is the volume of the box?

2 What is the volume of these boxes? (Please note: They are not drawn to their true size.)

a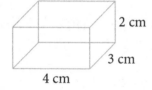
2 cm
3 cm
4 cm

b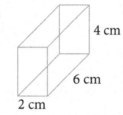
4 cm
6 cm
2 cm

c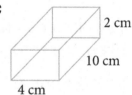
2 cm
10 cm
4 cm

d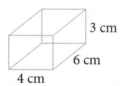
3 cm
6 cm
4 cm

e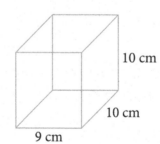
10 cm
10 cm
9 cm

f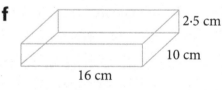
2·5 cm
10 cm
16 cm

3 We now know that Microsoft Excel can be used to make quick calculations. It can also calculate the volume of a rectangular prism. Using the prism from question 2a – let's call it "Box 1" – try the following.

- Open a new Excel file.

- Enter the following information in cells A2, A3, A4, A5, B1, B2, B3 and B4 by clicking on each cell in turn:

		Box 1
1		
2	Length	4
3	Width	3
4	Height	2
5	Volume (cm3)	

(continued)

4 Now you need Excel to calculate the volume. But you want Excel to calculate the volume of any rectangular prism, not just one that measures 4 cm × 3 cm × 2 cm, so the *formula* (calculation) you need to enter in cell B5 is:

- *=B2*B3*B4* (Excel uses * for a multiplication sign.)

	Box 1
Length	4
Width	3
Height	2
Volume (cm3)	=B2*B3*B4

- Press **Enter** and you should see 24 appear in cell B5. (If you do not see 24, ask your teacher for some help.)

5 Excel can calculate complicated dimensions just as quickly. Try changing the length to 3.9, the width to 3.2 and the height to 1.8. The volume is immediately recalculated. Try entering different dimensions for the box.

6 Another time-saving feature of Excel is that you can see the volumes of all the rectangular prisms in question 2 at one time. To do this you "drag" the information from one cell to other cells, using the following steps:

- Click in cell B1. (This is the cell that says *Box 1*.)

- Hover the mouse over the bottom right-hand corner of the cell until the icon changes to a black "plus" sign.

- Click and hold the mouse on the plus sign and drag the cursor to the right, going across to column G.

- Let go of the mouse on column G and you will see that the columns have been named *Box 2, Box 3* and so on.

- Single-click in cell B5. (This is the cell in which you typed the formula.)

- Drag the information across by repeating steps 2 and 3 (above).

All you need to do now is to enter the lengths, widths and heights of the other rectangular prisms in question 2 and Excel will calculate the volumes for you. This is a good way of checking that you got the correct answers.

Worth your weight in gold

If someone thinks a person is very precious, they might say that they are "worth their weight in gold". This is because gold is extremely valuable.

1. If 1 kg of gold is worth around $50 000, how much would these amounts of gold be worth?

   a 2 kg   **b** 5 kg   **c** 10 kg   **d** 20 kg

2. Long ago, the value of a coin depended on two things: the kind of metal it was made from and the mass of the metal.

   The most valuable coins were made of solid gold. Next came silver, and the least valuable coins were made of copper (or bronze).

   a If silver had half the value of gold, what would a silver coin with a mass of 1 kg be worth?

   b If copper had one-tenth the value of gold, what would a copper coin with a mass of 1 kg be worth?

3. Some 10c coins have twice the mass of some 5c coins, and the mass doubles again for some 20c coins. The mass of ten 10c coins is 56 g. What is the mass of:

   a ten 5c coins?   **b** ten 20c coins?

4. Ten 50c coins have a mass that is 99 g more than the mass of ten 10c coins.

   a What is the mass of ten 50c coins?

   b What is the mass of one 50c coin?

5. Some $1 coins weigh about 9 g, but some $2 coins only weigh about 6.5 g.

   a How much heavier than the $2 coin is the $1 coin?

   b What would be the mass of ten $2 coins?

6. If you were given the choice between 560 g of 10c coins and 99 g of $1 coins, which would you choose? Give a reason for your choice.

Keeping it cool and hot

1 Some foods need to be stored in a fridge. This keeps them cool and below room temperature.

   a Write four examples of foods that need to be kept in a fridge.

   b Why do some foods need to be kept in a fridge?

   c The temperature inside a fridge is normally about 5°C. If the room temperature is 21°C, by how many degrees does the fridge lower the temperature?

   d If a fridge cools water from a room temperature of 21°C by 4°C an hour, how long will it take until the water is 5°C?

   e Breakfast cereal does not need to be stored in a fridge. What other foods can be kept at room temperature?

2 Some foods need to be kept at a temperature colder than 0°C. These foods are kept in a freezer. Inside a freezer, the temperature is about 18°C *less* than 0°C. This temperature is written as −18°C.

   a How many degrees lower than a fridge temperature is a freezer?

   b Give three examples of things that need to be kept in a freezer.

   c Why do you think some items need to be kept in a freezer?

   d If an ice block was taken out of the freezer and left on the kitchen bench it would melt. Eventually it would be at room temperature. By how much would its temperature have risen at a room temperature of 21°C?

(continued)

3 Water boils when the temperature reaches 100°C.

   a Imagine a kettle is filled with water at 14°C. By how much will the temperature of the water have risen by the time it boils?

   b Why is it dangerous to drink a hot drink as soon as the boiling water has been poured into a cup?

   c What temperature do you think a hot drink should be before you can drink it safely?

4 Water that comes out of a hot tap has to be set at a safe temperature.

   a What temperature is shown on this gauge?

   b The actual temperature of hot water in a home is usually between 10°C and 25°C *higher* than this gauge. What is the temperature range of hot water in a home?

5 Many foods are cooked at temperatures higher than 100°C. Do some research and write the temperatures that are needed to cook some everyday foods, such as cookies, pies or roast meat.

6 What temperature do you think of when someone talks about a "cold day"?

Why do we have am and pm times?

We use the abbreviations *am* and *pm* to show times before noon and after noon. These abbreviations are from Latin words.

- *ante meridiem* (am) means *before noon*

- *post meridiem* (pm) means *after noon*

These terms were invented because, until recently, nearly all clocks showed only 12-hour times.

1 Write the following times as am or pm.

a Ready for school

b Playing outside

c Nearly bedtime

d Asleep in bed

2 This strange-looking clock shows how the face would look with all 24 hours.

a Fill in the numbers on the 24-hour clock face.

b What time does the clock show?

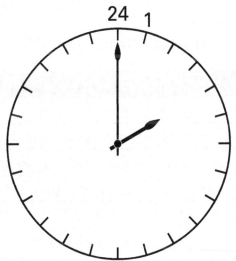

(continued)

3 Telling the *o'clock times* on the 24-hour clock is fairly easy. Try to work out the times that these clocks show.

a

b

4 Digital clocks can usually display either 12- or 24-hour times. It's easy to read 24-hour time because the day starts at 00:00, and when the hour reaches 12 it continues to count: 13, 14, 15, and so on.

This diagram shows a day split into 12- and 24-hour times. Fill in the gaps.

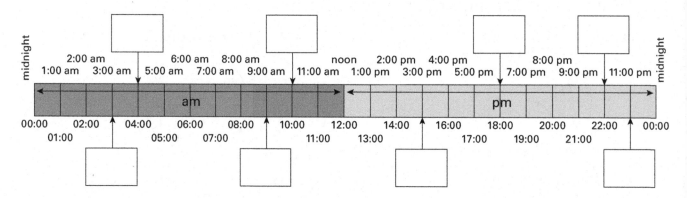

5 Convert these am and pm times to 24-hour times. For example, 1:30 pm becomes 13:30.

a 11:00 am   **b** 2:00 pm   **c** 2:30 am   **d** 10:15 am

e 6:55 am   **f** 2:58 pm   **g** 3:40 pm   **h** 6:19 am

6 Use am/pm times and 24-hour times to complete the following.

	am/pm time	24-hour time
I get up on a school day at …		
I go to bed on a school night at …		
I eat my lunch on a school day at …		
I have breakfast on the weekend at …		

A world of patterns

You will need

- grid paper
- a pencil and ruler
- a geoboard with nine pins
- an elastic band

A pattern is when something is repeated again and again.

1 Without using the word *rectangle*, write as many facts about this shape as you can. Think about features such as sides, diagonals, angles, types of lines, length, perimeter, area and so on.

2 This pattern is made from squares and triangles. When you stare at the square, what seems to happen?

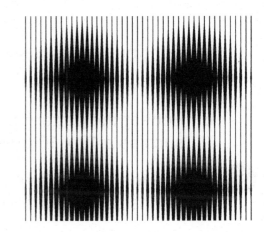

3 The pattern in question 2 is an optical illusion. This means your eyes see something that isn't really there. Here is another optical illusion.

a Describe what you see when you first look at the pattern.

b Are the black and white parts irregular quadrilaterals?

c Are the lines that go from left to right parallel to each other? Cover all but one row of the pattern to check.

d Draw another few rows of the pattern.

(continued)

4 Another type of optical illusion is when straight lines appear to curve. You can make straight lines appear to curve quite simply.

- On grid paper, draw two axes and label each of them from 0 to 5.

- Use a pencil and a ruler to join point 5 on one axis to point 1 on the other axis.

- Join point 4 on one axis to point 2 on the other axis.

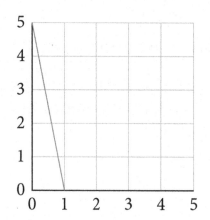 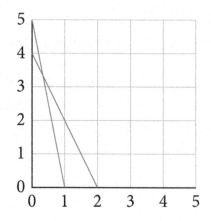

- Continue the pattern until points one to five have been joined.

a Where do you see a curved line starting to appear?

b Repeat the pattern using a square with more numbers on each axis, such as a 10 × 10 grid.

5 Extend the activity in question 4 so that the straight lines make a curved shape inside a square on a 5 × 5 grid or a 10 × 10 grid.

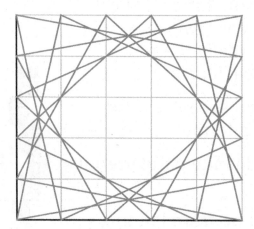

(continued)

6 A geoboard is usually made of wood with a pattern of nails on it. For this task, use a geoboard with nine pins, and an elastic band. (If you don't have a geoboard, you can do this activity with a piece of dotted paper.)

Position the elastic band on the geoboard so that it forms a polygon. Make a sketch of it.

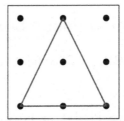

Make different polygons and sketch each one. Remember, the shape isn't different if it's turned sideways or upside down.

Packaging

You will need

- an empty, rectangular-shaped tissue box

From skyscrapers to tissue boxes, rectangular prisms are a very common part of our lives.

1 The tissue box shown on the right is based on a cube.

a Draw a small net (a flat shape that when folded up makes a 3D shape) for a cube in your book. Then, remembering to include the tabs, draw a larger one on a piece of paper and make it into a cube.

b Many tissue boxes are not based on cubes. What is the usual shape of a tissue box?

c In your book, draw a net that could make a tissue box like the one shown above.

2 Take your empty tissue box and, carefully, pull it apart. Try not to tear off any of the tabs.

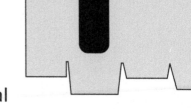

a What are the main differences between the net of the tissue box and the net of a normal rectangular prism?

b Why do you think the net of the tissue box is not the same as the net of a normal rectangular prism?

3 Why do you think we use rectangular prisms for so many things?

Angles in sport

1 When playing handball, you need a good knowledge of angles so you can send the ball in the right direction. The dotted line shows how the ball will leave the player's hand. In which picture will the ball not reach the other player in one bounce?

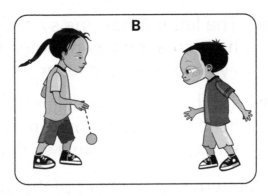

2 Alex invented a game that involves rolling a ball past obstacles in a box and trying to knock a skittle over. He made up the following rules:

- The ball must roll; it can't bounce.
- The ball must touch the obstacles.
- After you roll the ball, you can't touch it again.
- The ball can rebound off the edges of the box.

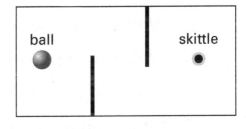

How could the ball get around the obstacles and hit the skittle? Draw a line on the diagram showing the direction the ball could roll in to knock over the skittle.

3 List five ball sports and explain how a knowledge of angles is important to each of them.

4 Design a game that involves a ball rebounding at various angles, similar to the one described in question 3. Make the game as simple or as detailed as you wish, and write out the rules so others know how to play. Draw a labelled diagram of your design. The game could be played in a large space, such as a hall or outside, or it could be a small-scale design using something like a marble and a shoebox. Be creative!

Line and rotational symmetry

1 There are two types of symmetry: line symmetry and rotational (turning) symmetry. The shape on the right has rotational symmetry – it fits on top of itself when it rotates around the centre (the white dot).

a The letter A has line symmetry but it does not have rotational symmetry. Draw the line of symmetry on the letter.

b The letter S has rotational symmetry because it would fit on top of itself if it rotated. You can show this by rotating a paper with the letter S written on it. Rotate it so that it turns upside down. What do you see?

2 Here are seven letters of the alphabet.

C D E F G H N

a Which of the letters are not symmetrical at all?

b Which of the letters have line symmetry?

c Which of the letters have rotational symmetry?

d Which letter has both line and rotational symmetry?

3 Look at these shapes. Shape A has rotational symmetry.

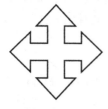
Shape A

Shape B

Shape C

a Which of the other two shapes has rotational symmetry?

b If you rotated shape A, counting the starting position as 1, how many times would it fit exactly on top of itself before it got back to the start?

Using grid references

Some people believe that grid references were invented by French mathematician René Descartes when he tried to describe the position of a fly as it crawled across his ceiling. Others say that grid references were first used by the English army hundreds of years ago, as a way of describing the enemy's position.

1 Today, grid references are used on most maps to refer to a specific point. Look at the key for Wonder Park. Follow the instructions to mark the entrance to each attraction on the map below.

Wonder Park

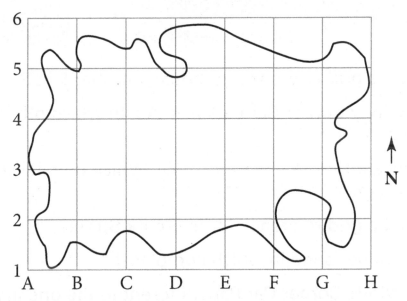

Symbol	Entrance to	Position on map
E	Eating World	E3 and E5
A	Adventure World	C3
F	Future World	F4
Y	Yesterday World	B4
T	Toddlers' World	E2
S	Science World	three squares east of Adventure World

(continued)

2 Grid references can also refer to regions on a map. Use the map of Falls Creek to complete the activities.

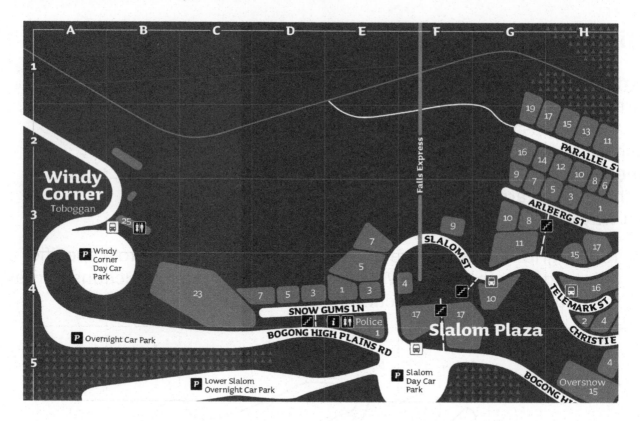

a What is the grid reference for house number 5 in Snow Gums Lane?

b Part of Windy Corner Car Park is in A3. In which other squares can it also be found?

c The Falls Express ski lift starts in F4. Which other squares does it pass through?

d What is the grid reference for Telemark Street?

e Toilets can be found in which two places?

f How is Windy Corner Car Park different to the one in A5?

g What is the grid reference for the entrance to house number 7 in Arlberg Street?

h Give directions to get from the Slalom Day Car Park to Windy Corner Toboggan.

The words we use

How many words do you think you know? Some people say that by the age of two, most children know 200 words. This increases to about 4000 by the time they start school. Some researchers believe that 10-year-old children have a vocabulary of 10 000 words. However, it is very difficult to collect reliable data about the number of words anyone knows.

1 Why do you think it might be difficult to collect reliable data about the number of words a 10-year-old knows?

2 Written words are easier to research than spoken words. Without doing any research, write down three words that you think are often used in writing.

3 It's time to do some research to see if you are correct.

- Find a text with 100 words in it.
- Skim through it and make a note of any words that you think are used frequently.
- Do a tally of the number of times each of these words is used.

a Which three words are most commonly used?

b Repeat the experiment with two other texts. If possible, use different books.

c Write a sentence or two about your findings.

d Compare your research with a partner. Were your findings similar?

e Look back at the three words you wrote down in question 2. How frequently did those words occur in the texts you've just looked at?

4 The five vowels are A, E, I, O and U. Almost every word we use contains one or more vowels.

a Can you find any words in your chosen text that do *not* contain a vowel?

b Do you think one of the five vowels is used more often than the other four? If so, which one do you think it is?

c Do you think one of the vowels is used less than the other four? If so, which one do you think it is?

What's in a name?

1 These graphs show the top 10 baby names in 2010.

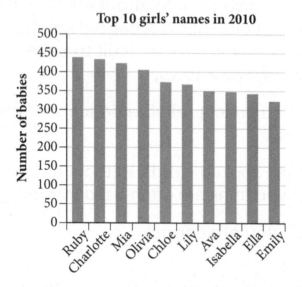

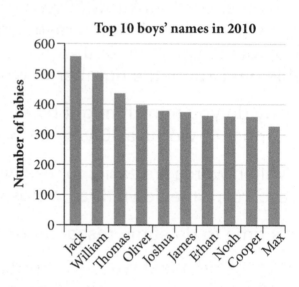

a What was the most popular boys' name and the most popular girls' name in 2010?

b The top boys' name was a single-syllable word. Which other single-syllable boys' names are in the list?

c How many girls' names in the list have one syllable?

d How many syllables does your name have?

e List the most common number of syllables for the top 10 girls' names in 2010.

f How many people in your class have names that were in the 2010 top 10?

2 Ten years earlier, the top 10 baby names were different. The graph on the right shows the most popular girls' names in 2000.

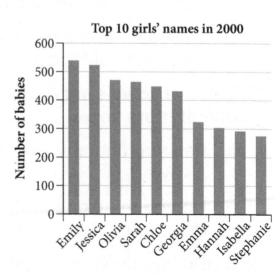

(continued)

These are the favourite boys' names in 2000.

Name	Number of babies
Joshua	759
Jack	735
Lachlan	713
James	656
Thomas	604
Matthew	575
Daniel	539
Nicholas	514
Benjamin	466
William	459

a   Make a graph, similar to the one for girls, showing the top 10 boys' names in 2000.

b   What was the most popular boys' name in 2000?

c   How did the popularity of the top two names for boys change from 2000 to 2010?

d   Which girls' names are in both top 10 lists?

e   Estimate the number of babies who were named Emily in 2000 and in 2010.

f   Did the most popular names have more or fewer syllables in 2010 than they did in 2000?

g   Which boys' names were in the top 10 at both the beginning and end of the decade?

3   One of the names in the top 10 in 2010 was also fashionable in 1930 – William. Try to find the top 10 names from over 80 years ago.

4   You'll have noticed that the graphs do not show the exact numbers. Do you think it matters that the exact numbers of the data aren't shown on graphs such as these?

What are the chances?

1 Some people say it's harder to roll a six on a dice than any other number. Explain why this is not true.

2 A coin has an equal chance of landing on heads or tails. We can say that there is half a chance that it will land on heads.

   a What fraction describes the chance of a 6-sided dice landing on 6?

   b A coin has a 1 in 2 chance of landing on heads. Fill in the gap in the following sentence:

    A 6-sided dice has a 1 in ⬚ chance of landing on 2.

3 For homework, Eva has to predict the results of rolling a 6-sided dice 12 times. Then she has to roll the dice 12 times and write the results. She knows there is an equal chance of rolling each number, so she expects to roll each number twice. This table shows the results.

Number on the dice	Number of times Eva expects to roll this number	Number of times this number was rolled
1	2	1
2	2	3
3	2	5
4	2	0
5	2	2
6	2	1

Why do you think the results were not as Eva expected?

4 Jack rolls a dice nine times, and every single time he rolls a five. Describe the chance of rolling a five with the next throw.

(continued)

5 When someone chooses a name for a baby, the last thing they think of is whether the name has an odd or even number of letters. But is there an equal chance of the name having an odd or even number of letters?

Try the following experiment to find out.

a Draw a table with space for 20 names. Write the first names of 10 people from your class *without* counting the number of letters in each name.

Name	Even number of letters (✓)	Odd number of letters (✓)

b Count the number of letters in each name and then tick the appropriate column.

c Write a sentence or two about what you found out.

d Add these names to your list, and tick for odd or even:
Amy, Sam, Jenny, Christopher, Betty, Nareish, Merna, Gabrielle, Zachary, Emily.

e Comment on the new results.

It's not fair!

Have you ever heard someone say "It's not fair!" after losing a game? If the game was organised properly and everyone played by the rules, the loss was just bad luck, but not unfair.

1 Consider the following: A group of children are about to play a game. They roll a 6-sided dice to see who should start – the child who rolls the highest number will start. Explain why each child has an equal chance of rolling the highest number.

2 Finlay wanted to play a board game with his friends. They couldn't find the dice. What could they use instead of a dice?

3 Ava's board game is called Prizes and Punishments. It is played by rolling two dice and adding up the numbers. You only have to move along 12 squares to win.

Starting position	1 Miss 1000 turns	2 Have 6 extra turns	3 Miss 4 turns	4 Have 3 extra turns	5 Miss 2 turns
					6 Have 1 extra turn
Finish You win!	11 Miss 4 turns	10 Miss 3 turns	9 Have 2 extra turns	8 Miss 1 turn	7 Nothing happens

(continued)

a Annie doesn't want to play because she doesn't want to miss 1000 turns. Why is the chance of that happening zero?

b Jack wins the game in less than three rolls of the dice. He does not land on any "extra turn" or "miss a turn" squares. How could Jack have won?

c Mia asks if it is a mistake that the prizes and punishments are lower for the numbers 6, 7 and 8. Ava says she did this for a reason, and asks Mia to think about the two dice. What do you think the reason is?

d In her first go Ava lands on 7. What combinations of numbers could she have rolled on the two dice?

4 Make up some rules for a board game in which there is *not* an equal chance of each number occurring. If possible, try to think of a method that does not involve rolling two dice.

5 **a** In the game described in question 3, it would be very difficult to land on "Finish" with one roll of the dice. There is one other square that you would have an equally poor chance of landing on. Which is it?

b Using words or fractions, describe the probability of rolling a 7 with two dice.

PRE- AND POST-ASSESSMENT TEST ANSWERS

UNIT 1: TOPIC 1

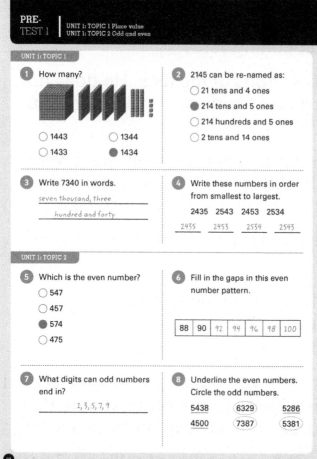

1 How many?

○ 1443   ○ 1344
○ 1433   ● 1434

2 2145 can be re-named as:
○ 21 tens and 4 ones
● 214 tens and 5 ones
○ 214 hundreds and 5 ones
○ 2 tens and 14 ones

3 Write 7340 in words.
seven thousand, three
hundred and forty

4 Write these numbers in order from smallest to largest.
2435 2543 2453 2534
2435   2453   2534   2543

UNIT 1: TOPIC 2

5 Which is the even number?
○ 547
○ 457
● 574
○ 475

6 Fill in the gaps in this even number pattern.

| 88 | 90 | 92 | 94 | 96 | 98 | 100 |

7 What digits can odd numbers end in?
1, 3, 5, 7, 9

8 Underline the even numbers. Circle the odd numbers.
5438   (6329)   5286
4500   (7387)   (5381)

UNIT 1: TOPIC 1

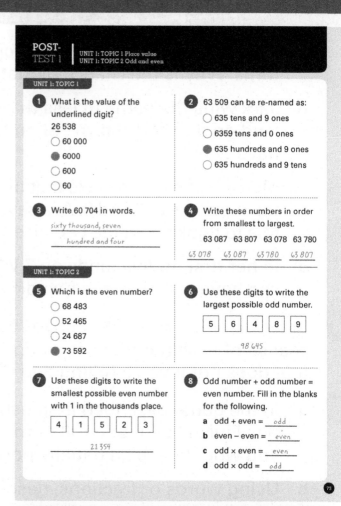

1 What is the value of the underlined digit?
26 538
○ 60 000
● 6000
○ 600
○ 60

2 63 509 can be re-named as:
○ 635 tens and 9 ones
○ 6359 tens and 0 ones
● 635 hundreds and 9 ones
○ 635 hundreds and 9 tens

3 Write 60 704 in words.
sixty thousand, seven
hundred and four

4 Write these numbers in order from smallest to largest.
63 087 63 807 63 078 63 780
63 078   63 087   63 780   63 807

UNIT 1: TOPIC 2

5 Which is the even number?
○ 68 483
○ 52 465
○ 24 687
● 73 592

6 Use these digits to write the largest possible odd number.

| 5 | 6 | 4 | 8 | 9 |

98 645

7 Use these digits to write the smallest possible even number with 1 in the thousands place.

| 4 | 1 | 5 | 2 | 3 |

21 354

8 Odd number + odd number = even number. Fill in the blanks for the following.
a odd + even = odd
b even − even = even
c odd × even = even
d odd × odd = odd

UNIT 1: TOPIC 3

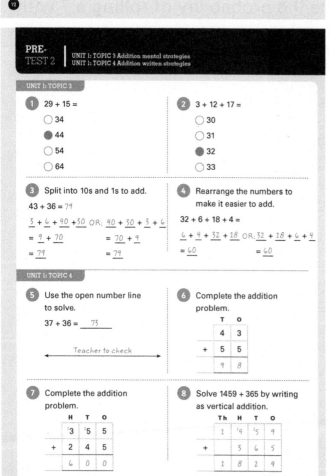

1 29 + 15 =
○ 34
● 44
○ 54
○ 64

2 3 + 12 + 17 =
○ 30
○ 31
● 32
○ 33

3 Split into 10s and 1s to add.
43 + 36 = 79
3 + 6 + 40 + 30 OR: 40 + 30 + 3 + 6
= 9 + 70   = 70 + 9
= 79   = 79

4 Rearrange the numbers to make it easier to add.
32 + 6 + 18 + 4 =
6 + 4 + 32 + 18 OR: 32 + 18 + 6 + 4
= 60   = 60

UNIT 1: TOPIC 4

5 Use the open number line to solve.
37 + 36 = 73
Teacher to check

6 Complete the addition problem.

	T	O
	4	3
+	5	5
	9	8

7 Complete the addition problem.

	H	T	O
	³3	¹5	5
+	2	4	5
	6	0	0

8 Solve 1459 + 365 by writing as vertical addition.

	Th	H	T	O
	1	⁴4	¹5	9
+		3	6	5
	1	8	2	4

UNIT 1: TOPIC 3

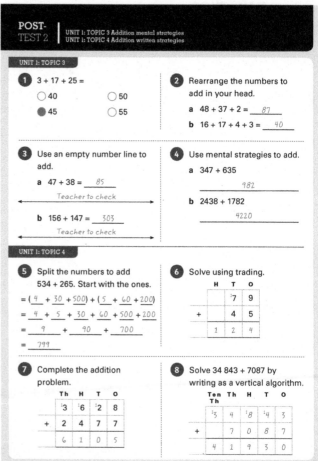

1 3 + 17 + 25 =
○ 40   ○ 50
● 45   ○ 55

2 Rearrange the numbers to add in your head.
a 48 + 37 + 2 = 87
b 16 + 17 + 4 + 3 = 40

3 Use an empty number line to add.
a 47 + 38 = 85
Teacher to check
b 156 + 147 = 303
Teacher to check

4 Use mental strategies to add.
a 347 + 635
982
b 2438 + 1782
4220

UNIT 1: TOPIC 4

5 Split the numbers to add 534 + 265. Start with the ones.
= (4 + 30 + 500) + (5 + 60 + 200)
= 4 + 5 + 30 + 60 + 500 + 200
= 9 + 90 + 700
= 799

6 Solve using trading.

	H	T	O
		¹7	9
+		4	5
	1	2	4

7 Complete the addition problem.

	Th	H	T	O
	³3	⁶6	¹2	8
+		2	4	7	7
	6	1	0	5

8 Solve 34 843 + 7087 by writing as a vertical algorithm.

	Ten Th	Th	H	T	O
	¹3	4	¹8	¹4	3
+		7	0	8	7
	4	1	9	3	0

UNIT 1: TOPIC 5

1 19 − 7 =
- ◯ 14
- ◯ 13
- ● 12
- ◯ 11

2 77 − 33 is the same as:
- ● 77 − 30 − 3
- ◯ 77 − 3 − 3
- ◯ 77 − 30 − 30

3 Complete the subtraction problem.

54 − 19 = __35__

4 Complete the subtraction problem.

175 − 26 = __149__

UNIT 1: TOPIC 6

5 Complete the subtraction problem.

74 − 22 = __52__

| 52 | 53 | 54 | 64 | 74 |

(−1, −1, −10, −10)

6 Complete the subtraction problem.

85 − 34 = __51__

7 What is 427 take away 214?

H	T	O
4	2	7
− 2	1	4
2	1	3

8 Rewrite 785 − 324 as a vertical algorithm and solve.

H	T	O
7	8	5
− 3	2	4
4	6	1

UNIT 1: TOPIC 5

1 54 − 19 is the same as:
- ◯ 54 − 20
- ◯ 54 − 20 then add 1
- ● 54 − 20 then take away 1

2 Circle one word for each.

a 745 − 198 = 647 | Correct / (Incorrect)

b 833 − 299 = 534 | (Correct) / Incorrect

3 Solve the subtraction problems.

a 734 − 728 = __6__

b 1953 − 1946 = __7__

4 Solve the subtraction problems.

a 734 − 199 = __535__

b 865 − 202 = __663__

c 1477 − 298 = __1179__

UNIT 1: TOPIC 6

5 Solve using the split strategy.

786 − 454 =

786 − __400__ − __50__ − __4__

= __332__

6 Solve 43 − 25 as a vertical algorithm.

T	O
³4	¹3
− 2	5
1	8

7 Solve 3625 − 2477 as a vertical algorithm.

Th	H	T	O
3	⁶6	¹²2	¹5
− 2	4	7	7
1	1	4	8

8 Solve 45 313 − 5578 as a vertical algorithm.

Ten Th	Th	H	T	O
⁵4	¹⁰5	¹²3	¹⁰1	¹3
−	5	5	7	8
3	9	7	3	5

---

1 Use the multiplication fact to write the division fact.

3 groups of 5 = 15

__15__ shared between 5 is __3__.

2 Use the division fact to write the multiplication fact.

20 shared between 4 is 5.

__5__ groups of 4 = __20__.

3 Make a turnaround multiplication fact to match the array.

__4__ × __3__ = __12__

__3__ × __4__ = __12__

4 Make a turnaround division fact to match the array.

__18__ ÷ __3__ = __6__

__18__ ÷ __6__ = __3__

5 Complete the fact family.

3 × 7 = 21

__7__ × __3__ = 21

21 ÷ __3__ = __7__

21 ÷ __7__ = __3__

6 Complete the fact family.

30 ÷ 5 = 6

30 ÷ __6__ = __5__

__5__ × __6__ = 30

__6__ × __5__ = 30

7 **a** Complete the multiplication fact.

8 × 3 = __24__

b Write a matching division fact.

__24__ ÷ __3__ = __8__

OR: 24 ÷ 8 = 3

8 **a** Complete the division fact.

24 ÷ 4 = __6__

b Write a matching multiplication fact.

__4__ × __6__ = __24__

OR: 6 × 4 = 24

---

1 This array shows that 6 × 4 = 24. It also shows that:
- ◯ 4 × 5 = 20
- ● 4 × 6 = 24
- ◯ 5 × 5 = 25
- ◯ 5 × 6 = 30

2 This array shows that 21 ÷ 3 = 7. It also shows that:
- ● 21 ÷ 7 = 3
- ◯ 28 ÷ 4 = 7
- ◯ 20 ÷ 4 = 5
- ◯ 24 ÷ 6 = 4

3 Write a multiplication fact and a division fact for this array.

__4__ × __8__ = __32__

OR: 8 × 4 = 32

__32__ ÷ __4__ = __8__

OR: 32 ÷ 8 = 4

4 Write a multiplication fact and a division fact for this array.

__5__ × __9__ = __45__

OR: 9 × 5 = 45

__45__ ÷ __5__ = __9__

OR: 45 ÷ 9 = 5

5 Which is true about the 6 times table facts?
- ◯ The last digit is always 6.
- ◯ The last digit is always odd.
- ● The last digit is always even.

6 Which is true about the 9 times table facts?
- ◯ The last digit is always 9.
- ● The digits in the number always add up to 9.
- ◯ The last digit is never even.

7 Use the numbers 7 and 9 in 2 multiplication and 2 division sentences.

__7__ × __9__ = __63__

__9__ × __7__ = __63__

__63__ ÷ __7__ = __9__

__63__ ÷ __9__ = __7__

8 Use the numbers 6 and 8 in 2 multiplication and 2 division sentences.

__6__ × __8__ = __48__

__8__ × __6__ = __48__

__48__ ÷ __6__ = __8__

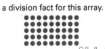

__48__ ÷ __8__ = __6__

PRE-TEST 5
UNIT 1: TOPIC 8 Multiplication written strategies
UNIT 1: TOPIC 9 Division written strategies

UNIT 1: TOPIC 8

1 3 × 14 is the same as:
- ○ 3 × 1 + 3 × 4
- ● 3 × 10 + 3 × 4
- ○ 3 × 10 + 2 × 40

2 2 × 35 is the same as:
- ● 2 × 30 + 2 × 5
- ○ 2 × 30 + 2 × 50
- ○ 2 × 3 + 2 × 5

3 Solve using the grid method.

×	20	4
3	60	12

3 × 24 = 72

4 Use your choice of written strategy to solve 5 × 37.

Answer: 185.

Teacher to check strategy.

UNIT 1: TOPIC 9

5 Solve the division problem.

12 ÷ 4 = 3

6 Divide the array into groups of 5 and solve the division problem.

20 ÷ 5 = 4

7 Draw an array to solve 28 ÷ 7.

Teacher to check

28 ÷ 7 = 4

8 Solve the division problem.

42 ÷ 6 = 7

Show how you got the answer.

Teacher to check

POST-TEST 5
UNIT 1: TOPIC 8 Multiplication written strategies
UNIT 1: TOPIC 9 Division written strategies

UNIT 1: TOPIC 8

1 Solve 3 × 32 using extended multiplication.

	T	O
	3	2
×		3
	6	← 3 × 2
9	0	← 3 × 30
9	6	

2 Solve 4 × 58 using extended multiplication.

	H	T	O
		5	8
×			4
		3	2
	2	0	0
	2	3	2

3 Solve 6 × 74 using contracted multiplication.

	H	T	O
		²7	4
×			6
	4	4	4

4 Rewrite 5 × 93 as contracted multiplication and solve.

	H	T	O
		¹9	3
×			5
	4	6	5

UNIT 1: TOPIC 9

5 Solve 84 ÷ 2.

```
   4 2
2) 8 4
```

6 Solve 72 ÷ 3.

```
   2 4
3) 7 ¹2
```

7 Rewrite and solve 96 ÷ 6.

```
   1 6
6) 9 ³6
```

8 Solve and rewrite.

```
   1 3
7) 9 ¹1
```

91 + 7 = 13

PRE-TEST 6
UNIT 2: TOPIC 1 Equivalent fractions
UNIT 2: TOPIC 2 Improper fractions and mixed numbers

UNIT 2: TOPIC 1

1 The shaded part is:
- ○ $\frac{1}{4}$
- ○ $\frac{1}{3}$
- ● $\frac{2}{4}$
- ○ $\frac{2}{3}$

2 Look at the rectangle in question 1. True or false?

The fraction of the rectangle that is white is $\frac{1}{2}$.

True

3 Shade $\frac{1}{4}$ of the rectangle.

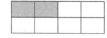

4 Shade $\frac{1}{5}$ of the rectangle.

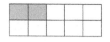

UNIT 2: TOPIC 2

5 Write the missing fraction on the number line.

0 $\frac{1}{5}$ $\frac{2}{5}$ $\frac{3}{5}$ $\frac{4}{5}$ 1

6 How far past 1 is the triangle?

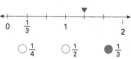

- ○ $\frac{1}{4}$
- ○ $\frac{1}{2}$
- ● $\frac{1}{3}$

7 Draw a triangle $\frac{4}{4}$ of the way along the number line.

8 How far along the line is the triangle?

- ○ $\frac{4}{7}$
- ○ $\frac{3}{4}$
- ● $\frac{7}{4}$

POST-TEST 6
UNIT 2: TOPIC 1 Equivalent fractions
UNIT 2: TOPIC 2 Improper fractions and mixed numbers

UNIT 2: TOPIC 1

1 Which fraction is equivalent to $\frac{3}{4}$?
- ○ $\frac{3}{5}$
- ○ $\frac{2}{3}$
- ● $\frac{6}{8}$

2 Label this pair of equivalent fractions.

$\frac{2}{3}$ $\frac{4}{6}$

3 Colour $\frac{4}{5}$ of the first rectangle. Colour and label an equivalent fraction of the second rectangle.

$\frac{4}{5}$ $\frac{8}{10}$

4 Which list has fractions that are all equivalent?
- ○ $\frac{1}{2}, \frac{2}{5}, \frac{3}{6}, \frac{4}{8}$
- ● $\frac{2}{4}, \frac{3}{6}, \frac{4}{8}, \frac{5}{10}$
- ○ $\frac{3}{6}, \frac{6}{12}, \frac{4}{8}, \frac{4}{9}$
- ○ $\frac{1}{2}, \frac{2}{4}, \frac{5}{8}, \frac{6}{12}$

UNIT 2: TOPIC 2

5 How far along the number line is the triangle?

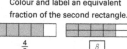

- ○ $\frac{5}{8}$
- ○ $\frac{6}{4}$
- ● $\frac{5}{4}$
- ○ $\frac{6}{8}$

6 Which pair describes the position of the triangle?

- ○ $\frac{5}{6}$ and $1\frac{2}{3}$
- ○ $\frac{5}{3}$ and $1\frac{1}{3}$
- ○ $\frac{4}{3}$ and $1\frac{1}{3}$
- ● $\frac{5}{3}$ and $1\frac{2}{3}$

7 Write the position of the diamond as:

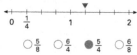

a an improper fraction. $\frac{7}{3}$

b a mixed number. $2\frac{1}{3}$

8 Look at question 7.

a How much further along is the diamond than the triangle? 2 or $\frac{6}{3}$

b Write the position of the circle as a mixed number. $1\frac{2}{3}$

OXFORD UNIVERSITY PRESS

1 The fraction shaded is:
- ○ $\frac{1}{10}$
- ○ $\frac{2}{10}$
- ● $\frac{3}{10}$

2 The fraction shaded is:
- ● $\frac{9}{10}$
- ○ $\frac{8}{10}$
- ○ $\frac{7}{10}$

3 Shade 4 columns and write as a fraction.

$\frac{40}{100}$ or $\frac{4}{10}$

4 Shade 7 columns and write as a fraction.

$\frac{70}{100}$ or $\frac{7}{10}$

5 There are 100 small squares. Write the shaded amount as a fraction.

$\frac{1}{100}$

6 There are 100 small squares. Write the shaded amount as a fraction.

$\frac{12}{100}$

7 Shade $\frac{15}{100}$ of the square.

8 Shade $\frac{50}{100}$ of the square.

---

1 The amount shaded is:
- ● $\frac{1}{10}$
- ○ $\frac{10}{10}$
- ○ $\frac{1}{100}$

2 As a decimal, $\frac{2}{100}$ is written as:
- ○ 0.05
- ○ 0.2
- ● 0.02
- ○ 0.20

3 Shade $\frac{3}{10}$ of the grid and write as a decimal.

0.3

4 Shade $\frac{7}{100}$ of the grid and write as a decimal.

0.07

5 Write the shaded amount as a common fraction and as a decimal.

$\frac{23}{100}$
0.23

6 Shade 0.09 of the grid and write as a common fraction.

$\frac{9}{100}$

7 Complete the number line.

0.7 0.8 | 0.9 | 1 | 1.1 |

8 Complete the number line.

0.08 0.09 | 0.1 | 0.11 | 0.12 |

---

1 Draw four coins that make 70c.

Student draws 3 × 20c coins and 1 × 10c coin.

2 Draw three coins that make 20c.

Student draws 1 × 10c coin and 2 × 5c coins.

3 How could you give the exact money for a 90c drink using the least number of coins?

50c and 2 × 20c

4 How could you give the exact money for a $1.80 item using the least number of coins?

$1, 50c, 20c and 10c

5 How much change from $1 would you get for something that costs 65c?

35c

6 How much change from $5 would you get for something that costs $3.85?

$1.15

7 Imagine that a drink costs 99c.
- **a** What is the lowest value coin you could use to pay for it?

  $1
- **b** How much change would you get? _____ none

8 Imagine that a snack costs $1.92.
- **a** What is the lowest value coin you could use to pay for it?

  $2
- **b** How much change would you get? _____ 10c

---

1 Round $1.67 to the nearest 5c.

$1.65

2 Round $1.68 to the nearest 5c.

$1.70

3 How much change would you get from $2 for a drink that costs $1.49?

50c

4 How much change would you get from $5 for a game that costs $3.97?

$1.05

5 How much change would you get from $5 for three toys at 99c each?

$2.05

6 How much change would you get from $10 for three pens at $2.02 each?

$3.95

7 How much change would you get from $50 for four items at $8.99 each?

$14.05

8 How much change would you get from $100 for six items at $9.89 each?

$40.65

PRE- AND POST-ASSESSMENT TEST ANSWERS

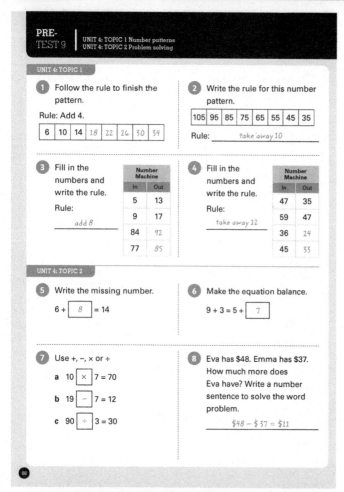

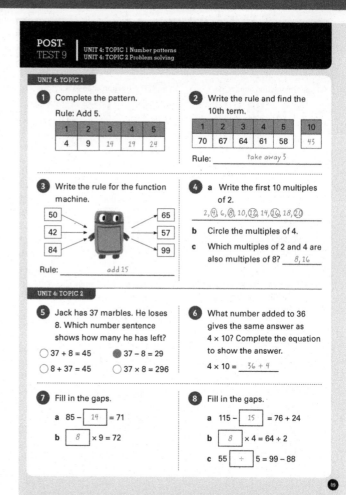

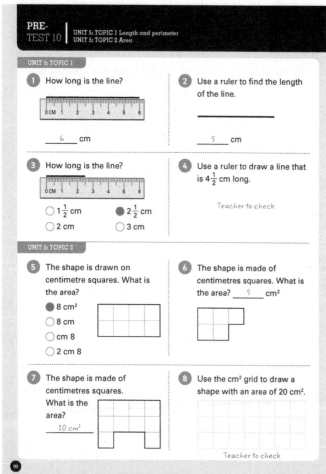

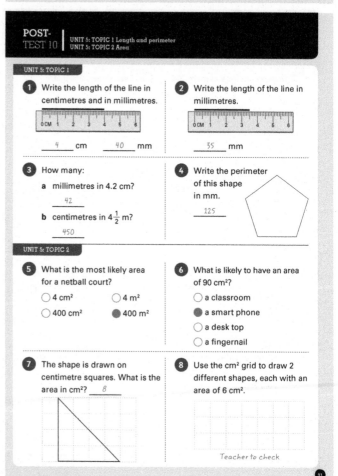

OXFORD UNIVERSITY PRESS

UNIT 5: TOPIC 3 VOLUME

1 The model is made from centimetre cubes.

The volume is ___8___ cm³.

2

The volume of this centimetre cube model is ___8 cm³___.

3 Which sentence is true?

A   **B**

● A has a bigger volume than B.
○ A has the same volume as B.
○ A has a smaller volume than B.

4 Look at the centimetre cube model.

a How many layers? ___4___

b How many cubes on each layer? ___4___

c What is the volume of the model? ___16 cm³___

UNIT 5: TOPIC 3 CAPACITY

5 A bucket holds:
● about 6 litres.
○ more than 6 litres.
○ less than 6 litres.

6 A teaspoon holds:
● about 5 mL.
○ about 50 mL.
○ about 5 L.

7

250 millilitres   1 litre   600 millilitres
A   **B**   **C**

Order the drink containers from smallest capacity to largest capacity.

___A C B___

8 Look at the drink containers in question 7.

a Which container holds ¼ of a litre? ___A___

b What is the total capacity of the 3 containers? _____

___1 L 850 mL or 1850 mL___

UNIT 5: TOPIC 3 VOLUME

1 The model is made from centimetre cubes.

The volume is ___10___ cm³.

2 Which is true?

A   **B**

○ Model A has a larger volume.
○ Model B has a larger volume.
● They have the same volume.

3 a How many layers?
___3___

b How many cm³ on each layer? ___6___

c What is the volume? ___18 cm³___

4 This box can fit 2 identical layers of centimetre cubes. What is the volume? ___16 cm³___

UNIT 5: TOPIC 3 CAPACITY

5 Which is true?

 550 mL   ½ L
A   **B**

○ A holds the same as B.
● A holds more than B.
○ A holds less than B.

6 Shade the jug to show the level after the 2 drink containers have been poured into it.

7

1150 mL   ¾ L   950 mL   1L 100 mL
A   **B**   **C**   **D**

Which of the jugs holds closest to 1 L? ___C___

8 a Order the jugs in question 7 from smallest to largest capacities. ___B, C, D, A___

b If 200 mL is poured out of jug B, how much is left? ___550 mL___

---

1 How many grams in 2 kg?
○ 20
○ 200
● 2000

2 a Is a melon likely to have a mass of 1 g or 1 kg? ___1 kg___

b Is a feather likely to have a mass of 1 g or 1 kg? ___1 g___

3 How heavy is a teddy likely to be?
○ 5 g
● 500 g
○ 50 kg

4 The cat has a mass of 1 kg. Write the same mass in a different way. ___1000 g___

5 How many 5 g weights would balance a 50 g weight? ___10___

6 How many 20 g weights would balance a 100 g weight? ___5___

7 Two identical books have a mass of 1 kg 500 g. What is the mass of one book? ___750 g___

8 What is the mass of one pencil sharpener?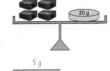

___5 g___

---

1 The box has a mass of 1 kg 500 g. This can also be written as:
○ 15 kg
● 1.5 kg
○ 1 kg 5 g

2 Another way of writing ¼ kg is:
○ 2500 g
○ 25 g
● 250 g

3 The box has a mass of 2.75 kg. This can also be written as:
○ 275 g
○ 2 kg 75 g
● 2 kg 750 g

4 How many grams in 3½ kg?
___3500___

5 Write the mass in 2 ways.
___4.25 kg, 4250 g___
___4 kg 250 g___
___4 ¼ kg___

6 Write the mass in 2 ways.
___1.4 kg, 1400 g___
___1 kg 400 g___

7 The box has a mass of 0 kg 650 g. Draw the pointer on the scale.

8 Draw the pointer on the scale.

PRE- AND POST-ASSESSMENT TEST ANSWERS

Answers given for questions 1 to 4 are probable. Student may be asked to justify different responses.

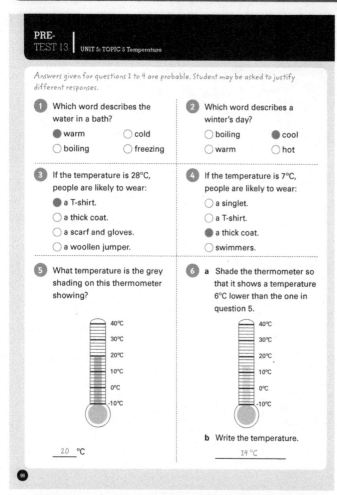

1. Which word describes the water in a bath?
   - ● warm
   - ○ cold
   - ○ boiling
   - ○ freezing

2. Which word describes a winter's day?
   - ○ boiling
   - ● cool
   - ○ warm
   - ○ hot

3. If the temperature is 28°C, people are likely to wear:
   - ● a T-shirt.
   - ○ a thick coat.
   - ○ a scarf and gloves.
   - ○ a woollen jumper.

4. If the temperature is 7°C, people are likely to wear:
   - ○ a singlet.
   - ○ a T-shirt.
   - ● a thick coat.
   - ○ swimmers.

5. What temperature is the grey shading on this thermometer showing?

   40°C / 30°C / 20°C / 10°C / 0°C / -10°C

   __20__ °C

6. a Shade the thermometer so that it shows a temperature 6°C lower than the one in question 5.

   40°C / 30°C / 20°C / 10°C / 0°C / -10°C

   b Write the temperature.

   __14 °C__

Answers given for questions 1 to 4 are probable. Student may be asked to justify different responses.

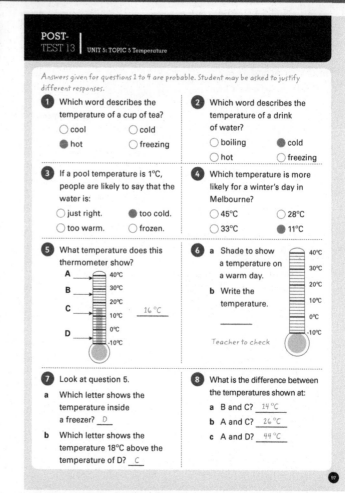

1. Which word describes the temperature of a cup of tea?
   - ○ cool
   - ○ cold
   - ● hot
   - ○ freezing

2. Which word describes the temperature of a drink of water?
   - ○ boiling
   - ● cold
   - ○ hot
   - ○ freezing

3. If a pool temperature is 1°C, people are likely to say that the water is:
   - ○ just right.
   - ● too cold.
   - ○ too warm.
   - ○ frozen.

4. Which temperature is more likely for a winter's day in Melbourne?
   - ○ 45°C
   - ○ 28°C
   - ○ 33°C
   - ● 11°C

5. What temperature does this thermometer show?

   A → 40°C
   B → 30°C
   C → 20°C / 10°C
   D → 0°C / -10°C

   __16 °C__

6. a Shade to show a temperature on a warm day.

   40°C / 30°C / 20°C / 10°C / 0°C / -10°C

   b Write the temperature.

   _____

   Teacher to check

7. Look at question 5.
   a Which letter shows the temperature inside a freezer? __D__
   b Which letter shows the temperature 18°C above the temperature of D? __C__

8. What is the difference between the temperatures shown at:
   a B and C? __14 °C__
   b A and C? __26 °C__
   c A and D? __44 °C__

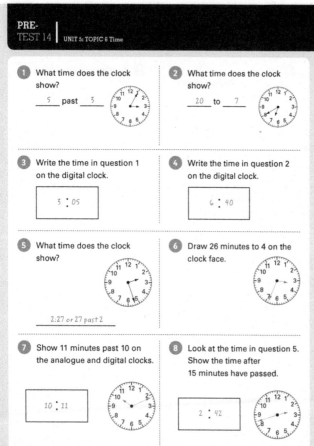

1. What time does the clock show?

   __5__ past __3__

2. What time does the clock show?

   __20__ to __7__

3. Write the time in question 1 on the digital clock.

   3 : 05

4. Write the time in question 2 on the digital clock.

   6 : 40

5. What time does the clock show?

   __2:27 or 27 past 2__

6. Draw 26 minutes to 4 on the clock face.

7. Show 11 minutes past 10 on the analogue and digital clocks.

   10 : 11

8. Look at the time in question 5. Show the time after 15 minutes have passed.

   2 : 42

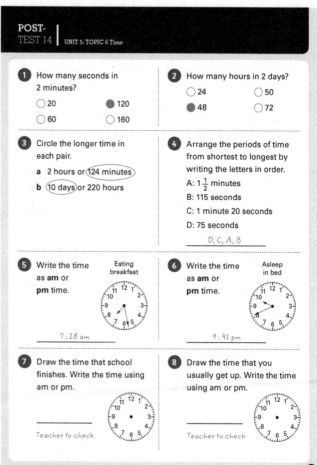

1. How many seconds in 2 minutes?
   - ○ 20
   - ● 120
   - ○ 60
   - ○ 160

2. How many hours in 2 days?
   - ○ 24
   - ○ 50
   - ● 48
   - ○ 72

3. Circle the longer time in each pair.
   a 2 hours or (124 minutes)
   b (10 days) or 220 hours

4. Arrange the periods of time from shortest to longest by writing the letters in order.
   A: $1\frac{1}{2}$ minutes
   B: 115 seconds
   C: 1 minute 20 seconds
   D: 75 seconds

   __D, C, A, B__

5. Write the time as **am** or **pm** time.   *Eating breakfast*

   __7:28 am__

6. Write the time as **am** or **pm** time.   *Asleep in bed*

   __9:41 pm__

7. Draw the time that school finishes. Write the time using am or pm.

   _____

   Teacher to check

8. Draw the time that you usually get up. Write the time using am or pm.

   _____

   Teacher to check

OXFORD UNIVERSITY PRESS

1. Another way to write 11 am is:
   - ○ 11 pm.
   - ○ 11 m.
   - ○ 11 o'clock in the evening.
   - ● 11 o'clock in the morning.

2. An hour after midnight, the time is:
   - ○ 11 pm.
   - ○ 1 pm.
   - ● 1 am.
   - ○ 11 am.

3. These are some special times from Tom's birthday.
   5:30 am 11:30 am 7 am 4:30 pm
   Which time came first?
   - ○ 4:30 pm
   - ● 5:30 am
   - ○ 7 am
   - ○ 11:30 am

4. Write the times from question 3 in order from earliest to latest.
   5:30 am, 7 am, 11:30 am, 4:30 pm

5. At which of the times from question 3 do you think Tom went shopping?
   11:30 am (Student could be asked to justify a different answer.)

6. At which of the times from question 3 do you think Tom's party started?
   4:30 pm (Student could be asked to justify a different answer.)

7. Below are some events from the morning of Tom's birthday.
   Breakfast: 8 o'clock
   Opened presents: $\frac{1}{2}$ past 7
   School starts: $\frac{1}{4}$ to 9
   Birthday snack: $\frac{1}{2}$ past 9
   Put the times in order from earliest to latest.
   $\frac{1}{2}$ past 7, 8 o'clock, $\frac{1}{4}$ to 9, $\frac{1}{2}$ past 9

8. Write the times, arrows and events from question 7 on the timeline.

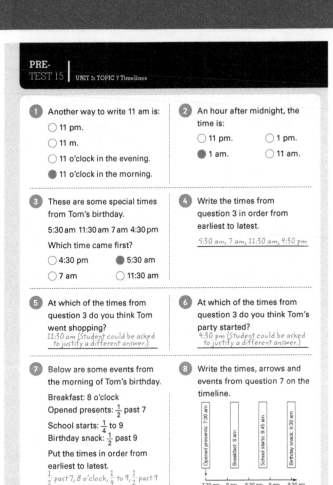

---

1. This is a timeline for Eva's party.

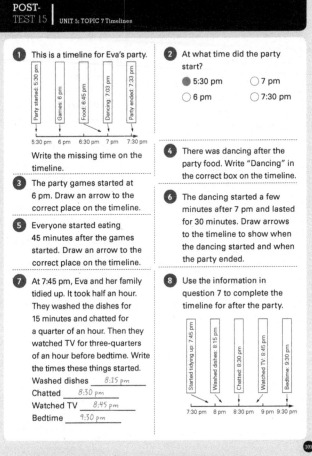

   Write the missing time on the timeline.

2. At what time did the party start?
   - ● 5:30 pm
   - ○ 7 pm
   - ○ 6 pm
   - ○ 7:30 pm

3. The party games started at 6 pm. Draw an arrow to the correct place on the timeline.

4. There was dancing after the party food. Write "Dancing" in the correct box on the timeline.

5. Everyone started eating 45 minutes after the games started. Draw an arrow to the correct place on the timeline.

6. The dancing started a few minutes after 7 pm and lasted for 30 minutes. Draw arrows to the timeline to show when the dancing started and when the party ended.

7. At 7:45 pm, Eva and her family tidied up. It took half an hour. They washed the dishes for 15 minutes and chatted for a quarter of an hour. Then they watched TV for three-quarters of an hour before bedtime. Write the times these things started.
   Washed dishes ___*8:15 pm*___
   Chatted ___*8:30 pm*___
   Watched TV ___*8:45 pm*___
   Bedtime ___*9:30 pm*___

8. Use the information in question 7 to complete the timeline for after the party.

UNIT 6: TOPIC 1

1. This shape is a:
   - ● trapezium.
   - ○ rectangle.
   - ○ parallelogram.

2. Which of these best describes this shape?
   - ○ pentagon
   - ○ hexagon
   - ● regular pentagon

3. What shape will be made if the two triangles are joined?
   square

4. What shapes can you see?
   2 triangles and a parallelogram

UNIT 6: TOPIC 2

5. Circle the pyramid.

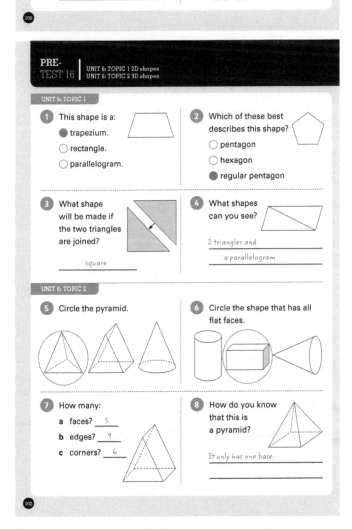

6. Circle the shape that has all flat faces.

7. How many:
   a faces? _5_
   b edges? _9_
   c corners? _6_

8. How do you know that this is a pyramid?
   It only has one base.

UNIT 6: TOPIC 1

1. If a shape has 6 sides and 6 angles, it is a:
   - ○ triangle.
   - ○ square.
   - ● hexagon.
   - ○ octagon.

2. a Name this shape.
   parallelogram
   b Draw a line that splits the shape into 2 triangles.
   Teacher to check

3. a This shape is a *pentagon*.
   b Draw a line to split it into a rectangle and a triangle.

4. a Draw an 8-sided shape that can be made from these shapes.
   b Name the new shape. *octagon*

UNIT 6: TOPIC 2

5. This shape is:
   - ○ a rectangular pyramid.
   - ○ a cube.
   - ● a rectangular prism.

6. a Join the base corners to the dot.
   b Name the shape. *Teacher to check*
   triangular pyramid

7. a Name the shape.
   triangular prism
   b The 2D shape from the side view is a *rectangle*

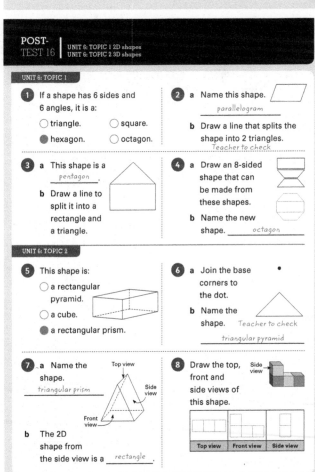

8. Draw the top, front and side views of this shape.

Top view	Front view	Side view

PRE- AND POST-ASSESSMENT TEST ANSWERS

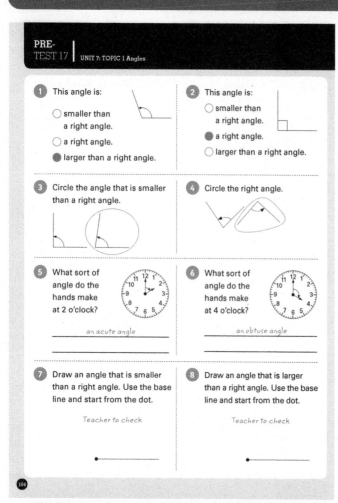

1 This angle is:
- ○ smaller than a right angle.
- ○ a right angle.
- ● larger than a right angle.

2 This angle is:
- ○ smaller than a right angle.
- ● a right angle.
- ○ larger than a right angle.

3 Circle the angle that is smaller than a right angle.

4 Circle the right angle.

5 What sort of angle do the hands make at 2 o'clock?
an acute angle

6 What sort of angle do the hands make at 4 o'clock?
an obtuse angle

7 Draw an angle that is smaller than a right angle. Use the base line and start from the dot.
Teacher to check

8 Draw an angle that is larger than a right angle. Use the base line and start from the dot.
Teacher to check

104

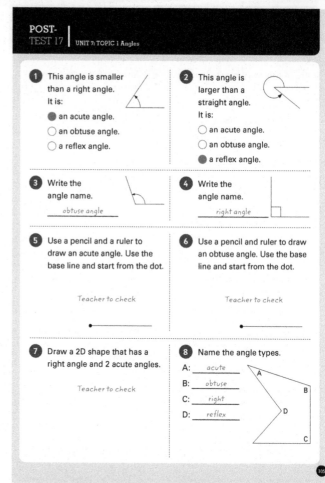

1 This angle is smaller than a right angle. It is:
- ● an acute angle.
- ○ an obtuse angle.
- ○ a reflex angle.

2 This angle is larger than a straight angle. It is:
- ○ an acute angle.
- ○ an obtuse angle.
- ● a reflex angle.

3 Write the angle name.
obtuse angle

4 Write the angle name.
right angle

5 Use a pencil and a ruler to draw an acute angle. Use the base line and start from the dot.
Teacher to check

6 Use a pencil and ruler to draw an obtuse angle. Use the base line and start from the dot.
Teacher to check

7 Draw a 2D shape that has a right angle and 2 acute angles.
Teacher to check

8 Name the angle types.
- A: *acute*
- B: *obtuse*
- C: *right*
- D: *reflex*

105

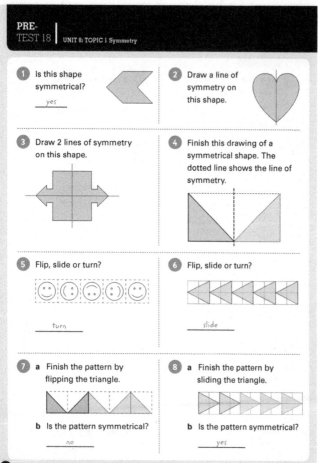

1 Is this shape symmetrical?
yes

2 Draw a line of symmetry on this shape.

3 Draw 2 lines of symmetry on this shape.

4 Finish this drawing of a symmetrical shape. The dotted line shows the line of symmetry.

5 Flip, slide or turn?
turn

6 Flip, slide or turn?
slide

7 a Finish the pattern by flipping the triangle.
b Is the pattern symmetrical?
no

8 a Finish the pattern by sliding the triangle.
b Is the pattern symmetrical?
yes

106

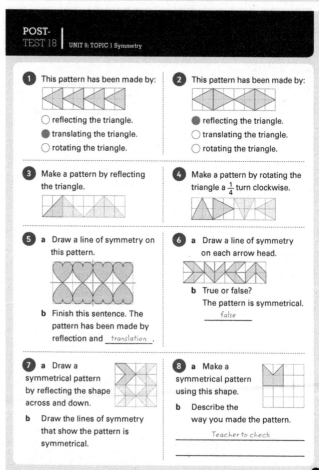

1 This pattern has been made by:
- ○ reflecting the triangle.
- ● translating the triangle.
- ○ rotating the triangle.

2 This pattern has been made by:
- ● reflecting the triangle.
- ○ translating the triangle.
- ○ rotating the triangle.

3 Make a pattern by reflecting the triangle.

4 Make a pattern by rotating the triangle a $\frac{1}{4}$ turn clockwise.

5 a Draw a line of symmetry on this pattern.
b Finish this sentence. The pattern has been made by reflection and *translation*.

6 a Draw a line of symmetry on each arrow head.
b True or false? The pattern is symmetrical.
false

7 a Draw a symmetrical pattern by reflecting the shape across and down.
b Draw the lines of symmetry that show the pattern is symmetrical.

8 a Make a symmetrical pattern using this shape.
b Describe the way you made the pattern.
Teacher to check

107

OXFORD UNIVERSITY PRESS

1 This is where Joe lives.

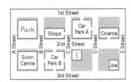

Sam lives on the corner of 2nd Street and C Street. Mark Sam's house with an "S" for Sam in the box on the map.

2 Look at the map in question 1. There is a park between A Street and B Street. Label the park on the map.

3 Look at the map in question 1. Is the Swim Centre closer to Sam's house or Joe's house?
Sam's house

4 Look at the map in question 1. Which car park has 4 entrances? _Car park B_

5 Look at the map in question 1. The entrance to the cinema is on:
○ 1st Street.
● 2nd Street.
○ D Street.
○ E Street.

6 Look at the map in question 1. The better exit from Car Park A for the cinema is the one on:
○ 1st Street.
○ 2nd Street.
○ C Street.
● D Street.

7 Look at the map in question 1. Start at Joe's house. Go along 3rd Street and turn right at C Street. Go along C Street until you pass 2nd Street. What is on your left? _Shops_

8 Write directions to get from Joe's house on 3rd Street to the cinema.
Teacher to check

108

1 The legend on a map tells us what:
● the symbols mean.
○ the map costs.   ○ to do first.

Legend
🚲 Bikes
🍴 Cafe
🚻 Toilet

2 This symbol tells us where to:
○ buy a table.   ○ meet a friend.
● find a picnic area.

3 This is a map for a bike track.

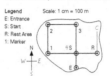

Legend
E: Entrance
S: Start
R: Rest Area
1: Marker

Scale: 1 cm = 100 m

Write S (South), E (East) and W (West) on the compass rose.

4 Look at the map in question 3. The 4th marker is also the start of the track. Write '4' by the 4th marker. _Teacher to check_

5 Use the map in question 3.
a In real life, how far is it from the Entrance to the start of the track? _100 m_
b If you went from the start to Marker 1, in which direction would you be going? _west_

6 Use the map in question 3.
a In real life, how far is it from Marker 3, past Marker 4 and to the Rest Area? _350 m_
b In real life, how far is it from the Start to the Rest Area and back again? _300 m_

7 Use the map in question 3. How far would you travel if you cycled from the Entrance to the Start, you did 4 laps, went to the Rest Area and then went back to the Entrance again?
_3.7 km or 3700 m_

8 Use the map in question 3.
a There is a cafe 150 metres north of the Rest Area. Mark the cafe with a C and a dot at the correct place.
b Draw a line to show the track from the Rest Area to the Café.

Teacher to check

109

UNIT 9: TOPIC 1

1 Choose the best question to find out how often people watch TV.
○ Do you like watching TV?
● How many hours a day do you watch TV?
○ What is your favourite program?

2 Evie made a tally of the number of pages she read each day. Write the totals.

Day	Tally	Total
Monday	ⅲ ⅲ II	12
Tuesday	ⅲ IIII	9
Wednesday	ⅲ III	8
Thursday	ⅲ ⅲ I	11
Friday	ⅲ IIII	9

3 The graph shows how many stickers Evie received. On Friday, she got 12. Finish the graph.

The number of stickers Evie got

☺ = 2 stickers

4 Look at the graph in question 3. On which day did Evie get 9 stickers? _Wednesday_

6 Look at the graph in question 3. What was the total number of stickers for the 3 days? _29_

UNIT 9: TOPIC 2

5 Look at the graph in question 3. What is the difference between the number of stickers on Friday and Wednesday? _3_

7 On Monday, Evie got 11 stickers. On Tuesday, she got 10. What was her total for the week? _50_

8 Draw a bar graph using the data in questions 3 and 7.

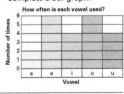

Number of stickers Evie got in a week

110

UNIT 9: TOPIC 1

1 Choose the best survey question to find out people's favourite sport.
○ Do you like to play sport?
○ Do you like to watch sport?
● What is the best sport?

2 Write a survey question about books for which the responses could range from "really dislike" to "really like".
Teacher to check

3 Tally the number of times you find each vowel used in this group of words.

a	e	i	o	u
2	6	4	6	4

UNIT 9: TOPIC 2

5 Look at the graph in question 4.
a Which vowel was used the least? _a_
b What was the total number of vowels used? _22_

7 The survey in question 3 showed that "a" is the least used vowel. Is that always true? Repeat the survey by tallying the vowels in this sentence: An apple is always an ideal food.

a	e	i	o	u
6	2	2	2	0

4 Use the data in question 3 to complete a bar graph.

How often is each vowel used?

6 Look at the sentence in question 3. True or false? More than half the letters used were vowels. _false_

8 a Compare the data in questions 3 and 7.
Teacher to check, e.g. use data from a whole page.
b What would be a good way to find out which vowels are used most and least?

111

UNIT 10: TOPIC 1

1 If you choose one bead without looking, how likely is it that you will choose black?
- ○ Impossible
- ○ Likely
- ● Unlikely

2 If you choose one bead without looking, how likely is it that you will choose white?
- ○ Impossible
- ● Certain
- ○ Unlikely

3 Imagine you pick a sock without looking. Describe the chance of taking a grey sock.

_____ Likely _____

4 Look at the socks in question 3. Show the possible outcomes when you take 2 socks without looking.

white and grey   OR   white and grey – 1
grey and grey   white and grey – 2
                         grey – 1 and grey – 2

UNIT 10: TOPIC 2

5 Imagine you have 3 pieces of paper turned over. "Yes" is written on 2 of them and "No" is on the 3rd. Is it **impossible** or **possible** that you will choose 2 with "Yes" written on them without looking? _possible_

6 What are all the possible outcomes when you choose 2 of the papers in question 5 without looking? Draw or write your answer.

yes and no   OR   yes – 1 and yes – 2
yes and yes   yes – 1 and no
                     yes – 2 and no

7 Colour the spinner red, yellow, blue and green so that each colour has the same chance.

Student colours 2 sections each for red, yellow, blue and green.

8 Follow these rules to colour the spinner red, blue, yellow and green. Half of the spinner is red. Blue and yellow have the same chance. Green has a better chance than blue.

Student colours 4 sections red, 1 yellow, 2 blue and 2 green.

UNIT 10: TOPIC 1

1 Which describes the chance of a 6-sided dice landing on 5?
- ● Unlikely   ○ Likely
- ○ Certain   ○ Impossible

2 Which describes the chance of you being asleep at midnight?
- ○ Unlikely   ● Very likely
- ○ Certain   ○ Very unlikely

3 Imagine you take a bead without looking. Describe the chance of choosing a black bead.

_____ equally likely _____

4 Write a likelihood term for this spinner landing on each number.

3: _____ likely _____
2: _____ unlikely _____
1: _____ very unlikely _____

UNIT 10: TOPIC 2

5 Follow the rules to write the numbers 1, 2, 3 and 4 on this spinner.
- 4 has very little chance.
- 3 has the same chance as 2.
- 1 has the best chance.

Student writes 4 on one section, 2 and 3 on two sections; 1 on three sections.

6 You need 4 small squares of paper that are the same size. Write "N" on 2 of them and "A" on 2 of them. What are the possible outcomes if you choose 2 without looking? Draw or write your answer.

N and N   OR   N-1 and N-2   N-2 and A-2
A and A   A-1 and A-2   N-2 and A-1
A and N   N-1 and A-1   N-2 and A-2

7 Turn over the papers from question 6. Shuffle them. Choose 2. Write the result in the table (e.g. A, N or A, A). Carry out the experiment 6 times.

Turn	1st	2nd	3rd	4th	5th	6th
Result						

Teacher to check

8 a Which outcome happened most often?

_____ Teacher to check _____

b Would it be the same if you repeated the experiment? Why?

Probably different because it relies on chance.

Unit 1 Topic 1: Place value

Activity sheet 1: Number facts and fun

1 Students will need to place USA at the top of the list. The numbers for the other countries are:

USA	79 695 000
Russia	17 800 000
Brazil	17 262 000
Japan	11 300 000
China	10 726 000
France	10 550 000
UK	10 450 000
Ukraine	8 895 000
Canada	8 583 100
Germany	8 050 000

2 a & d

	Country	Number of pet dogs	Rounded number
1	USA	65 791 000	66 000 000
2	Brazil	33 745 000	34 000 000
3	China	27 034 000	27 000 000
4	Mexico	17 859 000	18 000 000
5	Japan	13 618 000	14 000 000
6	Russia	12 270 000	12 000 000
7	Philippines	9 651 500	10 000 000
8	Ukraine	8 517 000	9 000 000
9	France	8 495 000	8 000 000
10	South Africa	7 449 000	7 000 000

b Philippines
c 9 651 000 or 9 652 000
e 51 000 (7 449 000 + 51 000 = 7 500 000, which rounds up to 8 000 000)

3 This task could be completed individually or in groups. Look for those who complete the activity in a systematic way, e.g. 2345, 2354, 2435, 2453, 2534, 2543 and so on.

24 possible numbers (in rising order) are:

2345	3425	4523
2354	3452	4532
2435	3524	5234
2453	3542	5243
2534	4235	5324
2543	4253	5342
3245	4325	5423
3254	4352	5432

Unit 1 Topic 2: Odd and even

Activity sheet 2: That's odd!

1

Number operation	Is the answer odd or even?	Proof
even + even =	even	Answers will vary.
odd + even	odd	
odd + odd	even	
even − even	even	
even − odd =	odd	
odd − odd =	even	
even × even =	even	
even × odd =	even	
odd × odd =	odd	

2 a Teachers may wish to begin this activity with a group discussion.
b Answers will vary. Some examples are shown below.

A number is even if ...	Test with an even number	Test with zero
the answer is even when it's added to even number.	2 + 4 = 6	0 + 4 = 4
there is no remainder when it's divided by 2.	10 ÷ 2 = 5	0 ÷ 2 = 0
the numbers either side of it are odd.	The numbers on either side of 4 are 3 and 5.	The numbers on either side of 0 are 1 and negative 1.
the answer is even when it's added to itself.	4 + 4 = 8	0 + 0 = 0
there is no remainder when the number is halved.	8 ÷ 2 = exactly 4	0 ÷ 2 = exactly 0
the answer is odd when the number is added to an odd number.	4 + 3 = 7	0 + 3 = 3
the answer is odd when the number is taken away from an odd number.	9 − 4 = 5	9 − 0 = 9

(continued)

c Again, this could form part of a group discussion. The likely answer is that zero can be counted as an even number because it passes all the "tests" for an even number.

3 a The only even prime number is 2.

b The difference between any square number and the next square number is always odd, e.g. the difference between 4 and 9 is 5; the difference between 9 and 16 is 7.

c The first 10 square numbers are 1, 4, 9, 16, 25, 36, 49, 64, 81, 100. The pattern of the list of square numbers is odd, even, odd, even, etc.

4 a The number 10 can be called even–odd because $10 = 2 \times 5$.

b Other even–odd numbers include: 2 $(2 = 2 \times 1)$, 14 $(14 = 2 \times 7)$, 18 $(18 = 2 \times 9)$.

c Some purely even numbers are: 4 $(4 = 2 \times 2)$, 8 $(8 = 4 \times 2)$, 12 $(12 = 2 \times 6)$, 16 $(16 = 2 \times 8)$, 20 $(20 = 2 \times 10)$.

5 This could be carried out as a group activity. Some other facts about the numbers 3 and 7 include:

- Number 3: Three is the first number that forms a geometrical figure – the triangle. Life is said to be in sets of three, e.g. past, present, future; birth, life, death; beginning, middle, end. People say "third time lucky". Fairy tales include three little pigs, three billy goats gruff and three bears. The octopus has three hearts. Camels have three eyelids. Cats have a third eyelid.

- Number 7: There are seven days in a week, seven notes on a musical scale, seven seas and seven continents.

Unit 1 Topic 3: Addition mental strategies

Activity sheet 3: Rounding, estimating and calculating

1 a This could be used as a discussion topic. Answers may vary. Hopefully students will note that the rounded answer should be around 3000.

b 3008

c Answers may vary, e.g. if 1003 + 205 were entered, the answer would be 1208.

2 Students may choose to round the numbers in other ways than shown below.

The problem	Round the numbers	Estimate the answer	Underline the likely answer
697 + 208	700 + 200	900	805 or <u>905</u>
1925 + 3064	2000 + 3000	5000	<u>4989</u> or 5989
4195 + 4827	4000 + 5000	9000	<u>9022</u> or 10 022
19 882 + 9968	20 000 + 10 000	30 000	<u>29 850</u> or 39 850
29 021 + 60 889	30 000 + 60 000	90 000	<u>89 910</u> or 99 910
103 465 + 99 332	100 000 + 100 000	200 000	102 797 or <u>202 797</u>

3 Ask students how they rounded the numbers. As the answer choices are not rounded to the nearest 10 000, the ideal method is to round the choices to the nearest 5000, i.e. 405 000 + 310 000 + 265 000 = 975 000.

The actual answer is 975 914.

4 Students may choose to round the numbers in other ways than shown below.

The problem	Round the numbers	Estimate the answer	Calculator answer
317 + 586	300 + 600	900	903
1214 + 827	1200 + 800	2000	2041
7835 + 4098	8000 + 4000	12 000	11 933
21 235 + 30 638	21 000 + 31 000	52 000	51 873
68 131 + 29 427	70 000 + 30 000	100 000	97 558
101 323 + 98 472	100 000 + 100 000	200 000	199 795
415 328 + 298 520	415 000 + 300 000	715 000	713 848
253 729 + 47 395	250 000 + 50 000	300 000	301 124

5 a Students might choose 69 000. However, newspapers would be more likely to round to 70 000.

b A newspaper (or online) report giving details of the crowds at the sport matches could be used for this activity. This could form part of a cooperative group activity.

Unit 1 Topic 4: Addition written strategies

Activity sheet 4: Working with large numbers

1 a The 2010 Australian Football League grand final

b 200 000

c 192 534

d 300 000

e 289 931

f 500 000

g 497 789

h More than one million (1 500 000)

i 1 474 500

Look for students who use the totals from questions 1e and 1f to begin the addition.

2 Look for students who apply appropriate strategies to solve the problem. For example, students could subtract one from the average for the first game and add one to the average for the second game and so on. Teachers may wish to make calculators available for this activity.

3 Look for students who recognise that digits totalling 10 are needed in each column. For example, 5373 + 5737 or 3573 + 7537 or 3735 + 7375.

4 The total is 123 456. Look for students who use the strategy of starting with the total and who then subtract two numbers in order to find the addends.

For example:

234 567 – <u>153 869</u> = 80 698.

80 698 – <u>8513</u> = <u>72 185</u>

153 869 + 8513 + 72 185 = 234 567

Unit 1 Topic 5: Subtraction mental strategies

Activity sheet 5: Unlocking your subtraction skills

1 Strategies used may vary. Teachers may wish to ask students to share the strategies they used with the rest of the group.
   a 900
   b 135
   c 383
   d 455
   e 990

2 Teachers could combine this activity with work on calculators or ask the students to use mental strategies to find the answer once a rounded answer had been correctly found. Students may also find ways to round the numbers other than those shown.
   • yes (170 – 140 = 30)
   • no (400 – 200 = 200)
   • yes (3000 – 1000 = 2000)
   • yes (2000 – 1500 = 500)
   • no (2000 – 400 = 1600)
   • no (3000 – 1000 = 2000, 2000 – 900 = 1100)

3 Students could round the numbers to find that Shop 2 has the better deal.

   Shop 1: $4000 – $1100 = $2900

   Shop 2: $4100 – $1300 = $2800

4 a $1.50 (possible steps are +50c to $9; +$1 to $10)

   b $2.25 (possible steps are +5c to $7.80; +20c to $8; +$2 to $10)

   c $7.50 (possible steps are +50c to $3; +$2 to $5; +$5 to $10)

   d $5.85 (possible steps are +5c to $4.20; +50c, 20c and 10c to $5; +$5 to $10)

5 These numbers were correct at the time of writing; however, teachers may like to direct students to do their own research into the five least-populated countries.
   a 68 – teachers may wish to ask students to share the strategy used.
   b 27 571 – teachers may wish to ask students to share the strategy used.
   c Teachers may wish to lead this activity to ensure that a town/city with an appropriate population is used.
   d Teacher to check.

Unit 1 Topic 6: Subtraction written strategies

Activity sheet 6: Using your subtraction skills

1 Teacher to check; the questions are self-correcting.

2 a 12 101 km
   b USA and Kazakhstan (22 km)
   c China and Mongolia (13 897 km)

d India and USA (2069 km)
e China and India (8014 km)
f China and Kazakhstan (10 105 km)

3 a 58 479 – 12 578 = 45 901
   b 45 138 – 23 129 = 22 009
   c 50 939 – 24 159 = 26 780
   d 85 004 – 13 221 = 71 783

4 a 7641
   b 1467
   c 6174
   d 9871 – 1789 = 8082
   Repeat the "largest and smallest" process:
   8820 – 0288 = 8532
   Complete the process: 8532 – 2358 = **6174**

   This could also form the basis of a group activity. Mathematicians believe that, no matter which digits are chosen, no more than seven repeats of the process are needed before an answer of 6174 is arrived at.

Unit 1 Topic 7: Multiplication and division facts

Activity sheet 7: Getting organised

1 a The eight possibilities are:

   1 × 30

   30 × 1

   2 × 15

   15 × 2

   3 × 10

   10 × 3

   5 × 6

   6 × 5

   b Answers may vary, e.g. I would choose five groups of six because six is a good size for a group.

2 There are eight possibilities:

   1 × 24

   24 × 1

   2 × 12

   12 × 2

   3 × 8

   8 × 3

   4 × 6

   6 × 4

3 Look for students who solve the problem by identifying 2-digit multiples of 4 that can be divided by a single-digit divisor to give an answer of 4:

   12 ÷ 3 = 4

   16 ÷ 4 = 4

   20 ÷ 5 = 4

   24 ÷ 6 = 4

(continued)

$28 \div 7 = 4$

$32 \div 8 = 4$

$36 \div 9 = 4$

4 The 12 factors of 96 are 1, 2, 3, 4, 6, 8, 12, 16, 24, 32, 48 and 96.
  a Look for answers that justify an appropriate group size. For example, four groups of 24 would mean the teams are too big, but would 24 teams of four be too many teams? Twelve groups of eight might be appropriate. Teachers could ask students to share their responses and reasons.
  b This could lead to a discussion on prime numbers, given that the only possible ways to group the students into equal groups would be one group of 97 or 97 groups of one.

5 Multiples of 4: 24, 36, 32, 40, 20

Multiples of 5: 15, 35, 45, 25, 20, 40

Multiples of 9: 18, 27, 36, 45, 54, 72

6 a Responses may vary. Although $5.33 rounds to $5.35, if they each have $5.35 the initial amount would need to be $16.05, and they have only $16.
  b Responses may vary, e.g. they could have $5.30 each and put the remaining 10c in a charity box.

Unit 1 Topic 8: Multiplication written strategies

Activity sheet 8: Using your multiplication skills

1 Look for students who use rounding as a time-saving strategy before doing written multiplications.
  a $25 \times 8 = 200$
  b $28 \times 9 = 252$
  c $52 \times 8 = 416$
  d $98 \times 5 = 490$
  e $59 \times 8 = 472$
  f $58 \times 9 = 522$

2 a 603
  b Answers may vary, e.g. because not every line will have nine words on it.
  c Teacher to check.

3 $704 \times 2 = 1408$

$352 \times 4 = 1408$

$176 \times 8 = 1408$

4 a 560
  b 180
  c 1 kg 799 g
  d Answers may vary, e.g. $4100 \times 6 = 24\,600$.
  e 236 800 km
  f Teacher to check. This could be carried out as a group activity.

5 a Answers may vary, e.g. $42 \times 5 = 210$ mL.
  b $94 \times 8 = 752$ mL
  c Answers will vary.

Unit 1 Topic 9: Division written strategies

Activity sheet 9: Share and share alike

1 1, 21, 3 and 7

2 a 19 r2
  b 24
  c 24 r1
  d 55 r1

3 Teachers could ask students to share their responses with the group, explaining how they dealt with the remainders. Likely answers are:
  a $3\frac{1}{2}$
  b 4 and 1 left over
  c $6.50

4 Teachers may need to discuss the meanings of the following before students begin this activity: *mean* (what is commonly thought of as "average"), *median* (the middle number when the list is arranged numerically) and *mode* (the most commonly occurring number).
  a $161 \div 6 = 26.8$
  b Answers may vary. Possible solution is:

Class	Number of students
3W	25
3/4D	26
4M	26
5S	27
5/6H	28
6T	29

  c Teacher to check. Using the figures above, the median number is 27, and the mode is 26.

5 $3000 \div 96 = 31.25$, $31\frac{1}{4}$ or 31 r24

If students think about the real-life situation being discussed, they should conclude that 32 boxes are needed.

6 Answers will vary. Teacher to check.

Unit 2 Topic 1: Equivalent fractions

Activity sheet 10: Half of a half

1 The pie that has been split into tenths has smaller pieces.

2 $\frac{1}{100}, \frac{1}{12}, \frac{1}{10}, \frac{1}{8}, \frac{1}{5}, \frac{1}{3}$

3 Teacher to check. Students need to identify that the larger the denominator, the smaller the fraction. Teachers to use their discretion in deciding how accurately the fractions need to be drawn.

(continued)

4 a 23

b 24

c 4

5 a Your friend would have more because one-fifth is larger than one-seventh.

b $5000

c $7000

6 Students will probably manage to cut out halves, quarters, eighths and sixteenths. It is unlikely, although possible, that they will manage to work with thirty-seconds.

7 In this challenge, it's doubtful that students will manage more than five (making 32 equal parts) or six (making 64 equal parts) folds of a sheet of A4 paper – but they could have fun trying!

Unit 2 Topic 2: Improper fractions and mixed numbers

Activity sheet 11: More than a whole one

1 a $\frac{12}{8}$ and $1\frac{1}{2}$.

b $\frac{11}{8}$ and $1\frac{3}{8}$

2 a Student shades and writes $\frac{13}{8}$.

b Student shades and writes $2\frac{2}{3}$.

3 Teacher to decide on level of accuracy required for splitting the shapes.

a Student divides the shapes into quarters and shades $\frac{7}{4}$.

b Student divides the shapes into eighths and shades $2\frac{1}{8}$.

c Student divides the shapes into halves and shades $3\frac{1}{2}$.

4 a Teachers may wish to discuss an appropriate shape and size for students to use, that will simplify the task. For example, four 2 cm × 2 cm squares would be appropriate.

b Students should shade $\frac{13}{4}$.

5 Multiple answers are possible. Students could work cooperatively in small groups. Possible answers are:

a $1\frac{1}{8}$ **b** $1\frac{3}{4}$ **c** $\frac{11}{4}$

6 A possible solution is to divide the list into those that are equivalent to $2\frac{1}{2}$ and those that are equivalent to $1\frac{1}{4}$.

List 1: $1\frac{1}{4}, \frac{5}{4}, 1\frac{2}{8}, \frac{10}{8}$

List 2: $2\frac{1}{2}, 2\frac{4}{8}, \frac{15}{6}, \frac{10}{4}$

7 This is a difficult task, so teachers may wish to ask students to work collaboratively. An alternative would be to complete the activity as a teacher-led shared task.

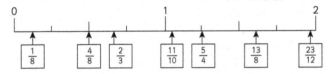

8 This could be undertaken as a think-pair-share activity, with individual students being asked to find as many solutions as possible in a limited amount of time. They then share their answers with a partner, and finally with the larger group.

Unit 2 Topic 3: Decimal fractions

Activity sheet 12: Working with decimals

1 a Students shade nine small squares on the first grid and eleven on the second.

b 0.11

c 0.91

2 Students shade:

a Red: 10 squares

b Blue: 25 squares

c Green: 27 squares

d Yellow: 5 squares

e Purple: 18 squares

f Students shade 15 squares and write 0.15.

g $\frac{27}{100}$, 0.25, 0.18, 0.15, 0.1, 0.05

3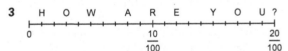

4 muffin: $1.70, bottle of water: $1.25, eraser: $1.05, sharpener: $0.90 or 90c, pen set: $2.90

5 Students may need assistance with using a stopwatch that has tenths and hundredths of a second.

a 0.16 seconds or $\frac{16}{100}$ of a second

b 0.86 seconds or $\frac{86}{100}$ of a second

c 9.77 seconds

d Practical activity. This would be ideal for a group activity.

Unit 3 Topic 1: Money and money calculations

Activity sheet 13: Money then, now and around the world

1 a £2
   b 24d
   c 12d × 20 = 240d
2 a 3s and 12d = 4s
   b 5s and 12d = 6s
   c 6d
3 Answers will vary.
4 a The symbol is €.
   b Answers will vary.
5 a rand
   b yen
   c baht
6 Nowadays, almost all countries use some form of decimal currency. However, there are two African countries that use non-decimal currencies: Mauritania (one ouguiya = five khoums) and Madagascar (one ariary = five iraimbilanja). In both cases, the value of the main unit is so low that the sub-unit is rarely, if ever, used.

Unit 4 Topic 1: Number patterns

Activity sheet 14: Patterns with numbers

1 Answers may differ from those given here, depending on how the calculator used has been programmed to deal with the order of operations. Teachers could use any discrepancies as a springboard for discussion. Likely answers are:
   a 12 – the calculator multiplied the answer by 2 again.
   b 24 – the calculator multiplied the answer by 2 again.
   c It's doubling the answer each time.
   d 48
   e The second answer is 18, then 54, etc. – the calculator keeps multiplying the answers by 3.

The next two questions could be used as an introduction to the order of operations.

2 a Students are likely to give the answer as 8.
   b Teacher to check.
   c It will continue to perform the last operation.
3 a Students are likely to give the answer as 10.
   b Depending on the way the calculator has been programmed, the answer will show as either 10 or 7. Students who have no experience with the order of operations are likely to predict the answer as 10. This could be used as a springboard for discussion.
   c It will continue to perform the last operation.
4 Practical activity. Teachers could photocopy the circle so students can experiment with various multiples.

Unit 4 Topic 2: Problem solving

Activity sheet 15: Mystery numbers

1 a 13
   b 14
   c 7
   d 27
   e 35
   f 6
2 a ★ = 6
   b ★ = 4
   c ★ = 7
   d ★ = 3
   e ★ = 5
3 a =
   b =
   c =
   d ≠
   e ≠
   f =
4 a

Number of tables	1	2	3	4	5	6
Number of people	4	6	8	10	12	14

   b 22, because 10 × 2 + 2 = 22
   c 13, because 13 × 2 + 2 = 28
   d (Number of students – 2) ÷ 2
5 a Number of glow sticks required = ★ × 2
      Number of sausage rolls required = ★ × 3
      Number of party favours required = ★ × 4 + 8
      Number of cakes required = ★ ÷ 8
      Teacher to check that the answers match up.
   b Number of sausage rolls required = ★ × 3 – 12

Unit 5 Topic 1: Length and perimeter

Activity sheet 16: The importance of accuracy

Teachers might choose to begin the activities with a discussion about the reason why some measurements need to be absolutely accurate (such as those taken by a jeweller) and others can be approximate (such as the length of a vegetable patch in a garden).

1 Answers may vary. Students could be asked to justify their answers. Possible responses are:
   a 20 cm and 1 mm; 19 cm and 9 mm
   b 60 cm
   c all lengths would be appropriate

(continued)

OXFORD UNIVERSITY PRESS

2 a If the person runs exactly along the lines, the length would be 300 m.

b Answers may vary. A possible answer would be "… more if the person kept to the outside of the lines and less if the person cut the corners."

3 Possible answers:

a Acceptable because 1 cm longer would hardly be noticeable.

b Not acceptable because the length and width are both far too long.

c Acceptable because the length and width are not very different to the regulation dimensions.

d The length would be acceptable but the width would not.

4 a 300 m and 2 cm

b 360 m

c 299 m and 10 cm

d 282 m and 20 cm

5 Answers may vary, e.g. Double the length and double the width and then find the total.

Unit 5 Topic 2: Area

Activity sheet 17: An even shorter shortcut

1 This could be carried out as an oral activity to remind students of the work they did in the Extended Practice activities from their Student Book. Answers may vary.

2 a 15 cm^2

b 16 cm^2

c 36 cm^2

d 30 cm^2

e 80 cm^2

f 140 cm^2

3 & 4 Teachers may wish to carry out these activities as part of a modelled lesson, depending on the ability levels of students.

Unit 5 Topic 3: Volume

Activity sheet 18: Volume of a rectangular prism

1 a Answers may vary. Teacher to check.

b 30 cm^3

2 a 24 cm^3

b 48 cm^3

c 80 cm^3

d 72 cm^3

e 900 cm^3

f 400 cm^3

3–6 Practical activities. Teachers may wish to begin this as a modelled activity, depending on the ability and experience levels of the students.

Unit 5 Topic 4: Mass

Activity sheet 19: Worth your weight in gold

1 a $100 000

b $250 000

c $500 000

d $1 million

2 a $25 000

b $5000

3 a Half of 56 g = 28 g

b Twice 56 g = 112 g

4 a 56 g + 99 g = 155 g

b $155 \text{ g} \div 10 = 15\frac{1}{2} \text{ g}$ (or 15.5 g)

5 a 2.5 g

b 10 × 6.5 g = 65 g

6 10 × 10c coins = 56 g, so 100 = 560 g, with a value of $10

11 × $1 coins = 99 g with a value of $11

The likely choice is, therefore, 99 g of $1 coins because that would be worth more money.

Unit 5 Topic 5: Temperature

Activity sheet 20: Keeping it cool and hot

1 a Answers will vary. Teacher to check.

b Answers may vary. Teacher to check, e.g. So that they do not go mouldy.

c 16°C

d 4 hours

e Answers will vary. Teacher to check.

2 a 23°

b Answers will vary. Teacher to check, e.g. frozen vegetables, ice-cream, ice cubes.

c Answers will vary. Teacher to check, e.g. So that they can be kept for a long time.

d 39°

3 a 86°

b Teacher to check, e.g. It would scald the mouth.

c Answers may vary, e.g. 50°C.

4 a 40°C

b 50°C to 65°C

5 Answers may vary. This could form part of a group research activity. Recipe books and websites would be a good starting point.

6 This could take the form of a group discussion. Teachers could also extend this by asking students to pretend that they are at various places, with an introductory question such as, "Would a cold day in Darwin be the same temperature as a cold day in Hobart?"

ACTIVITY SHEETS
ANSWERS

Unit 5 Topic 6: Time

Activity sheet 21: Why do we have am and pm times?

1 a 7:50 am
  b 1:16 pm
  c 7:24 pm
  d 1:48 am

Teachers may wish to discuss the times on the clocks in questions 2 and 3 with the group.

2 a

  b 4 o'clock

3 a 12:15 or quarter past 12
  b Every second marking represents five minutes, so the time shown is 5 to 4 or 03:55.

4

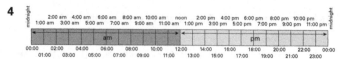

5 a 11:00
  b 14:00
  c 02:30
  d 10:15
  e 06:55
  f 14:58
  g 15:40
  h 06:19

6 Answers will vary. Teacher to check that the am/pm times match the 24-hour times.

Unit 6 Topic 1: 2D shapes

Activity sheet 22: A world of patterns

1 This could be carried out as a think-pair-share activity, with students working collaboratively to write descriptions of the 4 cm × 2 cm rectangle.

2 Teachers may wish to display the pattern on an interactive whiteboard and invite students to comment on it. (The four squares appear to become larger, then smaller.)

3 a Answers may vary. For example, at first glance, there appear to be no horizontal or parallel lines.
  b At first it is hard to decide whether the quadrilaterals are rectangles and squares, but isolating one shape by covering the others will show that the pattern is made from squares and rectangles.

  c Isolating one row reveals that the lines are parallel.
  d The pattern could be made by sliding rows of rectangles and squares sideways, as in the displayed image.

4 & 5 The lines appear to make a curve as they are drawn. This becomes easier to identify if the number of points along the axes is increased to ten or more.

    The activity could be extended to make a piece of 3D artwork using small nails along the axes on a board and stretching string, cotton or wool from one nail to the other in the same way that the lines were drawn.

6 This is ideal for a cooperative group activity with each new sketch being displayed on a board. Discussion could follow to ensure that the same polygon has not been repeated, e.g. the same triangle upside down, when counting the number of shapes that have been discovered.

Unit 6 Topic 2: 3D shapes

Activity sheet 23: Packaging

1 a Teacher to check that the nets are drawn correctly.
  b rectangular prism
  c Students should draw a net for a rectangular prism.

2 a Answers may vary, e.g. There are more/bigger tabs.
  b Answers may vary, e.g. It might be stronger that way.

3 This could form part of a group discussion. Students may decide that it's because we use right angles so often in our lives, or they may note that a rectangular prism stacks easily.

Unit 7 Topic 1: Angles

Activity sheet 24: Angles in sport

1 In Picture B, the ball will need to bounce several times before (if) it reaches the other player.

2

3 This could be carried out as a think-pair-share activity. There are countless games in which the players need to have a knowledge of angles, from basketball to billiards.

4 This activity can be as simple or as detailed as the teacher or student wishes. Students could share their ideas with each other.

ACTIVITY SHEETS
ANSWERS

Unit 8 Topic 1: Symmetry

Activity sheet 25: Line and rotational symmetry

1 a Students need to draw a vertical line down the centre of the letter A.

   b Students might think that there is a line of symmetry on the letter S, but this can be disproven with the aid of a mirror. If the shape is rotated half a turn, the letter S appears, showing that the letter has rotational symmetry.

2 a F and G are not symmetrical.

   b C, D, E and H have line symmetry.

   c H and N have rotational symmetry. (See the note about the letter S in question 2 if students identify the letter N as having line symmetry.)

   d H has both line and rotational symmetry.

3 a Shape C

   b four times

Unit 8 Topic 2: Scales and maps

Activity sheet 26: Using grid references

1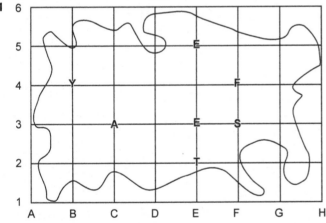

2 a D4

   b A4, B4, B3

   c F1, F2, F3

   d H4

   e B3 & E4

   f The other is an overnight car park.

   g G3

   h Answers may vary, e.g. Go west along Bogong High Plains Road past the overnight car park in A5. Go north past Windy Corner Day Car Park and Windy Corner Toboggan is on the left.

Unit 9 Topic 1: Collecting data

Activity sheet 27: The words we use

1 This could be an introductory discussion topic. Answers may vary, e.g. because it would take too long to ask even one 10-year-old to think of and say every word they know.

2 Answers may vary, e.g. a, the, to.

3 Practical activity. This could be carried out as a shared project or by pooling and comparing several students' findings.

4 This could form part of a discussion about how frequently certain vowels are used. A further discussion point could be the use of the letter *y* as a vowel substitute (e.g. 'cry').

Unit 9 Topic 2: Displaying and interpreting data

Activity sheet 28: What's in a name?

1 a Jack and Ruby

   b James, Max

   c None

   d Teacher to check.

   e Two: Ruby, Charlotte, Mia, Chloe, Lily, Ava, Ella

   f Answers will vary.

2 a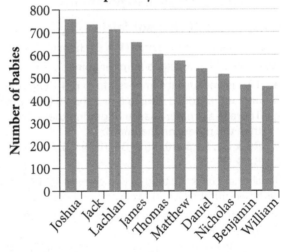

   b Joshua

   c Joshua moved from number 1 to number 5, and Jack moved to number 1, making William number 2.

   d Emily, Chloe, Isabella and Olivia

   e Answers may vary. Teacher to check.

   f fewer

   g Jack, James, Thomas, William and Joshua

3 Answers may vary. Teacher to check.

4 Answers may vary. Teacher to check.

Unit 10 Topic 1: Chance events

Activity sheet 29: What are the chances?

1 This could be carried out as an introductory group activity. Six has the same chance as the other numbers because the dice can land six ways.

2 a one-sixth

   b A 6-sided dice has a 1 in 6 chance of landing on 2.

3 Answers may vary, e.g. The way a dice lands depends on chance or "luck".

(continued)

4 1 in 6 – a 6-sided dice has a 1 in 6 chance of landing on any number, on any throw of the dice.

5 a–c Teachers could choose to carry out the first part of the activity as a modelled activity (possibly ensuring that there are five names with an odd number of letters and five with an even number of letters). The comments on the results will depend on the names chosen. If they were chosen at random it is doubtful (though this is by no means certain) that the vast majority will be either odd or even.

d–e Teachers will note that all 10 names have an odd number of letters. Students may comment that this is "not fair". The results could lead to a discussion about how data can be skewed in particular ways.

Unit 10 Topic 2: Chance experiments

Activity sheet 30: It's not fair!

1 Each number has the same (1 in 6) chance.

2 Answers will vary, e.g. a number spinner.

3 a This is because it's impossible to roll 1 with two dice.
 b Jack either rolled double 6 or 7 then 5 (or more).
 c There is a greater chance of getting these numbers than the others on the board.
 d R6 & G1, R1 & G6, R5 & G2, R2 & G5, R4 & G3, R3 & G4

4 Teacher to check. Instead of two dice, an 8-sided spinner with two number 2 and two number 4 could be used.

5 a The number 2 has the same chance as the number 12 (1 in 36).
 b Possible answers: $\frac{3}{36}$, $\frac{1}{6}$, 3 in 36 (or 1 in 6) chance.

OXFORD UNIVERSITY PRESS

TEACHER NOTES

TEACHER NOTES

OXFORD UNIVERSITY PRESS